Literature
in contexts

Manchester University Press

Literature
in contexts

Peter Barry

Manchester University Press
Manchester and New York
distributed exclusively in the USA by Palgrave

Copyright © Peter Barry 2007

The right of Peter Barry to be identified as the author of this
work has been asserted by him in accordance with the Copyright,
Designs and Patents Act 1988.

Published by Manchester University Press
Oxford Road, Manchester M13 9NR, UK
and Room 400, 175 Fifth Avenue, New York, NY 10010, USA
www.manchesteruniversitypress.co.uk

Distributed exclusively in the USA by
Palgrave, 175 Fifth Avenue, New York,
NY 10010, USA

Distributed exclusively in Canada by
UBC Press, University of British Columbia, 2029 West Mall,
Vancouver, BC, Canada V6T 1Z2

British Library Cataloguing-in-Publication Data
A catalogue record for this book is available from the British Library

Library of Congress Cataloging-in-Publication Data applied for

ISBN 978 0 7190 6454 8 hardback

First published 2007

16 15 14 13 12 11 10 09 08 07   10 9 8 7 6 5 4 3 2 1

Typeset in 10.5/12.5pt Plantin
by Graphicraft Limited, Hong Kong
Printed in Great Britain
by The Cromwell Press Ltd, Trowbridge

Contents

Illustrations

Acknowledgements

I was greatly helped in writing this book by a period of a year's research leave from the University of Wales, Aberystwyth in 2004–5, partly funded by the Arts and Humanities Research Council.

Parts of Chapter 2 were used as a seminar paper at the 'Condition of the Subject' conference at London University in 2005, and as a lecture at the conference of the European Society for the Study of English in 2006 (published in the journal *PN Review*, January–February 2007). An earlier version of Chapter 3 appeared in the *Review of English Studies*, and parts of Chapter 4 were used as a lecture at Liverpool Hope University, and as a paper at the 'Sustaining Romanticism' conference held at Liverpool University. Brother Ken Vance, S.J., Parish Administrator at SFX Church, Liverpool, gave me valuable information and help in connection with aspects of the Liverpool background of Chapter 5. Parts of Chapter 6 appeared in the journal *Cambridge Quarterly*, and parts of Chapter 8 appear on the British Council's web-pages for their anthology *New Writing 9*, and were used in presentations given to staff and students of Cadbury College, Birmingham, on their summer-term visits to Aberystwyth.

Professor Peter Middleton of Southampton University made a number of extremely valuable suggestions for re-thinks and re-visions, John Banks' eagle-eyed copy-editing saved me from several potential embarrassments, and Matthew Frost at MUP was, as always, helpful, encouraging, and convivial.

This book is dedicated to the memory of May Barry (1912–2006).

Introduction: half-acre tombs

This book addresses the question of context in literary study. How much importance should we attach to context in the academic study of literature in general, and of poetry in particular? What kinds of context are there, and how much weight should be attached to each? Is it possible to say where context might reasonably begin and end?

In the matter of context we have swung in recent years from one extreme approach to another. From the 1930s to the 1960s literary study was dominated by New Criticism in America, and by 'close reading' in the UK, while in the 1970s and 1980s post-structuralism and deconstruction were the dominant forces. What these two periods had in common was that they both (at least in their early 'high' revolutionary phases) effectively discounted history and context in the reading of literature.[1] Then, in the 1990s, with the growth of New Historicism, the pendulum swung to the opposite extreme, and historicism quickly became the default way of doing literature, bringing context so much to the foreground that the literary text itself became oddly sidelined to the margins of literary study. As James Chandler has put it: 'not even the briefest account of the way literary studies have been conducted in recent years, at least in England [sic] and America, could avoid coming to terms with the historicization of methods and objects of enquiry in the field'.[2] Thus, one extreme position replaced another. This book argues that it is time to reopen negotiations between the two extremes. Making 'Formalism' the demonised 'Other' of literary studies, and deceiving ourselves that studying context is the same thing as studying literature, is just as misguided as banning history and context from all consideration. One way forward is to subject the notion of context itself to detailed scrutiny, seeking to identify different kinds of contexts, and different ways of using them. The truism that 'literature must be studied in context' should not allow the notion of context to expand relentlessly until literary study becomes merely a sub-branch of history, and history becomes the new English. That is the argument of the book in brief. But just as it is impossible to challenge a stereotype without at the same time reinforcing it, so, while seeking to resist what James Chandler has called the 'regime of historicism', I am probably guilty in these pages of contributing to it.

For me, contrast between 'context-free' and 'context-saturated' approaches to literary study is encapsulated by Donne's lines in 'The Canonization' about the 'well wrought urne', the lines which provided the title of Cleanth Brooks's classic 1949 book *The Well Wrought Urn: Studies in the Structure of Poetry* (1949). In Donne's poem, the 'well wrought urne' has as its polar opposite the half-acre tomb. Donne says:

> As well a well wrought urne becomes
> The greatest ashes, as halfe-acre tombes

In this familiar poem the urn stands for the sonnet, and the sonnet is representative of the miniaturisation of literary form. The sonnet is small, but it provides all the room a writer needs – it offers 'infinite riches in a little room', to use Marlowe's familiar phrase from *The Jew of Malta*. The 'half-acre tomb', by contrast, stands for the epic, the poem in 'maximalist' rather than minimalist mode, and Donne's point is simply that the small-scale precision of the sonnet is as fine a thing in its own way as the full-blown pomp of the epic. He doesn't say (or doesn't say explicitly) that one is better than the other: he says they are as good as each other (one 'becomes' the greatest ashes 'as well as' the other), and it is only the hyperbole of the phrase 'half-acre tombs' which implies his preference for the personal intimacies of the sonnet over the pomp and circumstance of the epic.

Since the 1950s, however, the prime association for literary scholars of that phrase 'the well wrought urn' has arguably been with literary studies in general, rather than with any specific work of literature. Ask a dozen people in the discipline what the phrase suggests to them, and most will mention Brooks's book, which is the classic expression of New Critical principles, and has become synonymous with the 'Formalism' that dominated English studies from the 1940s to the 1970s. Of course, we don't believe in Formalism any more, and if you were to suggest to an English academic these days that it might sometimes be a good idea to concentrate on 'the words on the page', the reaction would probably be bafflement, disdain, or indignation, or some mixture of these. To go further: the very notion of the poem as a 'well wrought urn' or a 'verbal icon' would (I think) be regarded as distasteful by most people in the profession, for the contemplative and religious overtones of such terminology are widely disliked, and that kind of awe in the face of authorial achievement is no longer voiced in response to the work of poets, novelists, and playwrights (though it often is for that of literary and cultural theorists). Using phrases of that kind today about creative writers would bring a critic under suspicion of harbouring a preference for anti-materialist accounts of literature and ignoring its social context, or (worse) its 'politics'.

But *The Well Wrought Urn* is now more read about than read, and the title (in my experience) is usually thought to be an allusion to Keats's Grecian Urn, so that the implied contrast in the phrase between the mini-urn and the maxi-tomb is not widely understood. Yet, if the idea of the well-wrought urn, within our discipline, has come to signify the small-scale, eyes-down, critical activity of close reading, then what (if we extend the metaphor) are the half-acre tombs which are contrasted with that discredited activity? Asked in that way, the question seems to have only one possible answer: the half-acre tombs are the ever more elaborate historicist and contextualist approaches to literature with which almost every period of our discipline is currently being overlaid. Scholars in the early modern period, in Romanticism, and in Victorianism all increasingly devote their careers to the study of the literature 'in context'. The trend arises, as just suggested, out of the New Historicism of the 1980s, but it goes beyond it, and I will therefore call it 'New Contextualism', defining it for the moment as a context-based approach to literature which is not synonymous with New Historicism but in which the influence of New Historicism is an important foundational element. In our discipline today, sadly, it is a truth almost universally acknowledged that the construction of half-acre contextual tombs for literary works is a good thing.

New Contextualism, then, has become the right and natural-seeming way to do literature. Arguments against this approach are seldom advanced today, but if dissent in the discipline is to remain imaginable then we might imagine ourselves making the scandalous assertion that literary works 'can be understood only *outside* the detailed historical context in which they were produced'.[3] Naturally, to find somebody saying such a thing explicitly we have to go back a long way, and F.W. Bateson's way of putting this, in his *Essays in Critical Dissent* (1972), was that 'a degree of anti-historicism is the price that has to be paid for the continuing vitality of an English literary tradition'. This means that reading literature to some purpose may well mean reading it *outside* its own time and *into* our own – reading it, for instance, as Eliot read Donne. This is something quite different from the 'historicist/ archaeological' endeavour of currently dominant academic practice, which requires us to do precisely the opposite, to read much of Shakespeare back into the problem of 'the succession', for instance, or much of Restoration theatre back into the context of the Exclusion Crisis. The present book, to put it at its starkest, argues in favour of the current need for Bateson's 'degree of anti-historicism' in literary studies, as a counter-balance to the current dominance of broadly historicist approaches. It does not, however, advocate a return to decontextualised, or 'unseen' close reading, as will be evident in the chapters which follow on specific poets and poems. Instead, it argues that contexts are always selected and constructed by readers and critics, rather than ever being already there, and that we need to construct contexts which are (in the terms explained later) 'deep' rather than 'broad'.

The main body of the book begins with two chapters that discuss the issue of context and literature in broad terms, looking at both recent scholarly and recent pedagogical material. One unusual feature of the book is that, when appropriate, issues of teaching and curriculum are discussed alongside research matters. In other words, the book focuses both on how context might feature in academic writing about liter-ature and on its place in the teaching of literature. Hence, in the second chapter, for instance, the notion of context is discussed from two angles; firstly, how it is theorised in academic writing, and sec-ondly, how it is defined and prescribed in textbooks for students and materials which lay down such things as curriculum 'benchmarks', and in institutional documents which set out the curriculum for specific courses. Even in the discussion of academic writing, I do not always confine myself to the kind of material which is usually the focus of academic debate (essays in journals, chapters in books, and so on), but also take in such items as the formulations used in the editorial state-ments attached to series of academic books. My interest is in whatever is setting the agenda, in whatever contributes to the present situation whereby the notion of context remains largely un-critiqued in the dis-cipline, so that very few intellectual or procedural questions are ever asked about it. Usually, a clear demarcation is maintained between the two realms of research and teaching, in spite of the pervasive rhetoric which holds that the two 'go together'. Research as presented in acad-emic books is usually taken to be the 'cutting edge' at which funda-mental issues are debated, while teaching and curriculum are seen as operating at a more basic and passive level. I suspect that the opposite is often the case: career academics play safe in their research, sticking to a narrow conception of their 'field', but often do and say much more adventurous and wide-ranging things in the course of their teaching.

The best sense in which teaching and research can 'go together' is that we try to find a way of introducing that more open, and sometimes unguarded, kind of practice into our research. The discussion of pedagogical and curricular materials is mainly in Chapter 2.

All the material in the first two chapters is about literature generally, rather than just poetry, but the dilemma of context is always more acute in the case of poetry, so all six of the 'text-specific' chapters which follow are on poetry, Chapters 3 to 5 being on material from the 'long' nineteenth century, and 6 to 8 on the 'long' twentieth century (I adopt the privilege of stretching centuries as a way of asserting parity with earlier periods). Chapters 3 to 6, then, look at aspects of the work of Coleridge, Hemans, and Hopkins respectively. In each case, a distinct issue or procedure is brought into play, so that gradually a supplementary repertoire of approaches which are 'context-sensitive', but not 'context-saturated', is exemplified. In the Coleridge chapter the 'deep' context brought into play is the co-textual continuum of the 'conversation poems'. Instead of looking at the individual poems in isolation, the claim is made that all these poems are structured around the same four recurrent elements. Thus, the boundaries of the individual poem are breached, and a realm of 'co-textuality' is explored, which is made up of several cognate poems. A co-textual cluster in this sense is a group of pieces by the same author which derive from the same insight, situation, or feeling. The shorter the literary form, the more important co-textuality is. Sonnets and short stories especially have this 'clustering', co-textualising tendency, and usually come in groups or sequences. However, I make a distinction between '*co*-textuality' and '*inter*textuality'. Co-textuality designates a group of cognate items by the same author. It's not about allusions or quotations, and could better be described as a situation in which the Yeatsian 'quarrel with the self' is seen not *within* an individual poem but *between* the different poems in the cluster. Co-textuality recognises that textual boundaries are fluid, and that texts don't always end with the last full stop. Intertextuality, by contrast, can be defined as 'the presence of one text within another', or, more strictly, as 'the *words* of one text within another'. It refers primarily to texts by different authors, and to quotations and allusions. The texts explored in the Hemans chapter therefore represent a version of intertextuality rather than co-textuality, since they are by different authors, but the notion of 'text' is expanded to include both paintings and accounts of historical events. The context constructed for the Hemans poem 'Casabianca' acquires its 'depth' by the closeness of the parallel with the juxtaposed events, all featuring the boy, the cannon, and the deck of a ship.

The chapter on Hopkins, which is the most methodologically speculative of all, approaches the poet through another level of co-textuality, extending this notion to cover everything the poet has written, however seemingly remote from poetry. It seeks also a route to the poetry which is self-consciously personal, in active defiance of the 'affective fallacy' (the New Critical doctrine which proscribed any intermingling of our own concerns and those of the poem), but also (perhaps more significantly) taking issue with current norms of scholarly debate. The chapter seeks Hopkins in the locale of a significant phase of his professional life, positing a kind of symbiosis of word and world which is remote from the norms of literary critical writing, and more akin to those of biography, especially those of the 'romantic' or 'footsteps' approach adopted by the biographer Richard Holmes, in which there is a constant intermingling of questor and 'questee' (as seen in his *Footsteps: Adventures of a Romantic Biographer*). The context claimed in this chapter is 'deep' only if the claim made in the course of it is true, namely that what made Hopkins a poet also made him a priest.

The three remaining chapters concern examples drawn from the 'long' twentieth century, seeking entrances to poetry which are in some ways more overtly 'theorised' than those of the first section. Chapter 6, on 'ekphrasis', explores a form of 'multi-media' co-textuality, as does the Hemans chapter, but in a less open-ended way, since the poems discussed are unambiguously *about* paintings or photographs, and therefore have a context which is self-evidently 'deep', since it is 'built-in', so to speak. Chapter 7 looks at a 'cluster' of texts which are tentatively identified as examples of a new genre, one which can loosely be described as women's 'crime-fiction' poetry sequences, with the 'crime' being sometimes literal, sometimes metaphorical, sometimes incidental, but all of them questioning contemporary norms of behaviour in a fundamental way. The contextualisation is a form of 'inferred texuality' or 'transtextuality' (terms explained later), whereby the material is related to the generic archtype of detective fiction (p. 77). The final chapter revisits the question of the use of facts in poetry, a point to which the book is driven partly by its emphasis on seeing context as something *specific* outside the text, something, that is, which is uniquely relevant to the particular text under consideration (which is part of what I mean by 'deep' context).

There are several cross-groupings within the six 'case study' chapters which may usefully be mentioned. Three of them bring to the forefront aspects of the institutional context of literary study today. In the Coleridge chapter, for example, I make specific reference to the weighty body of relevant academic work which has to be negotiated by any critic wishing to write and publish on an 'inner-canonical' author. This is referred to as the 'tunnel' which we have to go through before we reach our 'target' author, which is a kind of imposed context of homogenising professionalism. The approach used in the chapter is a way of trying to escape the tunnel. In the Hemans chapter, likewise, I consider in overview the fluctuations in the reputation of this writer, and some of the professional issues which are currently brought into play when she is included on the curriculum. Again, these issues are an interposed context which has to be negotiated by the critic in some way. In the Hopkins chapter, finally, I frame part of the discussion with a reading of the current state of the discipline itself, seeking to relate that to aspects of Hopkins's own situation. These institutional considerations may not fulfil the criteria set out for *deep* context, but they are always a net from which none of us can entirely escape.

Another cross-grouping is the emphasis in some of the chapters on visual contexts. Thus, the Hemans chapter considers several images which are closely related to the material in the poems, while Chapter 6, on ekphrasis, is entirely devoted to that issue, and the final poem discussed in the book – *Lowlands Away*, by the poet and painter Adrian Henri – takes matters beyond ekphrasis to a text which has a 'deep' context of related images by the poet-artist himself, as well as the music of the oratorio for which it was written. The Hemans chapter also has affinities with Chapter 8 on contemporary women poets' 'crime-fiction' narratives, since both feature forms of 'novelisation' which avoid directly biographical writing. Two other chapters with a strong affinity are the Coleridge chapter and the ekphrasis chapter, both of which relate the literature under discussion to a tight and theoretical taxonomy, giving both of them a much more rigid outer frame than the others. Both have been previously published in an earlier form, and they are marked with the rigours of their editorial passage, and read rather differently from chapters (or parts of chapters) which began as lectures, and therefore have something of an underlying 'talking tone'. I haven't tried to produce an overall homogeneity of tone and treatment from end to end of the book, a task which would have been beyond me, since the oldest sections began life in 1995, while the most recent were completed about ten minutes before the final manuscript was printed off and sent to the publisher.

Notes

1 I argue the case for seeing close affinities between these periods in the section 'Seven types of continuity' in my *English in Practice* (Arnold, 2002), pp. 86–91.

2 This is the opening sentence of the first chapter of *England in 1819: The Politics of Literary Culture and the Case of Romantic Historicism*, by James Chandler (University of Chicago Press, 1999).
3 This inverts a quotation from John Barrell which is discussed later (in Chapter 2) – Barrell says 'inside', not 'outside', and I take his remark as representative of the current historicist orthodoxy in literary studies.

1

Contextuality in context

When was it, exactly, that context became so dominant in literary studies? So big a question cannot have a single definitive answer, but one plausible response would maintain that the pivotal year (when the 'turn' towards history and away from 'high' post-structuralist theory began) was 1986. Between New Criticism and New Contextualism had come deconstruction, which arguably reached the height of its influence in that year, and was poised for the final battle which would transform literary studies for ever. This ambition was both portrayed and enacted in the 1986 MLA presidential address of J. Hillis Miller, a speech entitled 'The Triumph of Theory, the Resistance to Reading, and the Question of the Material Base', published in *PMLA* (vol. 102, no. 3, May 1987), pp. 281–91. What theory had to do to ensure its total triumph was to deal with sudden and widespread outbreaks of historicism, for 'literary study in the past few years has undergone a sudden, almost universal turn away from theory in the sense of an orientation toward language as such and has made a corresponding turn toward history, culture, society, politics, institutions, class and gender conditions, the social context, the material base' (p. 283). Louis Montrose most prominently (but surely, too, almost everyone who heard or has read the speech) rejected this odd dichotomy between 'language' on the one hand and 'history, culture, society, politics', etc. on the other. Hillis Miller's view of language as separate from all these seems to see it as springing up ready-made out of nowhere, a point Montrose has no trouble in making (in 'Professing the Renaissance: The Poetics and Politics of Culture', reprinted in Rivkin Ryan, *Literary Theory*, pp. 777–85).

In *Professing English*, his fascinating institutional history of English, Gerald Graff cites an earlier relevant MLA presidential address, Helen Vendler's in 1980. Her more conservative call had been for members to remain in touch with their own 'unmediated' first experience of literature, the experience which (presumably) led them to take up the profession in the first place. She wanted them to recall how it felt to read *King Lear* for the first time, before it became for them part of a cultural formation and a professional field known as 'Renaissance literature'. The New Critics, in their innocence, had read *King Lear* 'itself', and, presumably, in some now long-distant professional primal scene, had once stood in awed contemplation of it, silent on a peak in Darien. By contrast, contemporary historicists seemed to disown that primal moment of 'peak' experience, seeing it as an embarrassing and naive irrelevance, and sought instead to construct a 'religious-historical-philosophical-cultural overview' of their new-found early modernist Pacific Ocean from down below on the contextual plain.[1]

Graff has some sympathy for Vendler's desire not to substitute a professionalised notion of 'the Renaissance' or 'the early modern' in the place of the New Critics' '*King Lear* itself', but he is well aware that the word 'itself' (or any equivalent of it) actually begs the question. The judicious poise of Graff's writing in this final chapter ('Tradition versus Theory') is admirable and enviable, but it too begs the question by assuming that the 'itself' is necessarily void of meaning, an assumption that now seems virtually universal, and provides the foundation for many a half-acre tomb. Graff, indeed, cites as the one point of agreement between all theoretical persuasions the fact that 'texts are not after all autonomous and self-contained, that the meaning of any text *in itself* [my italics] depends for its comprehension on other texts and textualised frames of reference' (p. 256). We may agree that this proposition is true in theory, but it is difficult to envisage any way of acting on it. By all means, let's study those other texts (if we have them to hand) on which the meaning of (say) Donne's 'The Canonization' depends, and its 'textualised frames of reference' while we are at it. But we surely need to recognise that counsel of the kind Graff offers here, if strictly adhered to, must in the end make literary study nearly impossible, for no critics acting on such principles could confine their tombs even to half an acre. When our professed aim is to study 'other texts and textualised frames of reference' we have set ourselves an object of study which is an intangible abstraction. Indeed, 'textualised frames of reference' could only ever be a *virtual* object of study – a concept I will come back to.

The contrary view to Graff's is that our sense of what and where the other texts might be which are in dialogue with a given one, and our reconstruction of what we imagine to be its 'textualised frames of reference', will have to emerge primarily from our engagement with that text ' " "itself" " ', and not from somewhere else. I place quadruple inverted commas round 'itself' to signify the intention of *ironising the irony* with which the phrase 'in itself' is now commonly used. The intention is both to register an awareness of the customary scepticism about the term and at the same time to signify scepticism about that scepticism: the intended effect is to place the *sous rature* itself *sous rature*.[2] So, to repeat, the 'relevant tacit knowledge' (p. 256) required by Donne's readers is mainly something they have to pick up by reading Donne – they certainly won't acquire it in any other way. We can readily agree with Graff that 'the historical circumstances that must be inferred in order to understand any text are not a mere extrinsic background, as positivist historians and New Critics supposed, but something presupposed by the work and thus necessary to intrinsic comprehension' (p. 257). But can a discipline sustain itself, as ours is now attempting to do, by setting out to study – as its primary aim – this realm which must always be 'tacit', 'inferred', and 'intrinsic'? The zeal to do so is pushing English into a kind of Platonic shadowland, where the text we see (those much disdained 'words on the page') is never as real as the 'text' we don't, that world of verbal virtuality which is for ever both everywhere and elsewhere. Graff concludes that 'the unit of study should cease to be the isolated text (or author) and become the virtual space or cultural conversation that the text presupposes' (p. 257). This is fine as a rhetorical flourish to end a fine book, but take it literally, and it is nothing less than a recipe for a showy and spectacular kind of disciplinary suicide – no method exists for the study of 'virtual spaces', and a lifetime won't be long enough even to get started if we refuse to recognise the validity of studying isolated texts or authors. Like it or not, English is nothing if not a positivist discipline.

On not choosing

The way these textualised frames of reference got into the picture in the first place can be traced back to the enormous influence (and, let's admit it, the enormous appeal) of notions of textual instability. This mighty river of contemporary thought, which irrigates literary theory, critical practice, and textual editing, arises from several different sources, but a particularly important one is Julia Kristeva's 1960s formulation of the notion of intertextuality, whereby, she says, 'Any text is constructed as a mosaic of quotations; any text is the absorption and transformation of another'.[3] The resulting 'deferral of text' is, says Mary Orr, 'then subsumed by the larger theoretical framework of postmodernism and deconstruction', and, indeed, she goes further than

I would and sees the Kristevan moment as 'the linguistic Big Bang, the deconstruction of "Text" into texts and intertexts *where these two terms ultimately became synonymous*'.[4] But deferring text is, among other things, deferring choice, for we seem to have a disciplinary inhibition about deciding, preferring to keep as much as possible in play for as long as possible, and seeing that as a mark of intellectual distinction. Thus, the rejection of the notion of the canon is not the result of a Leavisite conviction that we can make a better canon of hitherto neglected works: rather, it is the very notion of selecting (and, for that matter, rejecting) that we now reject. We are happy to study (say) literary representations of Napoleon, and we don't seem to worry much (it is surely right to say) about the literary quality of the works in which these representations occur. If our outlook is historicist, then this is entirely logical, for the best poem about Napoleon (the one with pace, subtlety, and impact which students might find memorable and thought-provoking) might not be the one which is the most historically accurate and representative (in fact, it almost certainly won't be). On the other hand, if our outlook is literary-critical, then we ought to regard it as a criminal act, in pedagogical terms, knowingly to subject students to second- or third-rate poems. Making choices and teaching literature belong together.

Cognate with this 'anti-choice' frame of mind is the attitude which refuses to express any preference between the literary text and its historical and political context as objects of study. We want to study the whole text/context continuum, even though we can't enrol our students for a lifetime. In its early days, New Historicism was content to make quirky and illuminating juxtapositions of literary texts with incidents or documents plucked (it often seemed) at random from the history of the relevant period (or even from some roughly adjacent one), but now it has become self-conscious about doing that, and it too seems reluctant to bear the responsibility of making choices. So, in their book *Practicing the New Historicism* (2000), Gallagher and Greenblatt seem to want 'protective regulation' to underwrite the choices they make of what to study:

> Similarly, we ask ourselves how we can identify, out of the vast array of textual traces in a culture, which are the significant ones, either for us or for them, the ones most worth pursuing. (p. 15)

Their question seems a strange one: obviously the textual trace to pursue is the one which turns out to have been significant, but you can't know which one that is until you have started to pursue it. If there existed a formula which could tell historians in advance where they should look, then there would also be one which told authors what rules to follow to be sure of writing a bestseller. Of course, Gallagher and Greenblatt go on to say this (in effect), admitting that 'it proves impossible to provide a theoretical answer, an answer that would work reliably in advance of plunging ahead to see what resulted' (p. 15). Only in 'the actual practice of teaching and writing', they say, can they be sure that the selected 'luminous detail' really is luminous. But it does seem symptomatic of that reluctance to make choices that they should express the desire to know in advance that there is treasure to be found at a given spot before they begin digging. The source of their difficulty is indicated in the next item in their list of the notional theoretical deficiencies of New Historicism, namely that 'If an entire culture is regarded as a text, then everything is at least potentially in play both at the level of representation and at the level of event'. The only sensible response to this is to say that it gives us a very good reason for *not* regarding an entire culture as a text, because if *everything* is in play then it will never be possible for us to read *any* text. The conviction that 'everything is in play', then, can only induce a debilitating professional anxiety, as perhaps it is designed to do. Once that proposition of everything being in play is accepted, then we are doomed as literary academics to spend our professional lives in futile attempts to harvest a limitless prairie of textuality. That is what our discipline suicidally attempts to do when it starts to regard whole cultures as texts and therefore refuses to make any (or make any hierarchical) distinction between text and context.

But New Historicism, as restated in this recent book, *is* determined to regard whole cultures as texts, and that drives it inevitably towards the virtuality which regards 'textualised frames of reference' as more important than actual texts. Since it is hopeless to try to describe a method for doing that, Gallagher and Greenblatt's introduction ends with one of those supposedly daring, but now actually quite routine 'negative theology' statements in which we are told that whatever the 'ism' in question might be, it is *not* a method:

> Writing the book has convinced us that new historicism is not a repeatable methodology or a literary critical program. Each time we approach that moment in the writing when it might have been appropriate to draw the 'theoretical' lesson, to scold another school of criticism, or to point the way towards the paths of virtue, we stopped, not because we're shy of controversy, but because we cannot bear to see the long chains of close analysis go up in a puff of abstraction. So we sincerely hope you will not be able to say what it all adds up to; if you could, we would have failed. (p. 19)

This moment of methodological denial is a familiar set-piece now in our discipline, as critics or theorists refuse to make *any* choices or identify *any* priorities. Gallagher and Greenblatt evidently see no incongruity between their title – *Practicing New Historicism* – and their proclamation that 'new historicism is not a repeatable methodology or a literary critical program'. How, we might wonder, can they practise something which is not a repeatable methodology? And if they *can* do it (even while saying they can't), then why can't we?

But the method-denying gesture, as just suggested, is commonplace in writing about any form of literary theory. Thus, in *Literary Theories: A Reader & Guide* (ed. Julian Wolfreys), the introduction to Martin McQuillan's section on reader-response theories is predictably entitled 'There is No Such Thing as Reader-Response Theory'. Likewise, introductory accounts of deconstruction often start with the denial that it is a method which can be practised, taking the lead in this from Derrida himself, who is vehement on the topic – see, for instance, his chapter 'Letter to a Japanese Friend' in the same book, which insists endlessly on the negative that 'Deconstruction is not a method and cannot be transformed into one . . . It is not enough to say that deconstruction could not be reduced to some methodological instrumentality or to a set of rules and transposable procedures . . . it must also be made clear that deconstruction is not even an *act* or an *operation*' (pp. 284–5). All these theorists, different though their views are, seem to share this peculiar horror of 'repeatable methodology' (Gallagher and Greenblatt) or 'transposable procedures' (Derrida), as if they cannot bear to imagine their 'blue sky' thinking being soiled by the grubby practicalities of application. This genteel disdain for the mere tradespeople of the discipline is disabling, for, once again, those to whom we might look for enlightenment seem to draw back with a grimace of distaste when it comes to the practical point. Asked the question 'What is deconstruction?', for instance, Derrida replies 'I have no simple and formalizable response to this question' (p. 285), as if 'formalizing' anything (the inevitable put-down word again) were a long way beneath him, and we should have known better than to expect it of him. Gallagher and Greenblatt, too, fastidiously distance themselves from anything as vulgar as a programme, or a method, or a lesson, leaving that kind of thing, in their aristocratic way, to academic menials like – well, like you and me, I suppose.

Inevitably, too, the result of this refusing to come to the point is to go on for too long, as if our time as readers were infinite. The essays in *Practicing New Historicism* certainly seem to dwell on their anecdote or their luminous detail (the Eucharist, or the potato, for instance), without ever quite seeming able to insert it into a wider picture. They say of their approach that it interrupts the official *grand narrative* of history with a 'counter-history' based on the anecdote or the luminous detail. They thus claim a part in a tradition which employs the 'effect of compression', as, for instance, in Auerbach's use of the detail of Ulysses's scar, at the start of his *Mimesis*, or as generally in Geertz's much-discussed technique of 'thick description' (in *The Interpretation of Cultures*, 1977). But the difference is, firstly, that Gallagher and Greenblatt's examples always have *the opposite* of compression – in fact they sprawl over twenty or thirty pages – and, secondly, that the framework into which the detail fits is precisely what they *don't* supply, and what they profess themselves unwilling to investigate, because they don't want their 'long chains of close analysis go up in a puff of abstraction'.

A less all-embracing form of contextualism is Paul Magnuson's (McGannian) 'historical close reading', advocated in his *Reading Public Romanticism* (1998, p. 5). This approach seeks to study the earliest published text of a Romantic poem within its original context of publication, or (in Foucault's words) 'in the exact specificity of its occurrence' (p. 23). Historical close reading seems to deny the literary text any autonomy at all, meaning, among other things, that the words on the page must be studied *on the page where they first appeared*, so to speak. Hence, for example, 'Coleridge first published "Reflections on Having left a Place of Retirement" in the *Monthly Magazine*, and "Dejection" in the *Morning Post*, and *one should read those poems in those contexts*' (p. 41 in Magnuson, my italics). This doctrine pushes the poem a long way beyond the reach of most readers, and even most critics, for the main endeavour at once becomes scholarly rather than critical – dates and places of publication, changes and revisions, variant readings, and so on, inevitably become the overwhelming focus of attention. A reader primarily interested in the poetry, and wanting critical discussion of it, is plunged into what seems at times an endless scholarly prelude. Indeed, while claiming to be historicist, the method always threatens to become merely antiquarian, for to argue that poems should *always* be read 'in the exact specificity of their occurrence' is to suspend them for ever in the amber of the 'archival continuum' in which they first occurred.

Further, the method establishes a contextual domain which is virtually limitless. Thus, if the essential context of 'Dejection' is the *Morning Post*, then what is the essential context of the *Morning Post*? If the poem's context is taken to be the adjacent *items* in that newspaper, then what is the essential context of those items? Where are the limits of the pond across which these contextual ripples spread? How can the archival continuum be prevented from reaching to infinity? Hence, these attitudes too pressure us into studying a realm of virtuality, insisting that vastly impractical ideals of contextualisation are carried out to the letter. The effect is, among other things, to widen the gulf between under-graduate and graduate study, and between elite universities and the rest, by making it nearly impossible to write even a journal article without travel grants and sabbatical time. Historicism, indeed, sometimes seems like a plot to 'North-Americanise' literary study for ever, by making mandatory an approach that only the world's richest nation can support and sustain.[5] It requires generous grants from foundations and trust funds willing to support scholars in a state of almost per-manent sabbatical to travel from one manuscript collection to another, producing intricate and time-consuming collations, and reducing the rest of the scholarly world to a state of academic coloniality. Magnuson accuses his opponents of preferring an 'idealised' text to a historicised one, but he himself is the textual idealist. He approvingly quotes Jack Stillinger's *Multiple Authorship and the Myth of Solitary Genius* (1991) which suggests that we 'drop the concept of an ideal single text fulfilling an author's intentions and put our money instead on some theory of versions'. Magnuson adds that Stillinger has challenged the idea that there is a 'single "best" or "most authoritative" text for each of Coleridge's poems' and notes that he has briefly detailed the several versions of some of Coleridge's major poems: 'sixteen or more manu-script and printed texts of "The Eolian Harp", twelve distinct texts of "This Lime-Tree Bower My Prison"', etc. (pp. 39–40). Instead of the textual 'idealisation' which he deplores, Magnuson proposes 'A theory of versions . . . [which would] take account, not only of the various versions of a work, but also of the work's location' (p. 40). Here again, then, is that reluctance to make choices which seems so characteristic of our discipline today.

But the argument, besides all else, is vulnerable: firstly, when Magnuson speaks of the 'location of the work' which 'version' is he talking about? If there are sixteen 'versions' of 'The Aeolian Harp', that means that sixteen locations have to be identified and discussed (since Magnuson's code of textual practice rules out 'idealising' any one of them and calling it the 'work'). So we had better make sure that we have plenty of funded study time on our hands. Secondly, which poem, really, is the idealisation? Is it the 'exact specificity' poem, which has remained for ever ageless, suspended in a time-warp at the moment of its birth? Or is it the poem which finally 'set' into a received text, based on the author's accumulated work on the poem through his lifetime, which has been the subject of critical debate through many generations? The latter, after all, in spite of all the rhetoric about the public sphere (the title of Magnuson's book is *Reading Public Romanticism*), is the one which is actually *in* the public sphere. As for the 'theory of versions' poem (or the 'synoptic' poem), that double octopus with sixteen arms, it is a poem that never was, as far as the reading public is concerned, for it is a mere scholarly abstraction.

'Textual synopticism' is a name we might give to this tendency to treat all extant versions of a text as equal, refusing to say that any one version is *the* poem. Consequently (and following the marked disciplinary preference for virtuality) a poem which is actually a hypothetical construct – the notional 'frame' of the multiple versions – is favoured above the poem 'itself'. There seems to be overwhelming support within the discipline today for that kind of thinking, but, again, such 'virtuality' actually makes literary study 'virtually' impossible. Thus, for J.C.C. Mays, editor of the new edition of Coleridge's poetry in 'synoptic format', 'some works, like the "Ode to Chatterton", moved through separate stages, each of which in effect constitutes a different poem' (Zachary Leader, *Revision and Romantic Authorship*, p. 136). Jack Stillinger, in *Coleridge and Textual Instability: The Multiple Versions of the Major Poems* (1994), holds similar views on the status of each 'stage' or 'version' of Coleridge's poems, believing (for instance) that each of the sixteen different versions of 'The Aeolian Harp' which he identifies changes 'the tone, the philosophical and religious ideas, and the basic structure' of the poem (quoted in Leader, p. 161). I share Leader's reservations about 'textual synopticism', which is that tendency to deny the existence of finished versions of poems and the attribution of equal provisionality of status to *all extant versions*. Leader argues that Stillinger 'overstates his case, here and elsewhere, presenting too complicated or indeterminist an account of Coleridge's practice as a writer' (p. 161). Thus, 'it is . . . perfectly sensible to see almost all the alterations to "The Eolian Harp", for example, as working towards intentions – thematic and formal – present from the poem's inception' (p. 131). Further, and seriously, synopticism involves 'the slighting of publication, or the equal weighting of published and unpublished versions' (p. 138). Synopticism always threatens to postpone discussion of poems in favour of discussion of what used to be called 'variant readings', and that always has the effect of disenfranchising the vast majority of readers. Textual synopticism may well prove to be the most tangible residue of post-structuralism, providing, as it does, the most concrete embodiment possible of the notion of the inherent instability and provisionality of all language, but especially texts. Synoptic editors are rather like football managers who refuse to select the team and insist that the whole squad is equally eligible and must play. It follows, too, that accepting synopticism must entail an exponential expansion of context.

The rise of context

In the 1970s and 1980s the New Critical 'literal formalism' was displaced by deconstructive 'rhetorical formalism', as it might be called, which now looks more a change of regime than a change of system, for the two agreed on the essential point that 'there is nothing outside the text', even if they understood that point differently, the one embodying it as the central characteristic of its critical practice, while for the other the pervasiveness of textuality was the key to its conceptual universe. Of course, 'politics' and 'history' were often evoked by rhetorical formalists, but often just as large generalisations, even when the generalisation took the form of insisting that every literary text is embedded in a 'specific' history or politics. The assertive presence of the word 'specific' in the pronouncements of the period was usually an indication of the fact that nothing specific was actually being evoked. Likewise, the closely related pronouncement that 'everything' is socially constructed is an implicit admission of the critic's inability or unwillingness to show how *anything* is. In the 1990s, therefore, part of the reaction against deconstruction took the form of a new and widespread historicist fervour in literary studies. Essentially, literary studies made a choice at this point between Derrida and Foucault, and chose the latter.

But Gallagher and Greenblatt, in the book discussed earlier, surprisingly describe the New Historicist approach as 'counter-historicist' – 'the histories one wanted to pursue through the anecdote might, therefore, be called "counter-histories"'' (*Practicing the New Historicism*, p. 52). The 'anecdote' is the 'potted instance' with which many essays of this type begin, and the notion of the anecdote deliberately rehabilitates a despised category of evidence in social and historical studies. This (for the New Historicists themselves) effectively disposes of the frequently heard charge that New Historicism isn't 'proper' history, for that is its whole point – it aims to counter the '*grands récits*' of mainstream history, 'which themselves began as counter-histories', they say (p. 52); hence 'the undisciplined anecdote appealed to those of us who wanted to interrupt the Big Stories' (p. 51). This 'countering' effect of the New Historicists has been very valuable, and their advantage has been that they were often good writers who knew about pace, impact, and appropriate detail, making them unusual as literary critics. Yet, it is odd that the New Historicists have not formulated any term for the 'countering' which they do, not in historical studies, but in literary studies – after all, 'historicism' is a method not of history but of literary studies. Attempting to do so on their behalf, we might say that the most revolutionary aspect of their literary critical practice can be described as a form of 'counter-textualism', whereby the historical anecdote is submitted to the kind of close textual analysis formerly reserved for the literary text. But counter-textualism is a double practice, and its other side is that the literary text itself is let off comparatively lightly, often with little more than a caution, as far as close textual analysis is concerned.

But the New Historicism was not the only kind of historicism which came to the fore in the 1990s. Increasingly, literary studies became dominated during that period by historicist approaches which emphasised the 'historical content' (as I will call it) of the literary text in what seemed a newly restricted way, bringing about a kind of 'internal colonisation' of literary studies. Broad non-literary notions such as 'power', 'culture', 'gender', 'politics', and 'history' began to set the agenda (in the titles of books and conferences), and, as the decade progressed, the literary work itself seemed to become merely the written context of items of historical content narrowly conceived. Thus, texts were trawled for (say) images and representations of Napoleon, or the East, or daughters, invalids, bachelors, teachers, or food (all these being the subjects of monographs on the novel during the period). At the end of the 1990s, a range of broader, more abstract, but still non-literary, concepts became frequent in the titles of articles and books, notions such as 'commerce', 'finance', and 'publicity'. These newly current terms mostly represent a range of concerns which had not previously been of great interest in literary studies, and their prevalence does seem to indicate that literary studies is increasingly less concerned about the literary than about a whole range of other matters. Much of the shift in interest is evident in changing fashions in book titles. For instance, the names of specific plays or playwrights (other than Shakespeare) seem to have been relegated from book titles to chapter titles. Instead, book titles seem to prefer a 'genericist' or 'generalist' approach, for instance mentioning the theatre, viewed as a social institution, and called 'the early modern stage', 'the English theatre', 'the London stage', and so on. The kind of book title which now seems inconceivable would simply name author and work – *Dickens the Novelist*, let's say – as it no longer seems enough for Dickens merely to have been a novelist. Recent books on Dickens tend to have an 'and' in the title, linking his writing with one of the 'cultural institutions', or areas of 'cultural production', which now dominate thinking in English departments, such as the construction of national identity, the representation of empire, or the culture of the stage. Almost the only 'stand-alone' literary topic left seems to be the Gothic, which seems widely regarded as the most important aspect of the literature of the late eighteenth and early nineteenth century period, displacing Romanticism which (following Jerome McGann) is increasingly seen as evading the political issues of its era, while the Gothic is regarded as facing up to them. Hence, a book like *Novel Reading and the Victorian Popular Theatre* (with its chapter on Dickens) would be the late-1990s equivalent of *Dickens the Novelist*. Also no longer imaginable, of course, are those book titles that envisage the act of reading literature as a kind of elevated meditation before a revered object (titles like *The Verbal Icon*, or *The Wheel of Fire*). Titles now are busier and fussier, always reminding us (with that ubiquitous 'and') that literature doesn't exist in that kind of contemplative vacuum at all. Hence, there have been innumerable 'and' books since the late 1990s, and, just as the very title *The Wheel of Fire* conjures up a long-vanished disciplinary past, so in the future these 'and' titles will instantly evoke the flavour of the present era in literary studies – *Samuel Johnson and the Culture of Property*, *George Eliot and Italy*, *Milton and Heresy*, *Henry James and the Culture of Publicity*. Permutating the parts of the title which follow the 'and' will produce books potentially as interesting and important – *Henry James and Italy*, *George Eliot and the Culture of Property*, *Johnson and the Culture of Publicity*. The rise of the 'and' book, then, is one of the indications that, in the late 1990s, historicism became the default way of doing literature.

That emphasis on history was consolidated with the rise of post-colonialism, and was built upon antecedents in the work of Michel Foucault, who had stipulated, in *The Archaeology of Knowledge* (1972), that in the analysis of the discursive field 'we must grasp the statement in the exact specificity of its occurrence'. It built too upon Raymond Williams's emphasis (in *Marxism and Literature*, 1977) on understanding 'the whole lived social process, as practically organized by specific and dominant meanings'. The somewhat intimidatory use of the word 'specific' in such proclamations drove us towards exhaustive historicist study, so that literary scholars became preoccupied by historical method, turning themselves into, if not historians exactly, then at least 'historianists'. By the late 1990s, historicism had (arguably) become the most prevalent form of what Paul de Man had called 'resistance to theory', and it seemed to be taken for granted that only an amateur reader of literature would deny that literature can best be understood through history. Talk of 'exact specificity', and the like, fosters the delusion that, if only we are relentless enough in the archival grind, we will one day recover the past, and again walk the streets of Shakespeare's London, making for the playhouse to see a performance of *Hamlet* (Stephen's intellectual fantasy in the 'Scylla and Charybdis' section of Joyce's *Ulysses*). Further, it's not the mere streets which are to be rescued by historicist archaeology but the mind-set. Hollywood and the Bankside Globe, after all, can give us the *mise en scène*, but it's the *mentalité* which is the Grail of historicists. Herein lies the main distinction between historians and historicists: the former are interested in finite *externals* – events, chiefly, and in what happened and why, who did or said what, and what the consequences were. Historicists, by contrast, are always primarily interested in *internals*, which are conceived as detachable abstractions – an 'identity', a 'mind-set', a mentality, a 'discourse', or, as Raymond Williams puts it in *Marxism and Literature*, 'the whole lived social process, as practically organized by specific and dominant meanings'.

Context – the privileged signifier

As will be evident form the foregoing section, an underlying issue throughout this book is the idea that the demise of the New Critical practice of 'unseen close reading', which solved the problems posed by the bad habit of reading poetry in a vacuum, left us with the opposite problem, that of how to contain and make coherent the potentially limitless ocean of contextual material which poured into the text once the dam of 'the words on the page' had been breached. Indeed, the potential vastness of this contextual field has had the effect of pushing literary criticism and literary theory towards a kind of self-dissolution, indeed, towards a voluntary academic secession in favour of a historicism whose territorial demands on the discipline of literary studies continue to expand This effect (whereby what is literary in literary study becomes the recessive gene, always retreating in the face of the claims made by historicist methods and concerns) is especially marked in the case of Romanticism, which in this respect has followed the lead set by the study of the early modern period, where the effects of the New Historicist revolution were first felt. But the liberating historicism which swept away the arid formalism of the old days has now in its turn become frozen into unexamined dogma and uninterrogated personal practice. For who is to say when the laboriously reconstructed context is 'detailed' and 'specific' enough? Fearful of a return of the Formalist repressed, we cross ourselves with yet more manorial rolls, Acts of Parliament, cases from Probate, lists of early modern household effects, and the like, for our appetite for the non-literary text has become insatiable. We seem to believe in a kind of primitivist magic whereby our understanding of what we deem to be the 'context' of the work will transform itself into the illumination of the literary text. What this enterprise leaves unexamined is, of course, the notion of 'context' itself, which has become the privileged, transcendent signifier of literary studies, universally assumed to be a good thing.

But 'context' is a floating signifier whose hard content is often minimal. The 'detailed historical context' of a given literary work can always be reconstructed in any number of different ways, a truth which the fraudulently singular usage of the word 'context' attempts to disguise. In the course of his polemical exchanges with F.W. Bateson in the 1950s, F.R. Leavis rebuts the contextualising enterprise which was then the emergent position in literary studies and is now the dominant. Bateson, says Leavis, 'starts from the commonplace observation that a poem is in some way related to the world in which it was written. He arrives . . . at the assumption that the way to achieve the correct reading of a poem – of, say, Marvell's or Pope's – is to put it back in its "total context" in that world'. But, he continues, any reader really focused on the poem would see the absurdity of this proposal at once, would see 'that the aim, in fact, is illusory'. He continues:

> What *is* this 'complex of religious, political and economic factors that can be called the social context' . . . How does one set to work to arrive at this final inclusive context, the establishment of which puts the poem back in 'its original historical setting', so that 'the human experience in it begins to be realised and re-enacted by the reader'?[6]

This posited totality, in Leavis's view, is an illusion, which will never amount to more than 'random notes from his [the critic's] historical reading'. Current debates have not gone beyond this; con*text* is always con*struct*, rather than something determinate (unlike the poem, says Leavis, which is 'something indubitably *there*'). The constructedness of all knowledge is something which the literary theory of the 1970s and 1980s surely taught (or re-taught) us, and, in wanting to problematise contextualism, I try to stay in touch with that new theoretical dawn of the 1970s. For theory at that time proclaimed the end of period specialism and announced a new 'democratic' age in which we would work as equals on newly theorised readings of literary texts. In this regard, the theory revolution made pedagogic sense, just as the earlier Cambridge revolution in literary studies had done, for, instead of being disenfranchised by their lack of literary history and period knowledge, students would be empowered, as close-readers had been, by their possession of a rudimentary theoretical tool-kit. In that sense, 'theory' made for pedagogic egalitarianism. It was a kind of battleship *Dreadnought* which, at a stroke, rendered all previous approaches to literature obsolete, including those of the professors, whose vast arsenals of literary-historical knowledge were suddenly worthless, so that they too had to begin again to re-equip themselves. By contrast, history, in literary studies, is always a disempowering force. Even at the graduate seminar, or the high-level international conference, virtually all participants will be effectively silenced and disenfranchised by one of these '*petit narrative*' papers, for how many in the room will feel themselves able to contribute, without exposing their ignorance, to discussion of a paper whose main focus is (say) nineteenth-century forensic science or Victorian property laws? Context is only ever a postulate, and the more you try to delineate it (getting away from that insulting charge of 'randomness') the more you are really just doing what Leavis says Bateson did – 'the wider he goes in his ambition to construct it from his readings in the period, the more it is *his* construction'.

'Deep' context

A suggested earlier, Leavis's view that context can never be definitively delimited is curiously similar to Derrida's beliefs on context. Leavis's 'words on the page' approach sees the poem as disembodied from everything which is *not* on the page: Derrida, likewise, when he tells us that there is nothing outside the text, isolates the text from everything it is not. Of course, a universe of dispute now surrounds the Derridean concept of the '*hors-texte*' outside of which there is nothing. In *The Ethics of Deconstruction* Simon Critchley quotes the 'Afterword' to Derrida's *Limited Inc.* where Derrida says (in effect, and of course less succinctly than this) that contexts can be opened, but they cannot be closed, that it is of the nature of context to be indeterminate:

> The structure thus described supposes that there are only contexts, that nothing *exists* outside context [*qu'il existe rien hors contexte*], as I have often said, but also that the limit of the frame or the border of the context always entails a clause of *non-closure* [*non-fermeture*]. The outside penetrates and thus determines the inside. (Critchley, p. 32)

Derrida here revises his original saying: whereas before there was nothing outside the text, now there is nothing outside the context ('nothing *exists* outside context'). Critchley chooses to see this as the 'ethical moment' in Derrida's thinking, and one can see what he means: whereas the older formulation suspends the text in a biosphere of its own, the revised form denies the possibility of any such insulation.

One of the distinctions which I am seeking to make is between the context which exerts a 'pressure' on the text, as if demanding consideration, and the context whose presence has to be willed into being by the specialist critic. The kind of context we should be interested in, then, is not 'broad context' but this kind that exerts a palpable pressure, which can also be called 'deep context'. And our aim should be to identify and activate *deep* contexts rather than *broad* ones, the deep variety being the kind which, in addition to the pressure they exert, have specific textual warrant *and are unique to the specific work of literature under discussion*. I will use an extended literary example to illustrate what I mean by 'deep context' and the pressure it exerts on content.

Edmund Spenser's *Amoretti* sonnet sequence uses the elevated rhetoric of Petrarchan convention, employing metaphors derived from contemporary warfare – battles, sieges, bombardments, and the like – to convey the devastating effect his beloved has on her admirer – the darts from her bright eyes pierce and wound the observer, sapping his will to resist, till he is overcome and sues for peace. But as soon as a truce is entered into, she disregards the terms of the treaty, and binds him into perpetual enslavement, so that he realises the truce was just a trap. The hyperbole is rich and sonorous, and, in spite of the deep-down rhetorical conventionality of this kind of poetry, the effect is moving, and the quaint-seeming antique spellings seem to reinforce it:

12

One day I sought with her hart-thrilling eies,
to make a truce and termes to entertaine:
all fearlesse then of so false enimies,
which sought me to entrap in treasons traine.
So as I then disarmed did remaine,
a wicked ambush which lay hidden long
in the close couert of her guilefull eyen,
thence breaking forth did thick about me throng,
Too feeble I t'abide the brunt so strong,
was forst to yeeld my selfe into their hands:
who me captiuing streight with rigorous wrong,
haue euer since me kept in cruell bands.
So Ladie now to you I doo complaine,
against your eies that iustice I may gaine.

The literary context is the tradition of hyperbolic Petrarchanism which 'licenses' rhetorical excess of this particular kind, and being aware of that context is an essential element in reading poems like this. But there is another context, for the writer is the Edmund Spenser who held the office of Secretary to Lord Grey de Wilton, Lord Deputy of Ireland, with whom he arrived there in August 1580 as part of a retinue of thirty. For a Cambridge-educated, but relatively poor, young man like Spenser, serving as Secretary to a member of the ruling class was the surest way to advancement, and Ireland offered the chance of considerably accelerating the process. But being a Secretary was not at that time a safe office job, but involved being in the thick of things. Richard Rambuss writes:

> It is quite likely, then, that Spenser was in attendance on his master during Lord Grey's infamous military assault on an enemy fortification at Smerwick. After the surviving garrison of 600 Spanish and Italian papal troops surrendered to Grey on the sole condition that their lives be spared, he summarily ordered them all executed. As Grey's secretary, Spenser scripted the official narrative of the Lord Deputy's victory and the massacre that followed in a letter he penned on 12 November 1580 from Grey to the Queen, and in another on 28 November from Grey to Lord Burghley. As a poet, Spenser approvingly retells the event in allegorical form in Book v, canto xii of *The Faerie Queene*.[7]

He defends it again in *A View of the Present State of Ireland*, and was a beneficiary of this action, in the sense that 'the land which was confiscated as a result of the Desmond Rebellion (1579–83) – of which the massacre at Smerwick was a significant incident – went to establish the Munster Plantation after 1584, where Spenser made his fortune'.[8] The massacre of those who had surrendered was not an accepted act of war, and Grey's action, and the extreme anti-Catholicism which seems to have motivated it, were seen as making the situation in Ireland worse, leading eventually to his being recalled. That Spenser should defend the action as the right policy, in spite of its cruelty, is not in itself anomalous or surprising, nor would it be even if he had not benefited from the campaign, but it is impossible not to be puzzled that he still found himself able to use notions of siege, surrender, and a broken treaty as a source of imagery in a sequence of courtship sonnets. Indeed, the contextual juxtaposition is so striking that, once it is known about, the sonnet becomes difficult to read. For the elegant variations on the notion of 'a truce and termes' which turn out to have been a treacherous entrapment of a 'disarmed' enemy are not (or not just) the fanciful, rhetorical word-spinning of a sophisticated scholar poet but the words of someone who had actually seen this done in real life, and had been to some degree complicit in the ensuing slaughter. For all we know, he had heard the screams and put in hand the arrangements for disposing of the bodies. It is difficult to imagine a modern parallel, but perhaps a modern love poem containing lines that described love as hitting the speaker 'like a bullet in the head', and written by a poet who had taken part in, or witnessed, acts of ethnic cleansing or genocidal slaughter might fit the bill. How would (or could) we read such a poem? What could cleanse the stench of ethnic cleansing from the words of that poem, and enable us to read it as literature? Time? Distance? Differences of sensibility and verbal convention? Or nothing at all?

Modern writers, of course, would not have made the juxtaposition of love and warfare in such graphic terms, no matter how personally depraved they might have been: such juxtapositions, if made at all (for instance, as in Sylvia Plath's juxtaposition of images of holocaust with aspects of her own personal life), would be made with an awareness of the provocative affront they offer to cultural sensibilities. But Spenser doesn't write in that way, and there is no sense of any awareness that norms of expression or decency being challenged. The juxtaposition confronts us with the kind of conceptual difficulty which George Steiner (in *On Difficulty*, 1978) calls 'Modal', this being the kind in which we have 'understanding [of basic terms and data], but no genuine comprehension', the kind in which 'the order of difficulty is not removed by clarification of word and phrase [because] it functions centrally'. For my purposes here, what is clear, though, is that Spenser's involvement in the Smerwick massacre is the *deep* context of Sonnet 12: adducing it is simply not the same as evoking the *broad* context of the colonisation of sixteenth-century Ireland. What is used as a metaphor in the poem was a brutal fact of the author's direct experience, and most readers, surely, couldn't ignore the link even if they wanted to. While we may be generally happy to accept a separation between 'the man who suffers' and the 'poet who creates', as the Eliot of 'The Dissociation of Sensibility' essay wanted us to do, it is not so easy to allow the same separation between the man who *inflicts* suffering and the poet who creates.

Contexts, to reiterate, are always plural, always a choice, and always a construct. When we say that we believe in studying literature in context, the statement is a meaningless piety unless we go on to say *which* contexts we mean and why we have chosen and constructed those ones rather than others. There are broad contexts and deep contexts, and, while the former tend to engulf the text and rob it of its individuality, making our literary studies more and more indistinguishable from historical studies, deep contexts are unique to the work in question, and have a 'warranty' or 'trigger' within the text, so that it becomes possible to assert that deep context is actually part of content.

What does it mean to say 'There is nothing outside the text'?

Returning, now, to Critchley's commentary on the notion of context: Critchley also identifies a much more familiar sense of the word 'context': 'Opening a dictionary, one might define context as those parts of a discourse which immediately precede or follow any particular passage or text and which can determine its meaning' (p. 32). This notion of 'context' is the one which operated in old-fashioned examination questions in which students were asked to consider a given speech from a Shakespeare play 'in context', which would involve saying what comes immediately before and immediately after, and what stage in the overall progress of the action has been reached at this point. Certain phrases in the speech, for instance, might be rendered ironic in view of earlier events, or might gain a retrospective element of irony in the light of subsequent events. When public figures in the news complain that their remarks have been quoted 'out of context' they nearly always seem to mean context in this sense: the phrase which the news reports quoted in isolation from the remainder of what was said in the speech is (they claim) misleading or apparently sensationalist – it lacks the qualifications, or the subtleties of emphasis, which this circumambient context would supply. All the same, 'context' in this sense is surely part of text – context here is content in the simple, literal sense, for the underlying idea of an *internal context* is really a contradiction in terms. Context is only such when it is some way *outside* the text as a whole, not just outside one quoted extract from it, no matter how familiar the above usage has become to us. Undoubtedly the act of quoting from a text (removing a part of the text from the rest of the text) brings into play a notion of *internal* context, or intra-textual context, which is distinguishable from the vast realm of *external*, or extra-textual context which the word context normally designates. Perhaps the politician who is quoted 'out of context' often has in mind some combination of the two – for example, that what was said in the same speech before and after what was quoted softens or balances the emphasis of the quoted bits – but also that the fact that the speech was being made to a specific audience in specific circumstances, which would help to explain the emphasis of the form of words chosen, and mitigate the apparent harshness. Anyway, my point here is simply to emphasise that I don't consider that internal context counts as part of context in the sense in question here, and consequently I have disregarded it in the present book.

As Critchley's discussion makes clear, a deconstructive approach to textuality has no option but to dissolve the text/context dichotomy into the endless flicker of difference/*différance*, since that is what it does to *all* distinctions. The sometime excitement of this once radical ploy has long since declined. Critchley goes on to cite Derrida offering 'one possible definition of deconstruction', using the notion of context as something which cannot be limited or closed, and describing deconstruction as 'the effort to take this limitless context into account *(la prise en compte de ce contexte sans bord)* . . . He then proceeds to redefine the axial proposition of deconstructive method . . . namely "*Il n'y a pas de hors-text*" . . . as "*Il n'y a pas de hors contexte*" ' (p. 39). The move is needed, he says, because the original word 'text' may be understood empirically, and thereby reduce the dictum to a 'refutable slogan', which of course (in his view) would never do. In my view, reducing it to a 'refutable slogan' would be an excellent thing to do, but then, it isn't really necessary, for it already is a slogan, and it is certainly refutable. The only way to make it irrefutable is to deny that it means anything definite at all, as Critchley effectively does. He reiterates, all the same, that 'the text is not the book', but denies that this generalising of the notion of 'text' is an attempt to 'turn the world into some vast library; nor does it wish to cut off reference to some "extra-textual realm" ' (p. 39). But what, then, *is* it an attempt to do? It certainly sounds as if this idea of the text not being the book is trying to textualise the whole of circumambient reality. It's like a fridge with the door left open, which immediately sets about the task of freezing the whole world down to its own internal temperature.

Derrida and his exponents now assure us that the originating slogan about there being nothing outside the text means something much more sophisticated than, they suppose, we had naively supposed: it 'does not mean that all referents are suspended, denied, or enclosed in a book, as people have claimed, or have been naïve enough to believe and to have accused me of believing' (Derrida, quoted by Critchley, p. 39). So, again, what *does* it mean then? He goes on:

> But it does mean that every referent and all reality has the structure of a différantial trace (*d'une trace différantielle*), and that one cannot refer to this 'real' except in an interpretative experience.

Well, let us try to see what this statement can mean. As it is about 'all reality', it would have to include the experience of, let's say, accidently banging one's knee on the door, an event which Derrida's formulation would require us to see as having 'the structure of a differential trace', which we would not be able to refer to as 'real' and would be required to see as an 'interpretative experience'. In what sense, then, is this *not* suspending or denying referents, *not* enclosing them in a book? In so

far as any significant meaning at all can be extracted from the formulation, we might see the event of banging one's knee on a door as
the product of the differential trace which distinguishes the state of
not being in pain from the state of being in pain, each being mutually
defined by its opposite, and each doubtless culturally conditioned to
some extent. But seeing *everything* as composed of differential traces
in that way (*'every referent and all reality'*, remember – my italics and
my exasperation) is like putting on a pair of orange-tinted glasses and
then endlessly proclaiming the fact that the world is orange. It would
be as logical to see the operations of (say) divine providence in everything ('God made me bump into that door in order to give me the
opportunity to exert self-control and not react by swearing, thereby
helping me to accumulate more divine grace'). Or we could see the
processes of the Freudian subconscious in the event ('I "accidentally"
bumped into that door to punish myself for acts of self-indulgence which
I now guiltily regret').

Critchley works hard to salvage something from Derrida's dissolving of text into context; for him (writing about ethics and deconstruction)
the crucial point about the Derridean shift from text to context is
that 'context contains a clause of non-closure'. The dissolution of the
one into the other is the ethical moment of affirmation, a 'Yes-saying
to the unnameable, a moment of unconditional affirmation that is
addressed to an alterity that can neither be excluded from nor included
within logocentric conceptuality' (p. 41). My own position, again, is
firstly to note the affinity between Leavis and Derrida, in that both
affirm that context is necessarily open-ended (a fact which Leavis,
of course, deplores and Derrida applauds). The gesture of embracing
'context' in the broad sense is always, in literary studies, a gesture of
claiming the moral high ground, and asserting one's ethical superiority over the textualists. Context colonises every corner of the textual
mansion and transforms it, sometimes, like floodwater, threatening to
sweep it away altogether. It is that kind of *limitless* context which is at
issue here.

The three points I wish to emphasise from this discussion of
Critchley's discussion of Derrida on context are these: firstly, the
notion of 'context' which sees it merely as intention has to be rejected
as inadequate; secondly, we have noted Derrida's alignment with
Leavis on the matter of how content is uncontainable and indeterminate and will always spill out and defy limitation – Leavis sees this
as a problem, while Derrida celebrates it as a (dis)solution; and,
thirdly, the notion of there being nothing outside the text (or the context) has to be countered, since otherwise a limitless domain of 'broad

context' is brought into play, with similar consequences to those which follow from the widespread acceptance of 'textual virtuality' as our object of study.

Notes

1 As an undergraduate I spent a great deal of time studying the text of *King Lear*. I now understand that Shakespeare never wrote any such play, and that I was studying a modern conflation of two texts, the Quarto *Historie of King Lear* and the Folio *Tragedie of King Lear*: see Graham Holderness 'Texts and Contexts: *King Lear*', chapter 5 in *Textual Shakespeare: Writing and the Word* is (University of Hertfordshire Press, 2003).

2 Derrida uses a word '*sous rature*' (under erasure) when it is printed on the page legibly, but crossed out. He does this (following a precedent set by Heidegger) when he regards the word or concept as invalid, but feels obliged to use it anyway. The device distances the user from normative usage of the word, and signals scepticism about its validity, just as speakers do when they signal that they are using a particular word in inverted commas. My device of doubled inverted commas is intended to signify not a bluff confidence in the generally accepted meaning of the word or concept but scepticism about the grounds for, or usefulness of, expressing scepticism in this manner.

3 In the essay 'Word, Dialog and Novel'; see *The Kristeva Reader*, ed. Toril Moi (Columbia University Press, 1986), pp. 34–61.

4 Mary Orr, *Intertextuality: Debates and Contexts* (Polity, 2003), p. 22, my italics. See the opening chapter, 'Intertextuality', for a brilliant exposition of the provenance and influence of notions of intertextuality.

5 But the veneer of North American historicism can sometimes seem a little thin. The section of James Chandler's *England in 1819* entitled 'The Week when Keats Wrote *To Autumn*' (pp. 425–32) reconstructs the week in question with an accumulation of small errors that collectively somewhat undermine the reader's confidence. Thus, the Winchester walk of Saturday 18 September 1819, which Keats describes in his letter to his brother George and Georgina, takes him, says Chandler (p. 426) 'past Westminster College', presumably meaning Winchester College, the error probably arising from the mention of Dilke's son at Westminster College (in London) a couple of pages earlier in the Winchester letter. The walk continues 'through the Abbey of St Croix', says Chandler (actually St Cross, then and now), 'and on to the sallows of the River Itchin' (actually Itchen). Keats had come to Winchester from the Isle of Wight (where he had been staying with Charles Brown), a place which Chandler seems to think was unpopulated in 1819 ('the unpopulated Isle of Wight', he calls it, p. 428). Perhaps he imagines this because Keats opens the letter by saying that he had come to Winchester from Shanklin (on the Isle of Wight) 'for the convenience of a library'.

6 See Leavis's essay 'The Responsible Critic or the Function of Criticism at any Time', *Scrutiny* (1953), vol. 19, pp. 173–4. The essay, with Bateson's response, is also in Leavis's compilation *A Selection from Scrutiny* (Cambridge, 1968), vol. 2, from p. 301.

7 Richard Rambuss, 'Spenser's Life and Career', pp. 13–36 in *The Cambridge Companion to Spenser*, ed. Andrew Hadfield (Cambridge University Press, 2001). This is the source of my Spenserian details here.

8 Andrew Hadfield in *Edmund Spenser's Irish Experience: Wilde Fruit and Salvage Soyl* (Clarendon Press, 1997), p. 18.

2

Contextuality contested

Cambridge and context

The key notion of historicist study has been the denial of the idea that the literary text is the 'foreground' which is to be studied against the 'background' of the history, sociology, and culture of its period. The 'privileges' of the literary text have been removed, and refusing this hierarchical binarism is the hallmark and essence of contemporary literary historicism. This is made explicit in the blurb to the influential 'Cambridge Studies in Nineteenth-Century Literature and Culture' series; the relevant sentences are worth quoting in full:

> In recent years theoretical changes and historiographical shifts have unsettled the assumptions of previous scholarly syntheses and called into question the terms of older debates. Whereas the tendency in much past literary critical interpretation was to use the metaphor of culture as 'background', feminist, Foucauldian, and other analyses have employed more dynamic models that raise questions of power and of circulation. Such developments have reanimated the field.

I want to critique this statement fairly closely, even though it is not the kind of material usually subjected to such attention (and indeed it seems not to have been drafted in anticipation of any close scrutiny at all). Firstly, taking the foreground/background distinction as invariably equivalent to a distinction between major and minor elements makes little sense. Hence, an academic choosing to study (say) Shakespeare's *Richard II* rather than Elizabethan anxieties about the succession is simply making a choice of what should be the primary object of professional attention, rather than putting forward a general assertion that, in culture, literature is always more important than 'visual arts, politics, social organization, economic life, technical innovations, scientific thought', that is, than all the things mentioned earlier in the

Cambridge blurb as the new foci of attention. If the series editors really believed in the equality of all these cultural spheres, then the members of the Editorial Board listed above the blurb would not all be Professors of English, engaged in tilling these 'rich fields for inter-disciplinary studies' without the aid of anybody who actually professes them. What is happening, then, is a unilateral extension of the empire of English, rather than any genuine interdisciplinary engagement. Just as it takes two to tango, so it takes at least two consenting academic disciplines to produce interdisciplinarity, and the other disciplines just aren't there.

But the keyword in the Cambridge blurb is probably 'circulation': the 'circulation' model implies that ideas and practices suffuse the totality of culture – literature, law, government, religion, and so on – rather than remaining confined within literature. Once the notion of 'circulation' is accepted, it follows that a work of literature can only ever be *part* of the picture, and hence that no true understanding (even of literature) can be had by studying literature alone. But if a true state of inter-disciplinarity actually existed, there would be historians maintaining that history cannot be understood without the simultaneous study of liter-ature. Where are they? Only literary studies (with our long-standing habit of embracing extreme statements of intent and attempting to live by them) has set the study of the *totality* of culture as its goal. Thus, the 'foreground' of study becomes the totality of 'culture in its broadest sense', and literature becomes part of the open field territory in which broad cultural ideas can be detected – the ideas which, as suggested in the previous chapter, are recurrent now in the titles of so many books in the field – 'empire', 'nationhood', 'technology', 'advoc-acy', 'domesticity', 'disease', 'masculinity', 'materialism', 'psychology', 'publicity', and so on.

However, one of the apparent advantages of applying this idea of 'circulation' to literature is that it enables an avoidance of both 'extreme active' and 'extreme passive' notions of literature and authorship. The 'extreme active' concept is the view that authors *invent* meanings and ideas, as in the 'transcendent' notions of literature which supposedly typified liberal humanism: on this view, literature is able to rise 'above' society. In the 'extreme passive' notion of authorship, by contrast, sup-posedly typical of unsophisticated forms of Marxism, literary content can do nothing but *passively reflect* the author's class position, and the socio-economic conditions by which it is determined. The idea of 'circulation' promisingly seems to avoid both extremes; literature is one of the many cultural forms by means of which ideas move through culture. It will nearly always be difficult to say where an idea originates,

and such knowledge, even if it were attainable, would be of less interest than an understanding of the processes by which it is taken up,
developed, refined, given currency, tested, put into practice, becomes
dominant, begins to decline, becomes merely residual, and eventually
is either revived and transformed or simply fades into extinction. Thus,
the 'circulation' model sees authorship neither as 'active' nor 'passive'
but as part of a process – it's a 'processual' model of writing that we
are offered by this concept of culture as circulation. The processual
model is, on the whole, a good thing, but it comes at a very high price,
for we have to accept along with it a view of culture (culture as a seam-
less garment) which ostracises the only kind of focus which is attainable within the restricted length of a postgraduate or undergraduate
course (or, for that matter, within the restrictions of a sabbatical term
overshadowed by the pressures of the Research Assessment Exercise)
and substitutes an ambitiously broad, culturally diffused form of study
which is a voracious consumer of institutional, financial, scholarly, and
human resources.

As the notion of the circle (the root of the word 'circulation') would
imply, the extent of the various areas (legal, literary, social, historical,
religious, etc.) demanding study in these diffused approaches to culture entails the need for a training in multiple disciplines. A scholar
who might be considered properly equipped for the task would need
an elite schooling, followed by undergraduate and postgraduate years
at a top university; then a couple of postdoctoral fellowships, followed
by a career pattern of frequent sabbaticals, minimal teaching, with
fellowships, and travel grants – that is just the going rate. It isn't
otherwise realistic to expect the kind of multi-competencies which alone
can sustain the ideal of culturally diffuse scholarship. In other words,
'full-on' interdisciplinary contextualism makes demands on our collective
scholarly resources which seem to be (as we might consider calling it)
ecologically unsound.

The cultural spheres to be studied in contextually oriented English
departments (that is, again, the essential quintet of areas – legal,
literary, social, historical, and religious) are not to be arranged into a
hierarchy, but all must have equal status, with no one sector being
'privileged'. This word 'privileged' is, of course, itself a metaphor with
a high emotional charge: effectively, what it says to us is that regarding literature as 'special', and 'foregrounding' it for our particular professional attention, is like sanctioning the privileges of an aristocracy
and supporting an elitist world view in which some groups are more
equal than others. The democratic and egalitarian way (the emotional
blackmail continues) is to regard *all* cultural sectors as equally worthy

of our attention. This is how we come to the point where books accepted for publication by editorial boards made up of eminent professors of literature are sometimes about Victorian tastes in domestic furnishings, copiously illustrated from contemporary shop and trade catalogues. It is undeniably interesting, but it isn't literary studies.

'Circulation', then, emphasises interconnections between various aspects of culture, with some good effects and some bad ones, but within the field of literature its effect is to introduce whole new layers of discontinuity: in a book entitled (to take a hypothetical instance) *George Eliot and the Culture of Medical Practice*, the declared subject necessarily separates novels by this author which feature representations of doctors and medical science (*Middlemarch*, for instance) from all the rest. The circulation which is cut off by the emphasis on notions of circulation is that between this novel and all the rest in the author's *oeuvre*. Whereas another hypothetical title like (say) *George Eliot and the Novelist's Craft* would require treatment of all the author's novels within the frame of some continuous narrative or theme (such as a notion of developing expertise, increasing diversification, or gradual decline), the 'commodity' or 'concept' titles which are now commonplace do not allow this, and enjoin a random slicing into the *oeuvre* at the whim of an overarching cultural concept from outside it. Precisely what literature cannot be allowed, within this approach, is the integrity implied by considering the literary work as an integral figure on a ground, as opposed to a series of dispersed fragments embedded in some always-more-important 'commodity' narrative about finance, or the legal system, or changing notions of governance. The Cambridge blurb, then, represents a strange surrender on the part of literary studies of its place in the academic community of independent disciplines.

Context and undergraduate English

In the late 1990s a number of influential works on the undergraduate teaching of English offered working definitions of the key terms 'text', 'context', and 'intertext', and these working definitions arguably achieve a much greater currency and influence than either 'philosophical' definitions of the kind put forward by Critchley, or even the kind of 'position' statements exemplified by the Cambridge blurb just considered. Hence, getting a broad sense of the discipline's current 'take' on the matter of context requires some consideration of these practice-led, rather than research-led, definitions.

One key set of definitions can be found in Rob Pope's widely used foundation text *The English Studies Book* (1998). Pope begins the

relevant section by offering two definitions of 'text': the first regards
text as simply 'recorded language', irrespective of the form the recording takes (whether it be writing, print, sound-recording, and so on),
seeing it as essentially any premeditated utterance which is made per-
manently available through some medium of recording, as distinct
from 'spontaneous speech and conversation' (p. 234), which usually
disappears as soon as spoken. By this definition, visual images from a
silent film, say, or a piece of sculpture, could not be called texts. The
second definition makes the notion of textuality much broader in
scope, seeing a text as 'a cultural object produced by people, rather
than a natural object untouched by human hand or mind' (p. 235).
By this definition, texts might be 'everything from poems, adverts
and films to paintings, photos, shopping malls and whole cityscapes'.
But the term 'cultural object' in the definition is problematical: for
instance, is a railway engine, or a suspension bridge, a cultural object?
Perhaps such artefacts are so when they achieve some kind of 'iconic'
status, like the streamlined, record-breaking *Mallard* steam locomotive
of the 1930s, which became an 'icon' of period style. But even the
humble shunting engine *means* something as well as *doing* something:
indeed, we might say that the *culturality* of such artefacts may be
defined as those attributes which remain when its *functionality* has been
deducted. If so, then everything 'produced by people' must to some
extent be a text, rendering the definition pretty well useless for practical purposes. On the other hand, if engines and bridges are *not*
cultural objects, then Pope would need to explain the difference in this
regard between a railway engine or a bridge, on the one hand, and a
shopping mall, on the other. But in any case, Pope rejects this own
definition, on the grounds that 'if virtually everything is a text, the concept has no analytical power at all'. This throws him back on his first
definition, but that, remember, is one which denies textuality to films
and advertisements, and therefore seems at odds with widespread
contemporary usage. Structural and semiotic analysis, for instance, pre-
suppose the existence of non-verbal forms of textuality, and structuralist
founding texts like Barthes's *Mythologies* put forward precisely this
expanded notion of textuality, by analysing advertisements, packaging,
film images, and so on, in a very illuminating manner. Pope, then,
offers one definition of text which is too narrow, and another which is
too broad.

He goes on, however, to seek to establish distinctions within the triad
of text, context, and intertext. His position might be called 'trinitar-
ian' rather than merely 'triadic', for he posits 'intrinsic and possibly
inextricable relations' amongst these three concepts, on the grounds

that their common root – 'text' – suggests essential defining attributes held in common between them. Since the Latin source of this word, he says, is *texere*, meaning to weave, and the noun *textus* meaning 'tissue', 'weaving', or 'web', then perhaps texts should be looked at as 'intermittent and extensible structures formed by a weaving together of strands.' But structures which are 'intermittent and extensible' already seem to have escaped the web of definition, and the tone becomes increasingly theological, as he goes on to argue as follows:

> Texts are wholes full of holes: always apparently somewhere and at the same time both everywhere and nowhere. In fact, the harder and closer you look *at* a text (paper or electronic), the more you find yourself looking *through, round* and *beyond* it. Its presence always implies and in a sense requires its absences. (p. 235)

But it is, surely, better to avoid falling back on quasi-religious formulations like these in literary studies, at least for as long as possible. Given that the dominant influence of deconstruction over two decades has been founded on such formulations, we have perhaps had enough for the time being. (Deconstruction's closest analogues are with rabbinical exegesis of the Torah, rather than Christian theology and devotional mysticism, but there are close parallels between these aspects of the two traditions.) Hence, when Pope begins to sound mystical ('Like a bell, it rings out by virtue of the space where it is not', p. 235) we might wish to be cautious. Of course, no one would dispute that texts which are 'set' for study on academic courses are far from 'solid and immovable'. Obviously, they were set *by* somebody, and for specific reasons, and both they and the reasons may change in the future. All the same, in spite of the emphasis on holes and absences and inextricable relations, we base our courses, precisely, on set *texts*, not on set *con*texts or set *inter*texts, so it must be possible to come up with some non-theological definition of what texts are. Doing so does not imply any naive conception of textuality (that it is all wholes and presences, for instance). No matter how difficult a problem in literary studies might turn out to be, let's set out with the aim of explaining it in the simplest possible way. For there are obviously a number of ways in which it is actually quite easy to extricate the relations between text, context, and intertext, but, if we start by assuming that they are inextricable, then we have made a fatal concession, and may quickly find ourselves spending most of our time reading and writing history, and we will be back in the realm of textual virtuality.

When he comes to context (the second item in his text-context-intertext set), Pope sees 'four kinds of interrelated context', each of which I want to query, in order to illustrate the kind of difficulty which is built into the very notion of 'context'. The first kind is context meaning the 'immediate situation' – 'whenever and wherever you are reading this book, a particular course'. It is clear, surely, that this kind of context is entirely contingent and elective, rather than in any sense 'set'. And yet Pope doesn't use this kind of language about it: while he is keen to emphasise that *texts* are not 'solid and immovable', he seems happy to present *context* as if it were. But the definition is extremely permeable: what can 'situation' mean here, and what aspects of situation are 'immediate'? For instance (on the 'whenever' and 'wherever'), if I am reading this book on 4 July, or on Christmas Day, or on the Great Wall of China, is that part of the context? Whether this question is answered positively or negatively, the implications for this 'immediate situation' model of context seem serious. If the 'immediate situation' is the course for which a given book is a 'set text', *then* what? Isn't the place of that course in the whole process of my education also significant? And what of my gender and my social-class position? Are they part of it too? My point is, firstly, that it seems impossible to decide where the 'immediate' part of our 'situation' ends and the rest of it begins, and, secondly, that it also seems impossible to decide where to stop in constructing this kind of context; for instance, if the fact that I am taking English Module 106 is part of the 'immediate situation', is the fact that I am a white man taking it part of its context too?

Pope might want to say that all *that* (gender, race, and so on) is part of his second contextual element, '*context meaning larger cultural frame of reference*, e.g. the society, language community, and general historical moment in which that reading is taking place' (p. 235). Again, though, this leaves a lot of constructing to do, making again the point that every con*text* is also a con*struct*. Notice, for example, that the 'historical moment' entailed here is something 'general', not any specific event (like the Peterloo Massacre of 1819 as the context of Shelley's *The Mask of Anarchy*). As its paradoxical designation would imply, a '*general* historical moment' might be reconstructed in any number of ways, to say nothing of the 'larger cultural frame of reference' – 'larger than what?' we might start by asking. Further, the breadth of the definition of context here (which takes in 'society', 'language', 'history', surely making us wonder what *isn't* context) seems to place it beyond the analytical reach of any conceivable academic competence, for we would need textual/contextual coroners with multidisciplinary qualifications to engage in such work, and they do not exist. To provide them, we would need to set up a double qualification system, with undergraduate degrees in both English and history, followed by the interdisciplinary investigation of a topic at doctoral level, and even this would leave out the sociological and linguistic elements.

The third envisaged strand of contextuality (*'contexts of (re)production*, e.g. when, where and by whom this book was sketched, drafted, read, redrafted, edited, published') has the problems of the first two combined, plus the fact that there will hardly ever be any adequate known route to or source of this kind of information. The fourth sub-category (*'contexts of reception*, e.g., who uses it when, where, how and why') is also problematical – it is difficult to distinguish from the first sub-category, for instance, and again it seems to lie beyond the scope of any kind of empirical investigation. Doubtless there can be rhetorical speculation (of a kind now very familiar in literary theory) about such matters as who uses a book and when and why they do so, but to what end, I wonder, except to reinforce the assumptions the researcher set out with? This whole approach to context, therefore, merely shows how ill-examined and ill-conceived the very notion of context usually is. The problem with the approach can be simply stated, which is that, as with all notions of context, it is impossible to be confident that contextual investigations along the four avenues indicated by the critic would turn up matters which are *specific* to the text under investigation – in my terms, these versions of context all seem inherently 'broad', leading to open-ended historical study.

However, Pope's treatment of the third element of his trinity, which is the notion of intertextuality, is extremely useful and suggestive; he defines it broadly as 'the relation between one text and another', distinguishing three kinds: explicit, implied, and inferred. The first kind 'comprises all other texts that are overtly referred to and all the specific sources that the writer has demonstrably drawn upon' (p. 236). The example given is Eliot's *The Waste Land*, with its 'unnotated references' and 'acknowledged debts'. The second kind (implied intertextuality) 'comprises all those passing allusions to other texts (including texts in the same genre) and all those effects (especially ironic and satiric) which seem to have been deliberately contrived by the writer so as to be picked up by the alert and similarly informed reader' (p. 236). The example used is again from *The Waste Land*, where the opening line 'April is the cruellest month' is an ironic inversion of the first line of Chaucer's *General Prologue*, in which the *'shoures soote'* of April have connotations of softness and ease, in contrast to the 'cruelty' of winter conditions. In both cases (that is, explicit and implied intertextuality), what could be said would necessarily be *specific to the text under investigation* – a cardinal principle of value in literary enquiry – and both concepts therefore seem sound.

The third sub-category is somewhat more general; '*Inferred intertext-uality*' refers to all those texts which actual readers draw on to help their understanding of the text in hand. These need not have been in the writer's mind – or even existed at the time' (p. 236). The example given concerns the way we might compare the fragmentary collage effects of *The Waste Land* with Cubist or Surrealist art, or contrast them with 'analogous postmodern techniques in TV advertising and pop videos'. The remaining example of inferred intertextuality is that of reading *The Waste Land* through Eliot's own essay-writing on Shakespeare, that is, to 'other words and images in the immediate vicinity of the text' (p. 235). 'Inferred intertextuality', then, is a particularly useful concept, and my chapter on Hemans, later, can be seen as a demonstration of the use of inferred intertextuality as part of the critical process.

Notions of intertextuality

Another prominent discussion of matters related to contextuality is found in Graham Allen's *Intertextuality* in the 'New Critical Idiom' series (2000), particularly the parts of the book in which Allen engages with Gérard Genette's ideas about intertextuality. Genette's approach has remained resolutely Structuralist, right through to our post-post-structuralist age. For him there is a literary 'system' or *langue* which is always the ultimate object of investigation, and the individual literary work is a *parole* which can only be properly understood within that dyadic rela-tionsip, just as the remark 'Hello, how are you?' is an utterance (a *parole*) which makes sense only within the generating 'context' of the English language. As a non-native speaker you might learn to cope with this utterance, and even learn how to respond to it correctly (you might learn to do so by using a phrase book, for instance), but this does not alter the fact of the complete dependency of this phrase on the larger structural-linguistic entity, and it is clear that learning to get by with a phrase book is a very impoverished and limited achievement in com-parison with actually learning English. Genette's attitudes are precisely like this: for him, the goal and the achievement is always that of learn-ing 'literariness' itself, and in comparison with that, merely being able to cope with *Jane Eyre* in order to answer exam questions on it, write books about it, or just enjoy a quiet night in with it, is very much a lesser achievement, something rather at the phrase book level. Genette, then, would agree with many historicist-leaning contemporary critics and theorists that literary works can be understood only in context, but with the difference that for him the context is itself literary, rather than socio-historical. He is not interested in moving on to the theorisation of a non-literary context, and in that sense he is a true structuralist, one who never followed the flowing of the 1970s tide into post-structuralism, continuing instead to regard the literary system as a complex, self-sufficient internal economy. An 'Anglo-American' take on his work would be to say that his conceptualisation of literature as a whole is a macro-version of the way New Critics in the 1950s and 1960s conceptualised the poem as (again) complex, free-standing, self-sufficient and with a rigorous and vigorous internal market-economy of sense.

However, it is Genette's notion of 'transtextuality' which is most relevant here; this term designates what might be seen as a super-charged version of intertextuality, the precise nature of the supercharge being that it takes in *both* relations between specific texts *and* those between specific texts and their generic archetypes (in the sense that, for example, *Mansfield Park* might be said to have a transtextual relationship with the cross-cultural Cinderella story). Genette continues to use the term 'intertextuality', but shrinks its sense, so that it designates, simply, 'the actual presence of one text within another' (quoted by Allen, p. 101), reducing its scope to such matters as 'quotation, plagiarism and allusion' (Allen).

Genette identifies five sub-categories of 'transtextuality', of which intertextuality is merely one (see Figure 1). For instance, 'architextuality, the fifth type of transtextuality in Genette's map, is described with that note of quasi-mysticism as being 'everywhere – above, beneath, around the text' (Allen, p. 100). Architexts are 'basic, unchanging (or at least slowly evolving) building blocks which underpin the entire literary system' (p. 100) – that is, not an *Ur*-text, but (so to speak) an *Ur*-textuality, generating the specific kind of 'literariness' which generates the text. Thus, the architext of Shakespeare's *Hamlet*, for instance, is the generic notion of tragedy, and what causes the 'slow evolving' of the architext is precisely the composition of *Hamlet* or *Death of a Salesman*, so that it makes as much empirical sense to see the text as generating the architext as vice versa. Only when 'rules' are explicitly formulated and consciously followed (like the 'Three Unities', for instance) does it seem sensible to posit an extra-textual *generating* force. Even here, of course, it is notorious that such 'rules' are often an inaccurate extrapolation from observable practice, and even when a group of artists formulate a manifesto or an explicit common programme (like the 'Preface' to the second edition to *Lyrical Ballads*, or Ezra Pound's 'A Few "Don'ts" for Imagists') the formula usually postdates the practice, and never accurately describes it anyway – more often, it offers a kind of notional idealisation of that practice.

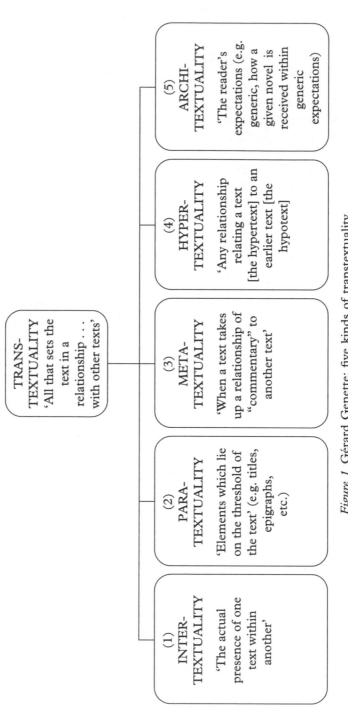

Figure 1 Gérard Genette: five kinds of transtextuality.

At the other extreme of classification, we move, so to speak, fi.... the theological, to the practical and the devotional. Thus, *paratextuality* (the second of the five types) marks 'elements which lie on the threshold of the text' (Allen, p. 103), including the *peritext* (book titles, epigraphs, chapter titles, prefaces, footnotes, and so on), and the *epitext* ('interviews, publicity announcements, reviews, private letters and other authorial and editorial discussions'). Yet another variant (the third type, called *metatextuality*) concerns a text taking up 'a relation of commentary towards another', as in literary criticism. Another type is *hypertextuality* (type 4 in the diagram), which is a transtextual relationship whereby one text (the *hypertext*) stands to another (the *hypotext*) as Joyce's *Ulysses* does to Homer's *Odyssey*. What is at issue here is a deliberate rewriting of the hypotext (the *Odyssey*) by the hypertext (*Ulysses*); the hypotext is a specific text, usually from the past, which a later text 'talks back to', whereas the architext (type 5) is not a specific text but a (literally) generic model with which the newer text is in dialogue. (This draws on Allen's formulation, p. 108.) Of course, having expressed scepticism about the absoluteness of the *langue/parole* distinction, we will find that all these apparently precise dichotomies are correspondingly problematised. For instance, one must wonder whether it is really possible for a writer to 'write back' to a 'generic model' without having any particular text in mind – any writer who wants to write a sonnet sequence will surely have read some sonnets, and will probably prefer some to others.

There are, too, some obvious problems with Genette's system for anyone who would want to use it merely as one element in a repertoire of concepts and approaches, rather than as a paid-up narratologist with a specific party allegiance. Firstly, it isn't universally accepted, so it has to be explained from basics every time it is used outside narratological circles. Further, a term like 'intertextuality' will be familiar to non-specialist readers, but Genette uses it in a much more restricted sense than is usual. Thus, Gerald Prince's *Dictionary of Narratology* defines interext as 'a text (or set of texts) that is cited, rewritten, prolonged, or generally transformed by another text that makes the latter meaningful. Homer's *Odyssey* is one of the intertexts of Joyce's *Ulysses* and intertextuality obtains between the two' (p. 48). For Genette, by contrast, the relationship would only be intertextual in so far as *Ulysses* quotes from *The Odyssey*, and he would describe the relationship between the two texts as hypertextual rather than intertextual. Likewise, whereas for Kristeva intertextuality connotes 'the sum of knowledge, the potentially infinite network of signifying practices that allows [any text] to have meaning' (Prince, p. 46), for Genette such networks would belong more to the realm of architextuality (type 5, concerning the reader's expectations of the text). This realm (of Genettian architextuality or Kristevan intertextuality) has that open-ended virtuality which is like the Derridean realm of open context, where the text expands to infinity. To reiterate, once we accept this notion of intertextuality, we introduce such a large speculative element into the discipline that it can hardly any longer *be* a discipline: it becomes imaginative, creative, constructive – perhaps quite exciting in some ways, but study needs an object, and objectives, held in common by large numbers of practitioners. The notion of a 'field' of study is precisely that of an area which has recognised boundaries, beyond which is another place, somebody else's property and domain. Take away the boundaries, and we are attempting to study everything – or nearly everything. But (to repeat some of the conclusions reached in the first chapter) nobody can cultivate the boundless wilderness, not even English studies academics.

Context prescribed: legislating curriculum in the UK

English in UK schools and higher education since the 1990s has become a highly regulated area of activity, and a contextualist approach is prescribed at both school level and university level. Thus, the subject guidelines for Advanced Level English in schools lay down that candidates are required to 'show understanding of the contexts in which literary texts are written and understood'. Likewise, at university level the subject Benchmarks[1] require us to offer students:

- a knowledge and appreciation of *contextual approaches* to the production and reception of literary and non-literary texts
- a knowledge of the linguistic, literary, *cultural and socio-historical contexts* in which literature is written and read
- an awareness of how different *social and cultural contexts* affect the nature of language and meaning
- breadth and depth of subject knowledge, including *relevant contextual knowledge* and the demonstration of powers of textual analysis as appropriate.

The key terms in these formulations shift about in apparently random ways: students have to know about 'contextual approaches' – but which ones, and what *are* these exactly? They have to know about 'cultural and socio-historical contexts': are those the same as the 'social and cultural contexts', which they have merely to be 'aware of'? In fact, they also have to be aware of how 'social and cultural contexts' 'affect the nature of language and meaning'. Finally, they have to have 'relevant contextual knowledge' as part of their 'breadth and depth of subject knowledge'. But contextual knowledge relevant to what? And what are the *criteria* of relevance in this area?

Those seeking some guidance in this area can turn to Rick Rylance and Judy Simons's *Literature in Context* (2001), which has authority, since Simons chaired the QAA Benchmarking panel for degree-level English and Rylance was one of the panel members. Further, the book has the approval of CCUE (the Council for College and University English), covering degree-level work, and the UK Qualifications and Curriculum Authority (covering A Level work). In Rylance and Simons's formulation, there are the seven strands of context, and I will list them here and comment on each in turn.

1. The context of period or era, including significant social, historical, political and cultural processes.

This represents what is most usually understood by the term 'context' when that word is used without qualification. Its potentially vast scope leads me to designate it as primarily the broad (or 'panoramic') kind of context. The wider the contextual panorama, the less likely it is that students will be able to say anything original about it, and the more likely it is that they will simply repeat what *we* have said to *them*. The coursebooks which have appeared since the year 2000, attempting to meet the need for broad or 'panoramic' contextualisation, are sometimes of questionable quality. The 'Authors in Context' series from Oxford World's Classics attempts to raise standards, but the series title seems paradoxical – a book entitled *Dickens in Context* alongside another called *George Eliot in Context* implies that the two authors have different contexts. Yet both are mid-Victorian British novelists. While mid-Victorian literature has a context which is different from that of late-Victorian literature, it is difficult to understand how two novelists of the same period can have different contexts. Likewise, the Cambridge Edition of the Works of Jane Austen has a volume entitled *Jane Austen in Context* (ed. Janet Todd, 2005), but it has no discussion or debate about what is meant by 'context' or what principles of exclusion or inclusion have been applied. It is divided into three parts, these being 'Life and works', 'Critical fortunes', and 'Historical and cultural context', the third being double the length of the first two combined. The chapters in that third section include 'Food', 'Manners', 'Medicine', 'Politics', 'Rank', 'Religion', 'Trade', and 'Transport'. But why not 'Marriage', 'Poverty', 'Property', 'Recreation', 'Science', 'Travel', 'War', etc. etc. instead or as well? The book, then, is indicative

of the fact that, in English studies, context is never taken to be a concept which requires any rigour of examination.

  2.   The context of the work in terms of the writer's biography or milieu.

This aspect of context is clearly specific rather than panoramic,
and tending towards what I have called 'deep' context: in this sense
Dickens and George Eliot do indeed have different contexts. This
reinstatement of biography is a major (and unexamined) shift in the
discipline – just when we have become accustomed to the Barthesian
'death of the author' we are confronted with the resurrection. But
at least there is a degree of specificity of context here which the first
sub-category lacks. But what exactly is envisaged? Will students read
a biography of Dickens, and, if so, do we really think this is better than
reading another Dickens novel? Or will they be given facts about
Dickens's life which they will be expected to link up with their readings of the text? My basic sense of broad or 'panoramic' contextuality
is that it tends to be *centrifugal*, tends to spin the student further and
further away from the text. By contrast, 'deep' contextuality should
be *centripetal*, spinning the reader closer in to the text. All the same, it
is admittedly difficult to be sure that this would *really* be the case with
this second kind of contextuality.

  3.   The context of a specific passage in terms of the whole work from
       which it is taken.

As already indicated, I don't think this is really contextuality at all:
*con*text has to mean something 'with' or 'beyond' the text, but this is
something *within* the text, so I will disregard this as not really being
'context' at all in any accepted sense of the term.

  4.   The context of a work in terms of other works, including works by
       the same author.

'Other works' seems to mean other works of the same type, or on the
same theme or topic: so in the case of Shakespeare's *King Lear* it might
mean *The True Chronicle Historie of King Leir* and Edward Bond's play
Lear, for instance. Students, presumably, won't actually be reading these
plays in most cases, so again the contextual emphasis is going to result
in a lot of absorbing of second-hand material.

  5.   The literary context, including the question of generic factors and
       period-specific styles.

Here students will read about relevant aspects of literary history, again
a very second-hand kind of study, since they would need much more
time than is available to read enough from a period to form judgements

and opinions about 'period-specific styles'. Again, the way such broad contextual emphasis results in the passivisation of students is very notable, and indeed inevitable in an era which has broadened the mandatory scope of courses while at the same time shortening them through modularisation and semesterisation.

6. The language context, including relevant episodes in the use and development of literary language, the question of demotic, colloquial, or dialect styles, and so on.

This is language study, not literary study, again moving out beyond the text with a strong centrifugal force. This seems to be a reinstatement of the old philological approaches to literary study, the kind which dominated the field in the nineteenth century and were eventually superseded by forms of close reading.

7. The different contexts for a work established by its reception over time, including the recognition that works have different meanings and effects in different periods. This might include an awareness of different critical responses. (*Literature in Context*, pp. xxii–xxiv)

This seems a very specialised and particular category: for modern works there would be little scope for study of the work's 'different meanings and effects in different periods'. In the case of historical works, there would only be a record of 'different critical responses' in the case of works which have been canonical for a long time. Though this is technically a context directly 'adjacent' to the work under study, one might wonder how suitable such material is for undergraduate study: the category would work well for many Shakespeare plays, where there is a detailed performance history, and (say) often several different film versions available of the same play. But the whole idea seems much thinner and much more tenuous in the case of most other writers.

These 'seven types of contextuality' can be related to my two basic types, that is, to 'broad' and 'deep' contextuality, though the 'deep' kind seems at best only marginally present. One, 5, 6, and 7 in the list, covering history, historical linguistics, and literary history or reception history, will certainly mean that students (using Rob Pope's terms) are looking '*through, round* and *beyond*' the text most of the time rather than at it. But two and four, covering 'the writer's biography and milieu' and 'the language context' will also fail to meet the 'deep' contextual ideal of providing a context which is text-specific, since much of the material studied in this way will necessarily have only a tangential bearing on any specific text. Hence, once these six variants of context become the focus of a significant part of undergraduate degree courses the primary focus of study becomes not knowledge *of* any specific literary work, or even knowledge *about* any specific work, but knowledge *about literature*. The change of focus could not be more fundamental, nor (in my view) could it be more detrimental to what is actually possible in English, for these vast topics can only be studied, given the time and resources available, by using predigested secondary materials, and operating in terms of large-scale generalisations about socio-politics, linguistics, and literary history. How could it be otherwise? Once the spirit of panoramic contextuality becomes dominant (and publishing trends discussed in the last chapter suggest that this has already happened), then the former focus of English studies on the student's detailed encounters with literary texts becomes impossible to maintain. Yet these panoramic contextual fields can be reconstructed in so many different ways that their character is always inherently speculative. Furthermore, teaching with an emphasis on this kind of context allows little scope for the demonstration of originality in thinking. Indeed, the paradox is that the more you *widen* the contextual focus, the more you *decrease* the scope for originality. For a student is far more likely to make an original and telling remark about a given line of *Jane Eyre* than about *Jane Eyre* as a whole. Hence, the more the contextual emphasis takes us out to those broad layers of history, politics, and culture, the more difficult it will become for a student to show 'conspicuous merit' as an English student.

Doing English, contextual-style

What will an English course look like which tries to put these QAA Benchmark principles into practice? The following descriptions, of a module called 'Contemporary Literature in Context' at a British university gives an indication. Students on the course will consider:

> How the contemporary British writer's personal history intersects with the collective social history of which she/he is a part. This will involve close consideration of biographical approaches and of sociological perspectives such as Marxism, feminism, neo-historicism and cultural materialism.

It is evident from this how far literature must recede when context rules: the students on this module will study 'the British writer's personal history' and how it 'intersects with the collective social history of which she/he is a part'. That will entail 'consideration of biographical approaches and of sociological perspectives'. But can the questions being posed here really be answered? What can any of us really say about how our own personal history interacts with collective social history?

Surely the former is not *just* the product of the latter – nobody could possibly believe that. The description goes on to say that students will also study:

> How language and literary form operate within specific historical and cultural parameters. Literary tradition and innovation. Structuralist and stylistic approaches.

Can teachers of literature really explain how language and literary form (literary *form*!) relate to broader historical and cultural parameters, showing the kind of pressures the former exert on the latter? A course offering to focus on such questions as its primary object of enquiry could never hope to 'deliver' its 'learning outcomes', but focusing on such inherently intractable objectives is one of the consequences of the current overemphasis on historicism and contextualism.

And yet, when prominent members of the profession state publicly what distinguishes their approach to literature they often speak of a commitment to studying 'literature in its context'. John Barrell, for instance, opened a *London Review of Books* piece in 2000 with the (I presume) regretful statement that:

> There is a large audience eager to read about literature, but one that is not to be persuaded that the works of their favourite authors can be understood only in the detailed historical context in which they were produced. (*LRB*, 2 November 2000, p. 18)

Something of this kind seems to be what most English teachers want to persuade their students of – that they can understand literature only in the detailed historical context in which it was produced. But what form should such 'persuasion' take? What argument will convince people that they have hitherto misunderstood their favourite authors? If the assertion were *entirely* valid, how could works of literature have survived from one age to the next (except in the minds of those who we would have to insist had misunderstood them)? If the assertion *is* valid, then there is nothing for us to do but become historians, like the author of *Imagining the King's Death*. But I have not quoted Barrell in full: the article in fact lists three things, not just one, which the large audience eager to read about literature is 'not to be persuaded of', these being that the works of their favourite authors can be understood '[*firstly*] only in the detailed historical context in which they were produced, [*secondly*] only in reference to some elaborate theory of writing or reading, and [*thirdly*] only in comparison with the work of dozens of other writers whose names are known only to professional scholars'. The tone is ironic, but it amounts to saying that it is difficult to persuade people that you have to be a professional to understand literature. It doesn't seem to me at all surprising that it is hard to persuade people of this. Naturally, those who read literature for pleasure imagine that they are quite capable of understanding it on their own. The implied position is like trying to persuade people that they should call in an electrician when they need to change a light-bulb. But my concern here is with the statement that we need to understand the 'detailed historical context' of literary works, for regarding this as indispensable condemns young literary academics to a lifetime of historicist 'archae-ology', as they attempt to reconstruct that 'detailed historical context' in which literary works are produced, an endless preliminary which will undoubtedly detain most of them for their entire careers.

In a recent book called *English in Practice* I considered two well-known contextual or historicist readings of canonical literary texts, namely the 'slavery' reading of *Mansfield Park* (Avrom Fleishman, Edward Said, and others) and the 'Peterloo' reading of Keats's 'Ode to Autumn' (Jerome McGann, Andrew Motion, Andrew Bennett, and others).[2] I don't need to elaborate on the details of these readings here, because they are so familiar, but the following were the grounds for my con-clusion that the 'slavery' reading is on the whole convincing, while the Peterloo reading isn't. There were three factors Firstly (as John Sutherland says in *Is Heathcliff a Murderer?*, p. 5), contextual reading is mainly about interpreting silence, that is, about reading the words *off* the page. But the silence shouldn't be total: *Mansfield Park* isn't *com-pletely* silent on the topic of Antigua and slavery, whereas the 'Ode to Autumn' *is* completely so on the matter of Peterloo. So we can offer the slavery reading while remaining within the bounds of the text. So this is the first principle: activating a context requires *some* textual or verbal warrant, however minimal. This amounts to saying, again, that true con*text* is always an aspect of con*tent*. Secondly, there should be a degree of *thematic congruity* between the claimed context and the overt or explicit content of the piece. Obviously this can't always be a hard-and-fast test, and it's essentially an expansion of the first criterion. In the case of *Mansfield Park*, the slavery issue and the matter of the West Indies estate have an evident congruence with the issues of morality, conduct, and silence which are the overt themes of the novel. But in the case of 'Ode to Autumn' it is difficult to see any such 'fit' between the claimed content (social unrest and injustice) and the overt matter of the poem (seasonal transition, coming to terms with loss and change, and so on). Thirdly, a contextual reading should be '*augment-ative*', which is to say that it should *add* something to the text, rather than introducing a mono-dimensionality into the reading of the work or denigrating the work's (or the author's) standing while flattering the reader's superior moral and social awareness. Thus, the Fleishman/ Said reading of *Mansfield Park* explicitly does *not* accuse the literary work of being culpably evasive and attempting to disguise the socially unacceptable by dressing it in high art. So the slavery reading *adds* a dimension to the work, whereas the 'Peterloo' reading seeks to *subtract* from the work's standing, indicting the author for supposed political evasiveness, and reducing the work to a new mono-dimensional level. The Peterloo reading flatters the critic's sense of moral superiority over the author and diminishes the status of the work. We should be cautious about readings which do that: a contextual reading, then, should be 'verbally-warranted', 'congruent' and 'augmentative', and something like these three grounds, suitably adapted, might provide a general basis for evaluating historicist readings of literary texts. What I am seeking overall are approaches which go beyond the text itself, but (while sometimes using localised aspects of history) don't open up the broad contextual highway which turns English into a form of history. So I am looking for the kind of contexts I call deep, which are text-specific, 'co-textual' or intertextual, or which consciously interrogate aspects of our own disciplinary practice. The chapters which follow are all attempts to achieve that elusive goal.

Notes

1 Published by the QAA (the Quality Assurance Agency) in 2002, they can be assessed at http://www.qaa.ac.uk/crntwork/benchmark/english.html.
2 For the Austen case see Avrom Fleishman's *A Reading of Mansfield Park: An Essay in Critical Synthesis* (Johns Hopkins University Press, 1970), and 'Jane Austen and Empire', pp. 95–116 in Edward Said's *Culture and Imperialism* (Vintage, 1995). Also, Brian Southam's 'The Silence of the Bertrams: Slavery and the Chronology of *Mansfield Park*' (in the *TLS*, 17 February 1975, pp. 13–14); Frank Gibbon, 'The Antiguan Connection: Some New Light on *Mansfield Park*', in *The Cambridge Quarterly*, vol. 11 (1982), pp. 298–305; and Moira Ferguson, '*Mansfield Park*, Colonialism, and Gender', in *The Oxford Literary Review*, vol. 13 (1991), pp. 118–39. For the Keats case see: Andrew Motion's *Keats* (Faber & Faber, 1997), p. 462; Andrew Bennett's *Keats, Narrative and Audience: The Posthumous Life of Writing* (Cambridge University Press, 1994), pp. 159–69; Vincent Newey's 'Keats, History, and the Poets' in *Keats and History*, ed. Nicholas Roe (Cambridge University Press, 1995); and Jerome McGann's essay 'Keats and the Historical Method' in his *The Beauty of Inflections: Literary Investigations in Historical Method and Theory* (Oxford University Press, 1988).

3

Mutual contextuality: Coleridge's conversation poems

A context is something specific outside the text which is activated and validated as an explicatory framework by something within the text. One of the 'deepest' kinds of contextuality occurs when a group of texts by the same author form a recognised 'cluster', so that the cluster as a whole constitutes a distinct 'textual domain' with its own integrity and cohesion, while the individual items in the 'cluster' contextualise each other, exhibiting a range of recurrent patterns, concerns, and motifs. This tissue of recurrences is the 'explicatory framework', the 'something specific outside the text', which facilitates the reading of the individual poems, and Coleridge's group of 'conversation poems' is one of the best-known instances of this kind of textual cluster. While not the same as Pope's 'inferred intertextuality', which is really a reading strategy applied to a group of items which do not emanate from the same source, it is certainly a form of Genette's transtextuality, even though it does not correspond precisely to any of his five sub-types.

If poetry is always primarily a form of self-address, then it is probably true that the most interesting poems are those in which the inner auditor seems not quite convinced by what the speaker says. In such poems, what has been said has to be reshaped and reiterated, often obsessively so, as it may seem to the reader. To say this is perhaps to do little more than again agree with Yeats that we make poetry out of the quarrel with ourselves. But I want to go a little beyond Yeats and suggest that the quarrel at its most interesting is often sustained, cross-textually, over long periods and over whole groups of poems – that is, throughout the whole of a co-textual cluster or constellation. The essence of the co-textual cluster is to go back again and again over the same argument or impasse, rewording and reworking it almost obsessively. These 're-visionary' tendencies are very marked in several of the great 'clusters' of poems (to call them 'sequences' implies a greater linear logic than they usually possess) which feature so strongly in the inner-canonical core of English poetry – Shakespeare's *Sonnets*, Keats's 'Odes', Tennyson's *In Memoriam*, Hardy's 1912–13 poems – all these constantly resay and recycle what has already been said. The 're-visionary' characteristic is especially marked in Coleridge's 'conversation poems', where in each poem, my contention will be, Coleridge goes further still, and gives the quarrel with the self concrete embodiment in an encounter between the speaking self and what I will call a 'surrogate' self.

These are large statements, and perhaps attempting to substantiate them would be enough for any chapter. But in discussing Coleridge there is another problem, one which confronts anyone who writes on material from that 'inner-canonicial core', namely that the poems themselves have become so 'overdetermined' by critical overlay that some means of radical defamiliarisation (of de-encrustation) is required. This is, I think, one of the services which literary theory can provide, for a theoretical angle of some obliqueness can enable the reader to clear ground for manoeuvre around the poems. The obliqueness in this case lies in the fact that, while following common practice in reading this group of poems cross-textually (or co-textually, as I prefer to call it), I enlist the aid of concepts and devices from narratology and stylistics (as explained later) which are more usually applied to prose.

The common structure of the conversation poems

The seven major conversation poems discussed here are: 'The Aeolian Harp' (1795), 'Reflections on Having Left a Place of Retirement' (1796), 'To the Rev. George Coleridge' (1797), 'This Lime-Tree Bower My Prison' (1797), 'Frost at Midnight' (1798), 'Fears in Solitude' (1798), and 'The Nightingale: A Conversation Poem' (1798). Of course, it is a commonplace of criticism to say that these seven poems are closely linked,[1] but my intention is to go a little further and argue that they have an underlying 'formula' which varies remarkably little from poem to poem. The formula, as I see it, is roughly as follows: firstly, there is usually a '*Locatory Prelude*', which describes the Coleridges' cottage and its immediate locale, setting the scene for the meditative, reflective main body of the poem. The locatory section is most often at the start, but can occur belatedly (lines 57–62 in 'To the Rev. George Coleridge', and 47–61 in 'This Lime-Tree Bower My Prison'). Secondly, the main body of the meditation then involves a '*Transposition*' of some kind, in which an aspect of the speaker's past self is recalled in a sustained and systematic way (as in 'To the Rev. George Coleridge', 'Frost at Midnight', and 'Reflections on Having Left a Place of Retirement'): alternatively, the transposition involves a 'parallel' scene imaginatively conjured up (for instance, the speaker's friends walking nearby in 'This Lime-Tree Bower', or the speaker lying on a nearby hillside in 'The Aeolian Harp'). Thirdly, the outcome of the reverie or meditation in all the poems is a *'Self-Reproof'* of some kind, and, fourthly, coupled with the Reproof is a *'Resolution'*, a determination to think or behave differently, or carry out some specific resolve in the future. These four 'stages' constitute the basic underlying structure of all these poems.

In the course of what follows I will refer to the four stages in discussing individual poems, but a central purpose is to explore a particular trope or device which always plays a major part in the crucial 'Transposition' section, and this is the trope, or motif, of surrogacy. By 'surrogacy' is meant that it is characteristic of these poems that the core of the central meditative episode is a transaction between the speaking persona and a 'surrogate' self, that is, another person on to whom are projected or transposed key elements of the speaker's own personality, dilemmas, or thought processes. In four cases the surrogate is the named addressee of the poem, these being Coleridge's brother George in 'To the Reverend George Coleridge', the 'dear Sara' of 'The Aeolian Harp', the 'tender-hearted Charles' of 'This Lime-Tree Bower My Prison, and the 'dear babe' of 'Frost at Midnight'; these figures can therefore be called *Nominated* Surrogates. In the other poems the surrogate is a more generalised figure: the 'wealthy son of commerce' of 'Reflections on Having Left a Place of Retirement', 'the humble man' of 'Fears in Solitude' and 'the night-wandering man' of 'The Nightingale'. These can be called *Generic* Surrogates. Both types have essentially the same result, which is to separate the self from itself, so to speak, and effect its displaced objectification within the person of another. The motif of surrogacy, it is argued here, is the key defining feature of the Coleridgean conversation poem. The unfolding dynamic of all these poems is that the surrogate figure is at first distinguished from and contrasted with the speaker, but then drifts into a kind of composite subjectivity as the poem progresses. This drift, as I will try to show, is indicated by shifts in linguistic register and by instabilities in verb tenses (both of which can be described using terminology drawn from stylistics) and by changes in what narratologists call 'focalisation'. It should be added that the Reproof at the end of the poem is usually attributed to, or 'read into', the silence of the surrogate (surrogacy in these poems is never a speaking role), and that the concluding Resolution takes as its implicit model for the reformed self the attitudes and behaviour of the surrogate. Of course, the surrogacy motif is stronger in some poems than in others, but, whether in strong or weak form, this motif is identifiable in all the poems in the series. I will start by tracing the four-part structure in the first poem, 'The Aeolian Harp', using this one as a paradigm for the whole group, and showing the initial emergence (in fairly weak form) of the surrogacy motif, before going on to concentrate mainly on the notion of surrogacy as seen in the remaining poems. From what has already been said, readers will probably have already surmised that the poem which most clearly manifests both the four-part structure and the surrogacy motif is 'This Lime-Tree Bower My Prison', but it seems sensible to begin with the first poem in the group, in which these matters need a little teasing out. For the reader's convenience, basic texts of the poems are reprinted in the order discussed in an appendix at the end of the chapter.

'The Aeolian Harp'

'The Aeolian Harp' opens, like most in the series, with the Locatory Prelude (lines 1–12), the description of the setting which is (in Stephen Bygrave's words) '*ostensibly* inhabited by the poet in the act of writing' (my italics).[2] The meditative core of the poem is the Transposition phase (lines 18–49), here centred upon the 'wind harp' which is placed in the window-frame so as to catch the breeze and emit plaintive notes which rise and fall with the wind. The bridge into the Transposition is that the 'witchery' (21) of the sounds of the lute takes the poem from the location dramatised at the start to an imaginary setting, a 'Faery-Land' (23), and thence to a remembered one – the 'midway slope / . . . at noon' (35–6). The description of the lute, as often noted, involves an explicit eroticisation of the scene as wind and lute are transposed into an image of two people engaged in love-making. The erotic fusion envisaged here is counterpointed with the interpolated lines about 'the one Life within us and abroad' (27–34) which images a single life-force as erotically suffusing all living things.[3] The Reproof follows and runs from lines 50–1 ('But thy more serious eye a mild reproof / Darts') to 58 ('On vain Philosophy's aye-babbling spring'), and the poem concludes with the Resolution, in which the speaker vows henceforth to adhere to orthodoxy ('For never guiltless may I speak of him', 59).

I am calling the Sara figure a surrogate here partly because she and Coleridge seem to reverse roles and gender stereotypes as the poem proceeds, so that the speaker is 'feminised' and Sara is 'masculinised'. Thus, at the start of this section the speaker evokes an image of himself on an unspecified previous occasion, stretched out in the sun, nearby ('on the midway slope / Of yonder hill', 35–6), thereby adopting the position of the 'reclining' Sara in the first part of the poem, this being the *third* version of the 'reclining' tableau with which the poem began (that is, counting the image of the lute caressed by the breeze as the second). In each case the feminised recliner is caressed by a masculine figure, or a masculinised force; so here the recliner on the midway slope is being 'caressed' intellectually as the lute was:

> And many idle flitting phantasies,
> Traverse my indolent and passive brain,
> As wild and various, as the random gales
> That swell and flutter on this subject Lute!
>
> (41–4)

The culminating vision is of a promiscuous divine force erotically engaged with 'all of animated nature' (45), awakening each being intellectually in a quasi-sexual initiation and making it 'tremble into thought' (47). But in the poem this is too much for Sara, whose 'more serious eye a mild reproof / Darts' (50–51). This completes the gender reversal mentioned earlier, for Sara here takes the 'masculine' role of the rebuking authority-figure, whose mind is 'serious' and resistant to fanciful musings, maintaining orthodoxy and reimposing the strict mental discipline which will rein in the speaker's 'idle flitting phantasies' (41). This is the culmination of the surrogacy motif in the poem, as the self-reproof is projected outwards, and becomes the reproof of another. This latter detail is fairly obvious and has often been noted before: Yarlott, for instance, sees Sara as 'a device for dramatizing the conflict within himself', and for Gerard, 'Sara is but a mouthpiece for something in Coleridge himself', and Rookmaaker (who quotes these two) agrees.[4] But to repeat, my point is that this 'projection device' – what I am calling the surrogacy motif – is not just a feature of the first poem in the series but is repeated in all the poems in the cluster. Further, as the word 'pensive' at the start of the poem implies, Sara, like all the surrogates in these poems, is silent, and merely has speech, and thought, attributed to her – obviously a necessary precondition if the surrogacy device is to work at all. Perhaps this appropriation of the surrogate by the persona has a slightly sinister edge: like the reanimated corpses of 'The Ancient Mariner', the named addressee, silently 'speaking' its attributed words, is not really an independent subjectivity at all.

'Reflections'

As with Sara in 'The Aeolian Harp', the surrogate figure in 'Reflections on Having Left a Place of Retirement' is at first firmly distanced through stereotyping but then seems to drift into that complicit surrogacy with the persona which seems to me the 'core' event in all these poems. The opening description presents the Coleridges' recently left cottage (lines 1–9) and its idyllic surroundings and the section which follows describes the reaction to the cottage and its setting of a passer-by, a 'wealthy son of Commerce' (11), as the speaker supposes, who is initially presented ('novelised', we might say), as a typical materialist consumed with 'thirst of idle gold' (13). But the speaker asserts the imagined meliorative effect of this environment upon the man – it 'made him muse', he says, 'With wiser feelings' (13–14). The drift into surrogacy is subtly indicated here in the register of the vocabulary which is applied to this figure. For instance, words like 'idle', 'muse', and 'gaze' are typically used in these poems to delineate the thought processes of the central subjectivity, that of the speaker. Usually they mark that crucial 'threshold' moment when the thought begins to shift out of focus, so to speak, assuming its own momentum, and drifting back to the past, or away to a distant setting.[5] But the representation of this surrogate figure also shifts from what narratologists like Genette call *external* focalisation (that is, presentation through elements observable to the senses, like spoken words, visible gestures, external appearances, and actions) to *internal* focalisation, where the focus is upon movements of the mind and the emotions, which have only the most approximate external indices.[6] For example, the man is said to be 'Hallowing his Sabbath-day by quietness' (10), a phrase which sits somewhat oddly as a description of somebody else's actions, and if true could be known only to the man himself. Thus, if he were to hallow his Sabbath by going to church this could be seen and observed, but if he does so merely by quietness, then his Sabbath observance is actually indistinguishable from that of a man walking along on a Sunday afternoon intently plotting a bank robbery. Hence the depiction of this person in the poem, in so far as it is internally localised, is in fact claiming a novelistic privilege, assuming the stance which used to be called authorial omniscience. The shift to internal focalisation is also suggested by phrases like 'and look'd / With a pleas'd sadness' (14–15), which surely indicate something which is more a felt quality than an observed quality.

The surrogacy episode as a whole is, significantly, initiated with the word 'methought', which will be seen occurring at the same 'threshold' point of entry into 'deep-level' subjectivity in other poems in the sequence: the lines 'Once I saw / . . . A wealthy son of Commerce saunter by, / Bristowa's citizen' (9–12) are externally focalised, but the phrases which immediately follow cross the threshold into internal focalisation:

'methought, it calm'd / His thirst of idle gold, and made him muse /
With wiser feelings' (12–14). Likewise, the boundary between this man's
pronouncements and the speaker's own avowals is somewhat ambiguously marked in linguistic terms: the son of commerce calls it a blessed
place; does he also call the inmates of the cottage blessed? Or is that
the speaker's own comment? We are told that he 'sigh'd, and said it
was a Blessed Place. / And we *were* bless'd' (17–18).[7] The sense seems
to shift according to whether the stress is on 'we' or 'were'. The implied
elision between this person and the speaker is compounded by the
fact that, though he is treated initially with some distaste, and rather
crudely stereotyped, it is this figure whom the speaker in the end
imitates, by continuing to derive moral and emotional sustenance from
this rural spot (as the poem testifies), but himself returning to urban
life. So, like the wealthy son of commerce, 'I was constrain'd to quit
you' he says of the cottage (45), and he now reproves the former
self who could 'dream away the entrusted hours' (47) – a powerful and
guilt-haunted phrase – 'On rose-leaf beds, pampering the coward
heart / With feelings all too delicate for use' (48–9). Thus he resolves
to engage henceforth in a fuller, more integrated life ('head, heart, and
hand', 61) and puts the cottage and what it represents firmly and un-
convincingly behind him. But he resolves, too, to revisit it mentally,
thus effectively becoming the surrogate self of the 'wealthy son of
commerce', for like him 'I shall sigh fond wishes – sweet Abode!' (69).
Hence the surrogacy motif seems to be present here in a more developed form than in the first poem, and there is an implicit return of
the surrogate as 'end-figure', a being whose actions or attitudes are
imitated, or aspired to, by the speaker – a frequent occurrence in these
poems. Like him, the speaker will from now on strive for fulfilment
in the wider world beyond, though in a spirit not capitalistic but
communistic and egalitarian, for he looks to a time when *all* will have
the comfort of such a cottage and *none* will have more than that
('Ah! – had none greater! And that all had such!', 70). The rhetorical
vehemence of this resolution suggests that a decision already taken on
grounds of instinctive preference is being provided with a rationalisa-
tion rooted in the powerful resources of this new kind of 'talking' poetry,
a genre which is itself proleptic of the mechanisms, and the dangers,
of the 'talking cure'.

'To the Rev. George Coleridge'

A similar process of 'surrogate drift' is seen in 'To the Rev. George
Coleridge', as a figure firmly 'othered' at the start of the poem (in this

case Coleridge's brother George) becomes curiously aligned with the speaker's own subjectivity as the poem progresses. The first section addresses Coleridge's brother George, as 'my earliest Friend' (9). The 'rootedness' of George and his other brother is praised, since they have returned to the parental home ('To the same dwelling where his father dwelt', 5) in early manhood and now bring up their own children there. They are envied for this 'blessèd lot' (1) by the brother who, 'from the spot where first I sprang to light / Too soon transplanted' (17–18), is now an outsider to this scene, and can only recognise it from without as 'blessèd' and observe it with a sense of exclusion; the parallels with the man of commerce in the previous poem are obvious – it is as if the 'Place of Retirement' scenario has been turned inside-out, so that the speaker is now the figure who expresses envy of the domesticity of others.

There is already an incipient element of surrogacy in relation to George, viewed as a potential self, a Coleridge-as-he-might-have-been had he returned home like his brothers. The blurring of the boundary between self and other is indicated in small pronominal details: thus in summarising the situation the speaker says 'Such, O my earliest Friend! / Thy lot, and such thy brothers too enjoy' (9–10). But one of George's brothers – Coleridge himself – does *not* enjoy this lot or fit into this category. Hence, the unqualified use of this pronoun (unqualified, for instance, as it would be in a phrase like 'thy *other* brothers') is peculiarly empathetic with George's subject position, with its effective disowning of Coleridge as a true brother. Effectively, the grammatical form chosen is an act of self-disowning. Likewise, when Coleridge says of his brothers 'At distance [from each other] did ye climb Life's upland road' (11), the 'ye' again strangely excludes himself from the brotherhood, since 'we' would make better sense in the utterance than 'ye'. Thus, though Coleridge is the speaker of these utterances, the subject-position seems to be George's, so that the speaker's painfully felt separation from the 'cheered and cheering' band (12) is repeated in his chosen grammatical forms.

The recall of childhood in this section has centred on the father-role of George. The next section asks George to recollect the past, as the speaker has done, and invites him to recall the 'joy of hope' (64) with which he greeted his brother's earliest poetic efforts. Again, however, the grammatical 'blur' of the writing, and the drift into an internally focalised representation of George Coleridge, is indicative of the underlying surrogacy motif. Firstly, the exact illocutionary force of the opening line is unclear: is it a question (though it doesn't have a question mark), a request, an invitation, or a statement?

Nor dost not thou sometimes recall those hours,
When with the joy of hope thou gavest thine ear
To my wild firstling-lays.

                                                              (63–5)

Secondly, the phrase 'with the joy of hope' (64), though grammatically
linked to George, seems strangely transferred from the poet's own remembered feelings. He is touchingly keen to assure his brother that his art
has since developed ('Since then my song / Hath sounded deeper notes',
65–6). Yet he is unable to be other than apologetic: the moods in which
the poems (now offered to George) were composed have varied, and
a reproof is anticipated. What is anticipated, in fact, is a repetition
of the past; that is, not the ear given 'with the joy of hope' (64) but
the parental eye boding evil, and rebuking each fault. Poetically, the
moment reiterated here is that with Sara at the end of 'The Aeolian
Harp', when his effusions elicited from her 'more serious eye' a 'mild
reproof'. Likewise here, he anticipates, in a response as yet unspoken,
a brotherly reproof, assuming that among the poems 'some perchance
/ Will strike discordant on thy milder mind' (72–3). In both cases,
the 'mildness' is attributed to the reprover and the 'wildness' to the
reproved self ('wildered', he – punningly? – calls himself, at the end
of 'The Aeolian Harp'). The resolution, by implication, is to allow
'riper Age' (75) to calm the residual wildness, in so far as it has resulted
in poetic error and intemperateness. Throughout this section, the
thoughts attributed to the brother are remarkably detailed and specific,
and again indicative of an ambivalent subjectivity. In short, the surrogacy device enables Coleridge to 'hive off' his own dissatisfactions
with his writing, to attribute the perception of discord within his work
to another's habitually 'rebuking' eye.

'This Lime-Tree Bower My Prison' and 'Frost at Midnight'

For the surrogacy motif at its most overt, however, we must turn to
'This Lime-Tree Bower My Prison', where the transposition element
is very clear, as the speaker takes part in a walk by imaginative proxy,
mentally placing himself within the group of walkers in an act of
sustained vicarious reverie ('Now, my friends emerge / beneath the wide
wide Heaven – and view again / The many-steepled tract magnificent
/ Of hilly fields and meadows', etc., 21–4). At this early stage, the transposition is to the *collective* experience of the group of walkers. Later,
it moves from the penumbra of the group and homes in, from line
29, on 'My gentle-hearted Charles'. Paradoxically, the 'homing in'

corresponds with the scenic opening up, as the walkers move from the dell to 'the wide wide heaven' ('they wander on / In gladness all; but thou, methinks, most glad, / My gentle-hearted Charles', 27–9). Again, the internal focalisation is notable ('in gladness all', he says of his friends, as if he had access to the inner self of each of them). Again, too, the word 'methinks' heralds the glide into, or the appropriation of, another's subjectivity. As before, the overall effect is perhaps slightly eerie, as 'Lamb' is evacuated by Lamb and occupied by Coleridge. As before, the key words used elsewhere in the conversation series to delineate the Coleridgean subjectivity – 'swimming', and 'gazing' (40) – are now used of Lamb. The process of constructing Charles into a surrogate self thus proceeds very clearly, with Coleridge's distaste for the city being transposed to Charles (who didn't actually think this way at all), and his own reactions on previous similar occasions being now imaginatively attributed to Charles, as the perceptions of the two, self and surrogate, are fused: 'So my friend / Struck with deep joy may stand, as I have stood' (38–9). The result is Coleridge's experiencing these imagined feelings as his own – 'A delight / Comes sudden on my heart, and I am glad / As I myself were there!' (45–7). As the whole willed, sustained, almost auto-erotic process seems to lead to this moment of possessing the scene, the word 'sudden' my seem disingenuous.

A kind of coda completes the fusion of speaker and surrogate, as the former spontaneously blesses the homeward-flying rook while the latter stands gazing (70–5): this unites the two lines of perception, the scene imaginatively created, and the scene of the dramatic present, which all along had been simultaneously, yet separately taken in. For it is now, as he looks around with freshly enlightened eyes, that he marks 'much that has sooth'd me' (49). Here the verb is in the perfect tense, delineating a process which has been working within him all along while his mind was elsewhere. In line 70 it moves back to a recollective mode, and to the past tense ('when the last rook / Beat its straight path . . .'). But in line 73 the description flickers briefly back into the present ('Now a dim speck, now vanishing in light'), and the speculative re-creation of another's experience is signalled by the word 'deeming' (72) – the speaker 'deems' that the rook's wing had crossed the setting sun as Lamb stood gazing at it. But immediately an alternative scenario is offered – 'or when all was still, / Flew creeking o'er thy head' (75–6) – so that the process of the fictionalisation (or 'novelisation') of Lamb is boldly laid bare, as the author presents us with alternative endings from which to choose. For the surrogate, too, the bird has a 'charm', since for him 'No sound is dissonant which tells of Life' (78). Hence the two

are fused in (as is often said) an Ancient-Mariner-like act of spontaneous and redemptive benediction of life.

The moment in these poems when the surrogate's subjectivity is
about to be invaded or appropriated is, as we have seen, often cued by
the word 'methinks'. In the next poem, 'Frost at Midnight', at line 17,
it interestingly prefaces the analogous moment of identifying the flame
in the grate as a 'companionable form' (19) to the speaker. The
flame is also the emblem of the 'reproof', here placed unusually near
the beginning of the poem, almost as a bridging passage into the 'transposition' section which follows. What the speaker reproves himself
for is a certain directionlessness in his thinking: like the flame, his
own intellectual spirit is puny, unable to achieve 'lift-off', purposeless,
narcissistic, and prone to interpret everything as a reflection of itself,
so that thought becomes an idle plaything rather than a purposeful
instrument.

The remaining verse paragraphs directly address the 'Dear Babe,
that sleepest cradled by my side' (45). This is the figure which will drift
into surrogate complicity with the speaker as the poem goes on, but,
as with the others, it is initially starkly 'other' – the troubled speaker's
untroubled infant child. But the babe's association with the speaker soon
becomes peculiarly intimate – *his* breathings fill up the 'interspersed
vacancies' (47) in the speaker's thought, breaking the intellectually
incapacitating total silence described at the start of the poem. Again,
too, the transitional points between the different subjectivities, are, as
so often, grammatically marked: here the marker is the curious lack of
a possessive pronoun ('*the* thought' rather than '*my* thought'), and the
missing pole of the comparison in 'thou shalt learn far other lore' (51),
to which the obvious response is 'other lore than what?' The answer,
presumably, is 'other than the lore I learned'. A few lines later the
child will 'wander like a breeze' (55), and these associations of the
child with breath, breeze, and spirit recall the 'intellectual breeze' of
'The Aeolian Harp', which is intimately implicated with individual
identity ('at once the Soul of each, and God of all'). Hence, the projected eidetic image of his child wandering 'by lakes and sandy shores'
(58) is, like the similar passage in 'This Lime Tree Bower', strongly
suggestive of the motif of the surrogate whose experience repeats, or
corrects, or replaces that of the speaking persona.

The sign of this happening is again the subtle shift from 'external'
to 'internal' focalisation as the 'pictorialised' representation in 55 to
59 of the child which 'shalt wander like a breeze / By lakes and sandy
shores' gives way in 59–65 to internalised, expressive writing which envisages and represents a movement of the heart, as things seen and heard

in nature operate on the spirit in a quintessentially Coleridgean manner ('so shalt thou see and hear / The lovely shapes and sounds intelligible / Of that eternal language, which thy God / Utters, who from eternity doth teach / Himself in all, and all things in himself'). In fact, the attribution of the sentiment is difficult: is it how Coleridge now reads these things, or how the grown-up babe will in the future? The now familiar use of the surrogacy motif produces a peculiar composite subjectivity – two companionable forms sharing one identity.

The general effect at the end of the poem is, on first sight, like that of the theological 'reining in' at the end of 'The Aeolian Harp'. Though in future wandering free 'like a breeze' by the lakes and mountains, the babe will correctly interpret the landscape he sees as the language by which God is revealed. The difference, of course, is that the thought being reined in here is supposedly someone else's. If the main resolution is to make his baby's childhood different from his own, exposing it to the benign influences of nature which (he claims) were denied to him, then the reproof concerns the by-now familiar self-accusation about intellectual self-indulgence and passiveness: Coleridge's reaction against the implied intellectual narcissism mentioned earlier is to emphasise the otherness of the sleeping child ('thou shalt learn far other lore / And in far other scenes'), but there is then (as with the 'humble man' of 'Reflections on Having Left a Place of Retirement', the Lamb of 'This Lime-Tree Bower', and the Sara of 'The Aeolian Harp') the inevitable glide back into his own subjectivity.

'Fears in Solitude'

A similar kind of 'glide' or 'drift' between subjectivities is again seen in 'Fears in Solitude'. Here, as in 'The Aeolian Harp', the speaker views nature from a recumbent position, or recalls doing so, lying amongst 'the unripe flax, / When, through its half-transparent stalks, at eve, / The level sunshine glimmers with green light' (9–11): as often, what is half-seen, or half-heard, indicates the attainment of a stage of liminality, imminence, or transition, when the sense 'swims' (though Coleridge doesn't use that word in this poem) and a threshold is crossed into a new way of seeing. Again, too, the word 'methinks' signals the start of the transition, the moment when the external scene dissolves and the meditation 'engages': all should love this 'spirit-healing nook' (12), 'but chiefly he, / The humble man, who, in his youthful years, / Knew just so much of folly, as had made / His early manhood more securely wise!' (13–16). And of this hypothetical man the speaker goes on to say that 'Here he might lie on fern or withered heath' (17), listening to the skylark. This reintroduces the recumbency motif, but shifts the location of the perceiving subjectivity from the silent dell to the open heath. The imagined surrogate is thus a version of the self only slightly displaced, rather as if the speaker is doing little more than referring to himself in the third person, since these second dozen or so lines mirror the content of the first: in the first the setting is the 'small and silent dell' (2), and the speaker is envisaged as lying there, so that the level sunshine of evening glimmers through the stalks of ripening corn, and listening to the skylark above. Likewise, of the imagined 'humble man', his youthful follies behind him, and now in his early manhood 'more securely wise' (16), it is said that 'Here he might lie . . . / While from the singing lark . . . / Sweet influences trembled o'er his frame' (17–21). This is, again, externally focalised, for the most part, which is to say that it is restricted to what an observer might see of this figure. But the succeeding lines slip into a mode which is internally focalised. Thus the section ends:

And so, his senses gradually wrapt
In a half sleep, he dreams of better worlds,
And dreaming hears thee still, O singing lark,
That singest like an angel in the clouds!

                                                                    (25–8)

Here the imagined and the actual seem to fuse – self and surrogate intermingle curiously, as the alternative self merges with the speaking self. The depersonalised self ('such a man', 30) now envisages the rapid transformation of this place which would be the result of military invasion, contrasting the calm so far described with the 'uproar and . . . strife' (34) which will overtake it, and the whole country, if the feared invasion by the French takes place.

Much of the subject matter of this poem, prompted as it is by the national emergency, rather than by the more usual personal crises of feeling, seems at first very remote from the concerns of the other poems in the series. But the crucial ideas of surrogacy and empathy, as just explicated, constitute a strong common bond. The speaker expresses the hope that the threat may pass away like the gust of wind which passed overhead, leaving untouched the dell in which he meditates. He then leaves the dell and winds up the 'heathy hill' (214) to the 'burst of prospect' (220) where the 'shadowy main' (220) and the 'amphitheatre of rich / And elmy fields' (222–3) are seen again. He now, literally, 'homes in' towards his own cottage, wife, and child, as frequently in these poems. He takes the peace of the dell with him, as nature's restorative gift, his heart now 'softened, and made worthy to indulge

/ Love' (236–7). It is significant, I think, that the locale of the meditation is not the cottage itself, as in 'The Aeolian Harp, 'Reflections on
Having Left a Place of Retirement', 'This Lime-Tree Bower', and 'Frost
at Midnight', but a separate spot dedicated solely to the speaker's
meditations; *this* is the spot with the 'sacramental' associations from
which he returns refreshed and renewed to the venues of day-to-day
life. Between this and the previous poems in the sequence, then, the
domestic has been quietly marginalised, and again the use of the surrogate figure of 'the humble man' has facilitated this process.

'The Nightingale: A Conversation Poem'

In the final piece, 'The Nightingale: A Conversation Poem', Coleridge's
personal domestic circumstances are written out of the poem altogether.
The occasion described is a night-time walk with the Wordsworths:
when the call of the nightingale is heard the speaker calls it a ' "Most
musical, most melancholy" bird' (13), but this response is at once disowned and attributed to a kind of double-layered surrogate, firstly to
Milton, to whom Coleridge's note attributes the thought, and then to:

> some night-wandering man whose heart was pierced
> With the remembrance of a grievous wrong,
> Or slow distemper, or neglected love,
> (And so, poor wretch! filled all things with himself,
> And made all gentle sounds tell back the tale
> Of his own sorrow) he, and such as he,
> First named these notes a melancholy strain.
>
> (16–22)

The closed-loop reflexivity whereby the 'poor wretch' 'filled all things
with himself' is a restatement of the notion of thought as 'Echo or
mirror seeking of itself', the habit of mind for which the speaker was
self-reproved in 'Frost at Midnight'. But the reflexivity disowned and
condemned here is, of course, a highly ambivalent quality in these poems.
Though the speaker condemns such reflexivity, the inner auditor
remains unconvinced. Sometimes, for instance, this kind of projection
is seen as the essence of the poetic act, like the intellectual breeze which
blows from without in 'The Aeolian Harp', and yet is simultaneously
the essence of the self ('at once the soul of each' and 'God of all').
Further, it is the inevitable product of the characteristic 'projective
perception' of the Romantics, which tends to down-grade the 'outward
forms' and elevate the life 'whose foundations are within' (to adopt
Coleridge's formulations in 'Dejection: An Ode').

Hence, the night-wandering man, and the over-zealous poet who is working at his versification when he ought to be surrendering his spirit 'to the influxes / Of shapes and sounds and shifting elements' (27–8), is, again, clearly a projected, partly disowned, aspect of Coleridge himself. He then turns to a kind of doubled, or composite, surrogacy – 'My Friend, and thou, our Sister!' (40) – William and Dorothy Wordsworth – whom he 'collectivises' and within which created entity he then includes himself, calling Dorothy 'our Sister' and claiming that 'we have learnt / A different lore' (40–1). This phrase, of course, echoes the one applied to the babe in 'Frost at Midnight' ('thou shalt learn far other lore'), the operative difference in both poems being between cultured or urban learning and 'natural' lore. As in all the others, the poem now enters 'deep reverie' with the detailed reconstruction of a transposed scene set somewhere other than in the place denoted in the locatory prelude. The 'grove / Of large extent, hard by a castle huge, / Which the great lord inhabits not' (50–2), and the 'most gentle Maid, / Who dwelleth in her hospitable home / Hard by the castle' (71–3) are images highly stylised and literary of immediately recognisable generic affiliations with the fairy tale. The insertion of the speaking 'I' into this quasi-fictionalised setting ('never elsewhere in one place I knew / So many nightingales', 56–7) has the effect of deconstructing both the actual and the fictional. The great Lord and the gentle Maid are clearly in some sense avatars of William and Dorothy, and the nightingales which 'answer and provoke each other's song' (59) are Coleridge and Wordsworth, often writing for each other, working on common themes, sending each other poems for comment (as this one was sent to Wordsworth, accompanied by Coleridge's own half-serious verse critique).

The second stage of the poem turns from the song of the nightingales to the 'most gentle maid' who hears them. She is 'a Lady vowed and dedicate' (74) who 'knows all their notes' (76), but seems most arrested by the 'pause of silence' (79) 'What time the moon was lost behind a cloud' (78). To note something silently or musingly or inwardly is always, as has already been suggested, the essence of what the surrogate does in these poems, providing the blankness, the *textlessness* we might call it, into which the speaker writes himself. When the moon re-emerges the song bursts out again, 'As if some sudden gale had swept at once / A hundred airy harps' (83–4). The Lady's susceptibility to the moment of silence, and her habit of emerging 'at latest eve' (73), link her closely with the habits and preferences of the speaker in the conversation poems. The 'suspended' moment, between dream and reality which is vicariously experienced as projected through her, is similar to the climactic moment in these poems of 'swimming sense' when past and present, self and other, here and elsewhere, dream and actuality seem to merge, as the mesmerised, 'dedicate' Lady watches the nightingale perched on the swinging twig 'Like tipsy Joy that reels with tossing head' (88).

The partial surrogate identification between the Lady and the speaker is confirmed at the start of the next section, when having described her experience of the nightingale he says farewell to it ('Farewell! O Warbler! till tomorrow eve', 89) and then breaks off with 'That strain again! / Full fain it would delay me!' (92–3) before turning finally to 'My dear babe' (93). The resolution which follows, concerning the nature of the child's planned upbringing, is the same in substance as the corresponding section of 'Frost at Midnight'. Again the babe is associated with varieties of silence; he 'laughs most silently' (105), and addresses the speaker without language ('capable of no articulate sound', 94), bidding him listen with a gesture, rather than a word, just as Sara, the corresponding 'end-figure' of 'The Aeolian Harp', darts a mild reproof with her eye rather than verbally, as if merely validating what the speaker already feels. Again the child's projected 'natural' education curiously projects the father's own life into the future – 'Well! / It is a father's tale: But if that Heaven / Should give me life, his childhood shall grow up / Familiar with these songs' (107–10). That invasion of the other by the self, then, which is the mark of the surrogacy motif, is seen in a peculiarly rich and complicated way in the last of these poems.

Conclusion

Where, then, does a reconsideration of this group of poems leave us? In one sense I have done very little, for, although previous writers have not used the term 'surrogate', many of them have been highly conscious of the interaction between self and other which the surrogacy motif implies. Likewise, although previous writers have not asserted that the poems in the group share an underlying four-part structure, many of them have discussed the elements which these poems have in common, often commenting on elements which overlap with aspects of the structure identified here.[8] So any claim I could make here is necessarily modest. Firstly, I would say that, the method used highlights the 'revisionary' element in Coleridge. His constant dissatisfaction with the limitations of his own mental powers, and the consequent and obsessive revising of what he has already said, is a vital part of his appeal – his strength is that he lacks precisely that grand rhetorical

Wordsworthian certainty. The approach highlights repetition, reitera-
tion, permutations of the same elements in varying forms, obsessive
returns to a particular kind of moment, and so on. It draws attention
to what cannot be resolved – to the poet's perennial dissatisfaction with
himself, and his desire to possess the qualities he sees in others.[9]

Secondly, employing this schema has enabled me to imagine as I write
a kind of co-ownership of the poems, something criticism can never
do entirely without. By 'co-ownership' is meant a sense of close liaison
with the poems, rather than with the critical community in whose domain
they ordinarily lie. As academic readers, our most pressing need is
sometimes to distance ourselves from this community, to shake off its
accusing presence (it will always know of a book or article we haven't
read), and conduct our primary negotiations with author and text rather
than critic and commentary. Critical theory (paradoxical though this
statement is) can enable us to achieve this distance, so long as we don't
buy our theory off-the-peg, but adopt a cut-and-paste attitude to it.
Theory just 'applied' is seldom rewarding or enlightening; it has to be
'used', losing its pristine ideality and dissolving into the kind of ad hoc
bricolage (as Lévi-Strauss would call it), which is the fate of any pre-
made 'Method' once it reaches the field. Here I have used terminology
and ideas from elsewhere (chiefly prose narratology and the kind of
precise linguistic description typical of stylistics) which seem to 're-angle'
the texts, so that they are not approached through the long tunnel
of the critical tradition they have generated. All competent critics, it
goes without saying, must visit the tunnel, but must also guard against
ceasing to be a visitor and becoming a confirmed tunnel-dweller. In
another way, of course, this is beside the point. I hope I have actually
discovered something objectively true about the poems – that they really
do all share the same four-stage structure, and that the notion of surrogacy is the best way of describing the character of their self-address.

Though the tightness of the patterning of motif and structure in a
co-textual cluster will seldom equal that of this particular Coleridgean
group, examples of such clusters in the canon readily come to mind,
and indeed, it could even be said that some form of 'clustering' is the
norm for short texts such as the individual lyric poems in a single-author
poetry collection, or the short stories published by a writer as a single
volume. The items in the co-textual 'cluster' provide context for each
other, and that context is indisputably a *literary* context, as well as being
one which is highly specific and not transferable to any other text or
set of texts. It's a context in which each item in the cluster exerts a
'palpable pressure' on all the others, and in that sense it is unambiguously
a case of *deep* context.

Appendix: Coleridge's 'conversation poems'

The Aeolian Harp

My pensive SARA! thy soft cheek reclined
Thus on mine arm, most soothing sweet it is
To sit beside our Cot, our Cot o'ergrown
With white-flower'd Jasmin, and the broad-leav'd Myrtle,
(Meet emblems they of Innocence and Love!)   5
And watch the clouds, that late were rich with light,
Slow saddenning round, and mark the star of eve
Serenely brilliant (such should Wisdom be)
Shine opposite! How exquisite the scents
Snatch'd from yon bean-field! and the world *so* hush'd!   10
The stilly murmur of the distant Sea
Tells us of silence.

           And that simplest Lute,
Plac'd length-ways in the clasping casement, hark!
How by the desultory breeze caress'd,   15
Like some coy maid half-yielding to her lover,
It pours such sweet upbraiding, as must needs
Tempt to repeat the wrong! And now, its strings
Boldlier swept, the long sequacious notes
Over delicious surges sink and rise,   20
Such a soft floating witchery of sound
As twilight Elfins make, when they at eve
Voyage on gentle gales from Faery-Land,
Where Melodies round honey-dropping flowers,
Footless and wild, like birds of Paradise,   25
Nor pause, nor perch, hovering on untam'd wing!
O! the one Life within us and abroad,
Which meets all motion and becomes its soul,
A light in sound, a sound-like power in light,
Rhythm in all thought, and joyance every where   30
Methinks, it should have been impossible
Not to love all things in a world so fill'd;
Where the breeze warbles, and the mute still air
Is Music slumbering on her instrument.
   And thus, my Love! as on the midway slope   35
Of yonder hill I stretch my limbs at noon,
Whilst thro' my half-clos'd eye-lids I behold
The sunbeams dance, like diamonds, on the main,
And tranquil muse upon tranquillity;
Full many a thought uncall'd and undetain'd,   40
And many idle flitting phantasies,
Traverse my indolent and passive brain,

As wild and various, as the random gales
That swell and flutter on this subject Lute!
      And what if all of animated nature 45
Be but organic Harps diversly fram'd,
That tremble into thought, as o'er them sweeps
Plastic and vast, one intellectual breeze,
At once the Soul of each, and God of all?
      But thy more serious eye a mild reproof 50
Darts, O belovéd Woman! nor such thoughts
Dim and unhallow'd dost thou not reject,
And biddest me walk humbly with my God.
Meek Daughter in the Family of Christ!
Well hast thou said and holily disprais'd 55
These shapings of the unregenerate mind;
Bubbles that glitter as they rise and break
On vain Philosophy's aye-babbling spring.
For never guiltless may I speak of him,
The Incomprehensible! save when with awe 60
I praise him, and with Faith that inly *feels*;
Who with his saving mercies healéd me,
A sinful and most miserable man,
Wilder'd and dark, and gave me to possess
Peace, and this Cot, and thee, heart-honour'd Maid! 65

Reflections on Having Left a Place of Retirement

Low was our pretty Cot: our tallest Rose
Peep'd at the chamber-window. We could hear
At silent noon, and eve, and early morn,
The Sea's faint murmur. In the open air
Our Myrtles blossom'd; and across the porch 5
Thick Jasmins twined: the little landscape round
Was green and woody, and refresh'd the eye.
It was a spot which you might aptly call
The Valley of Seclusion! Once I saw
(Hallowing his Sabbath-day by quiteness) 10
A wealthy son of Commerce saunter by,
Bristowa's citizen: methought, it calm'd
His thirst of idle gold, and made him muse
With wiser feelings: for he paus'd, and look'd
With a pleas'd sadness, and gaz'd all around, 15
Then eyed our Cottage, and gaz'd round again,
And sigh'd, and said, it was a Blesséd Place.
And we *were* bless'd. Oft with patient ear
Long-listening to the viewless sky-lark's note
(Viewless, or haply for a moment seen 20

Gleaming on sunny wings) in whisper'd tones
I said to my Belovéd, 'Such, sweet Girl!
The inobtrusive song of Happiness,
Unearthly minstrelsy! then only heard
When the Soul seeks to hear; when all is hush'd,   25
And the Heart listens!'
                But the time, when first
From that low Dell, steep up the stony Mount
I climb'd with perilous toil and reach'd the top,
Oh! what a goodly scene! *Here* the bleak mount,   30
The bare bleak mountain speckled thin with sheep;
Grey clouds, that shadowing spot the sunny fields;
And river, now with bushy rocks o'er-brow'd,
Now winding bright and full, with naked banks;
And seats, and lawns, the Abbey and the wood,   35
And cots, and hamlets, and faint city-spire;
The Channel *there*, the Islands and white sails,
Dim coasts, and cloud-like hills, and shoreless Ocean –
It seem'd like Omnipresence! God, methought,
Had build him there a Temple: the whole World   40
Seem'd *imag'd* in its vast circumference:
No *wish* profan'd my overwhelméd heart.
Blest hour! It was a luxury, – to be!
  Ah! quiet Dell! dear Cot, and Mount sublime!
I was constrain'd to quit you. Was it right,   45
While my unnumber'd brethren toil'd and bled,
That I should dream away the entrusted hours
On rose-leaf beds, pampering the coward heart
With feelings all too delicate for use?
Sweet is the tear that from some Howard's eye   50
Drops on the cheek of one he lifts from earth:
And he that works me good with unmov'd face,
Does it but half: he chills me while he aids,
My benefactor, not my brother man!
Yet even this, this cold beneficience   55
Praise, praise it, O my Soul! oft as thou scann'st
The sluggard Pity's vision-weaving tribe!
Who sigh for Wretchedness, yet shun the Wretched,
Nursing in some delicious solitude
Their slothful loves and dainty sympathies!   60
I therefore go, and join head, heart, and hand,
Active and firm, to fight the bloodless fight
Of Science, Freedom, and the Truth in Christ.
  Yet oft when after honourable toil
Rests the tir'd mind, and waking loves to dream,   65

My spirit shall revisit thee, dear Cot!
Thy Jasmin and thy window-peeping Rose,
And Myrtles fearless of the mild sea-air.
And I shall sigh fond wishes – sweet Abode!
Ah! – had none greater! And that all had such!   70
It might be so – but the time is not yet.
Speed it, O Father! Let thy Kingdom come!

To the Rev. George Coleridge

A blesséd lot hath he, who having passed
His youth and early manhood in the stir
And turmoil of the world, retreats at length,
With cares that move, not agitate the heart,
To the same dwelling where his father dwelt;   5
And haply views his tottering little ones
Embrace those agéd knees and climb that lap,
On which first kneeling his own infancy
Lisp'd its brief prayer. Such, O my earliest Friend!
Thy lot, and such thy brothers too enjoy.   10
At distance did ye climb Life's upland road,
Yet cheered and cheering: now fraternal love
Hath drawn you to one centre. Be your days
Holy, and blest and blessing may ye live!

To me the Eternal Wisdom hath dispens'd   15
A different fortune and more different mind –
Me from the spot where first I sprang to light
Too soon transplanted, ere my soul had fix'd
Its first domestic loves; and hence through life
Chasing chance-started friendships. A brief while   20
Some have preserved me from life's pelting ills;
But, like a tree with leaves of feeble stem,
If the clouds lasted, and a sudden breeze
Ruffled the boughs, they on my head at once
Dropped the collected shower; and some most false,   25
False and fair-foliag'd as the Manchineel,
Have tempted me to slumber in their shade
E'en mid the storm; then breathing subtlest damps,
Mix'd their own venom with the rain from Heaven,
That I woke poison'd! But, all praise to Him   30
Who gives us all things, more have yielded me
Permanent shelter; and beside one Friend,
Beneath the impervious covert of one oak,
I've rais'd a lowly shed, and know the names
Of Husband and of Father; not unhearing   35
Of that divine and nightly-whispering Voice,

Which from my childhood to maturer years
Spake to me of predestinated wreaths,
Bright with no fading colours!

                  Yet at times   40
My soul is sad, that I have roam'd through life
Still most a stranger, most with naked heart
At mine own home and birth-place: chiefly then,
When I remember thee, my earliest Friend!
Thee, who didst watch my boyhood and my youth;   45
Didst trace my wanderings with a father's eye;
And boding evil yet still hoping good,
Rebuk'd each fault, and over all my woes
Sorrow'd in silence! He who counts alone
The beatings of the solitary heart,   50
That Being knows, how I have lov'd thee ever,
Lov'd as a brother, as a son rever'd thee!
Oh! 'tis to me an ever new delight,
To talk of thee and thine: or when the blast
Of the shrill winter, rattling our rude sash,   55
Endears the cleanly hearth and social bowl;
Or when, as now, on some delicious eve,
We in our sweet sequester'd orchard-plot
Sit on the tree crook'd earth-ward; whose old boughs,
That hang above us in an arborous roof,   60
Stirr'd by the faint gale of departing May,
Send their loose blossoms slanting o'er our heads!

   Nor dost not thou sometimes recall those hours,
When with the joy of hope thou gavest thine ear
To my wild firstling-lays. Since then my song   65
Hath sounded deeper notes, such as beseem
Or that sad wisdom folly leaves behind,
Or such as, tuned to these tumultuous times,
Cope with the tempest's swell!

               These various strains,   70
Which I have fram'd in many a various mood,
Accept, my Brother! and (for some perchance
Will strike discordant on thy milder mind)
If aught of error or intemperate truth
Should meet thine ear, think thou that riper Age   75
Will calm it down, and let thy love forgive it!

This Lime-Tree Bower My Prison

Well, they are gone, and here must I remain,
This lime-tree bower my prison! I have lost

Beauties and feelings, such as would have been
Most sweet to my remembrance even when age
Had dimm'd mine eyes to blindness! They, meanwhile,   5
Friends, whom I never more may meet again,
On springy heath, along the hill-top edge,
Wander in gladness, and wind down, perchance,
To that still roaring dell, of which I told;
The roaring dell, o'erwooded, narrow, deep,   10
And only speckled by the mid-day sun;
Where its slim trunk the ash from rock to rock
Flings arching like a bridge; – that branchless ash,
Unsunn'd and damp, whose few poor yellow leaves
Ne'er tremble in the gale, yet tremble still,   15
Fann'd by the water-fall! and there my friends
Behold the dark green file of long lank weeds,
That all at once (a most fantastic sight!)
Still nod and drip beneath the dripping edge
Of the blue clay-stone.   20
                         Now, my friends emerge
Beneath the wide wide Heaven – and view again
The many-steepled tract magnificent
Of hilly fields and meadows, and the sea,
With some fair bark, perhaps, whose sails light up   25
The slip of smooth clear blue betwixt two Isles
Of purple shadow! Yes! they wander on
In gladness all; but thou, methinks, most glad,
My gentle-hearted Charles! for thou hast pined
And hunger'd after Nature, many a year,   30
In the great City pent, winning thy way
With sad yet patient soul, through evil and pain
And strange calamity! Ah! slowly sink
Behind the western ridge, thou glorious Sun!
Shine in the slant beams of the sinking orb,   35
Ye purple heath-flowers! richlier burn, ye clouds!
Live in the yellow light, ye distant groves!
And kindle, thou blue Ocean! So my friend
Struck with deep joy may stand, as I have stood,
Silent with swimming sense; yea, gazing round   40
On the wide landscape, gaze till all doth seem
Less gross than bodily; and of such hues
As veil the Almighty Spirit, when yet he makes
Spirits perceive his presence.
                         A delight   45
Comes sudden on my heart, and I am glad
As I myself were there! Nor in this bower,

This little lime-tree bower, have I not mark'd
Much that has sooth'd me. Pale beneath the blaze
Hung the transparent foliage; and I watch'd 50
Some broad and sunny leaf, and lov'd to see
The shadow of the leaf and stem above
Dappling its sunshine! And that walnut-tree
Was richly ting'd, and a deep radiance lay
Full on the ancient ivy, which usurps 55
Those fronting elms, and now, with blackest mass
Makes their dark branches gleam a lighter hue
Through the late twilight: and though now the bat
Wheels silent by, and not a swallow twitters,
Yet still the solitary humble-bee 60
Sings in the bean-flower! Henceforth I shall know
That Nature ne'er deserts the wise and pure;
No plot so narrow, be but Nature there,
No waste so vacant, but may well employ
Each faculty of sense, and keep the heart 65
Awake to Love and Beauty! and sometimes
'Tis well to be bereft of promis'd good,
That we may lift the soul, and contemplate
With lively joy the joys we cannot share.
My gentle-hearted Charles! when the last rook 70
Beat its straight path across the dusky air
Homewards, I blest it! deeming its black wing
(Now a dim speck, now vanishing in light)
Had cross'd the mighty Orb's dilated glory,
While thou stood'st gazing; or, when all was still, 75
Flew creeking o'er thy head, and had a charm
For thee, my gentle-hearted Charles, to whom
No sound is dissonant which tells of Life.

Frost at Midnight

The Frost performs its secret ministry,
Unhelped by any wind. The owlet's cry
Came loud – and hark, again! loud as before.
The inmates of my cottage, all at rest,
Have left me to that solitude, which suits 5
Abstruser musings: save that at my side
My cradled infant slumbers peacefully.
'Tis calm indeed! so calm, that it disturbs
And vexes meditation with its strange
And extreme silentness. Sea, hill, and wood, 10
This populous village! Sea, and hill, and wood,

With all the numberless goings-on of life,
Inaudible as dreams! the thin blue flame
Lies on my low-burnt fire, and quivers not;
Only that film, which fluttered on the grate,   15
Still flutters there, the sole unquiet thing.
Methinks, its motion in this hush of nature
Gives it dim sympathies with me who live,
Making it a companionable form,
Whose puny flaps and freaks the idling Spirit   20
By its own moods interprets, every where
Echo or mirror seeking of itself,
And makes a toy of Thought.

                        But O! how oft,
How oft, at school, with most believing mind,   25
Presageful, have I gazed upon the bars,
To watch that fluttering *stranger*! and as oft
With unclosed lids, already had I dreamt
Of my sweet birth-place, and the old church-tower,
Whose bells, the poor man's only music, rang   30
From morn to evening, all the hot Fair-day,
So sweetly, that they stirred and haunted me
With a wild pleasure, falling on mine ear
Most like articulate sounds of things to come!
So gazed I, till the soothing things, I dreamt,   35
Lulled me to sleep, and sleep prolonged my dreams!
And so I brooded all the following morn,
Awed by the stern preceptor's face, mine eye
Fixed with mock study on my swimming book:
Save if the door half opened, and I snatched   40
A hasty glance, and still my heart leaped up,
For still I hoped to see the *stranger's* face,
Townsman, or aunt, or sister more beloved,
My play-mate when we both were clothed alike!
  Dear Babe, that sleepest cradled by my side,   45
Whose gentle breathings, heard in this deep calm,
Fill up the interspersèd vacancies
And momentary pauses of the thought!
My babe so beautiful! it thrills my heart
With tender gladness, thus to look at thee,   50
And think that thou shalt learn far other lore,
And in far other scenes! For I was reared
In the great city, pent 'mid cloisters dim,
And saw nought lovely but the sky and stars.
But *thou*, my babe! shalt wander like a breeze   55
By lakes and sandy shores, beneath the crags

Of ancient mountain, and beneath the clouds,
Which image in their bulk both lakes and shores
And mountain crags: so shalt thou see and hear
The lovely shapes and sounds intelligible   60
Of that eternal language, which thy God
Utters, who from eternity doth teach
Himself in all, and all things in himself.
Great universal Teacher! he shall mould
Thy spirit, and by giving make it ask.   65
        Therefore all seasons shall be sweet to thee,
Whether the summer clothe the general earth
With greenness, or the redbreast sit and sing
Betwixt the tufts of snow on the bare branch
Of mossy apple-tree, while the nigh thatch   70
Smokes in the sun-thaw; whether the eave-drops fall
Heard only in the trances of the blast,
Or if the secret ministry of frost
Shall hang them up in silent icicles,
    Quietly shining to the quiet Moon.   75

Fears in Solitude

A green and silent spot, amid the hills,
A small and silent dell! O'er stiller place
No singing sky-lark ever poised himself.
The hills are heathy, save that swelling slope,
Which hath a gay and gorgeous covering on,   5
All golden with the never-bloomless furze,
Which now blooms most profusely: but the dell,
Bathed by the mist, is fresh and delicate
As vernal corn-field, or the unripe flax,
When, through its half-transparent stalks, at eve,   10
The level sunshine glimmers with green light.
Oh! 'tis a quiet spirit-healing nook!
Which all, methinks, would love; but chiefly he,
The humble man, who, in his youthful years,
Knew just so much of folly, as had made   15
His early manhood more securely wise!
Here he might lie on fern or withered heath,
While from the singing lark (that sings unseen
The minstrelsy that solitude loves best),
And from the sun, and from the breezy air,   20
Sweet influences trembled o'er his frame;
And he, with many feelings, many thoughts,
Made up a meditative joy, and found

Religious meanings in the forms of Nature!
And so, his senses gradually wrapt   25
In a half sleep, he dreams of better worlds,
And dreaming hears thee still, O singing lark,
That singest like an angel in the clouds!
   My God! it is a melancholy thing
For such a man, who would full fain preserve   30
His soul in calmness, yet perforce must feel
For all his human brethren – O my God!
It weighs upon the heart, that he must think
What uproar and what strife may now be stirring
This way or that way o'er these silent hills –   35
Invasion, and the thunder and the shout,
And all the crash of onset; fear and rage,
And undetermined conflict – even now,
Even now, perchance, and in his native isle:
Carnage and groans beneath this blessed sun!   40
We have offended, Oh! my countrymen!
We have offended very grievously,
And been most tyrannous. From east to west
A groan of accusation pierces Heaven!
The wretched plead against us; multitudes   45
Countless and vehement, the sons of God,
Our brethren! Like a cloud that travels on,
Steamed up from Cairo's swamps of pestilence,
Even so, my countrymen! have we gone forth
And borne to distant tribes slavery and pangs,   50
And, deadlier far, our vices, whose deep taint
With slow perdition murders the whole man,
His body and his soul! Meanwhile, at home,
All individual dignity and power
Engulfed in Courts, Committees, Institutions,   55
Associations and Societies,
A vain, speach-mouthing, speech-reporting Guild,
One Benefit-Club for mutual flattery,
We have drunk up, demure as at a grace,
Pollutions from the brimming cup of wealth;   60
Contemptuous of all honourable rule,
Yet bartering freedom and the poor man's life
For gold, as at a market! The sweet words
Of Christian promise, words that even yet
Might stem destruction, were they wisely preached,   65
Are muttered o'er by men, whose tones proclaim
How flat and wearisome they feel their trade:
Rank scoffers some, but most too indolent

To deem them falsehoods or to know their truth.
Oh! blasphemous! the Book of Life is made   70
A superstitious instrument, on which
We gabble o'er the oaths we mean to break;
For all must swear – all and in every place,
College and wharf, council and justice-court;
All, all must swear, the briber and the bribed,   75
Merchant and lawyer, senator and priest,
The rich, the poor, the old man and the young;
All, all make up one scheme of perjury,
That faith doth reel; the very name of God
Sounds like a juggler's charm; and, bold with joy,   80
Forth from his dark and lonely hiding-place,
(Portentious sight!) the owlet Atheism,
Sailing on obscene wings athwart the noon,
Drops his blue-fringéd lids, and holds them close,
And hooting at the glorious sun in Heaven,   85
Cries out, 'Where is it?'
                      Thankless too for peace,
(Peace long preserved by fleets and perilous seas)
Secure from actual warfare, we have loved
To swell the war-whoop, passionate for war!   90
Alas! for ages ignorant of all
Its ghastlier workings, (famine or blue plague,
Battle, or siege, or flight through wintry snows,)
We, this whole people, have been clamorous
For war and bloodshed; animating sports,   95
The which we pay for as a thing to talk of,
Spectators and not combatants! No guess
Anticipative of a wrong unfelt,
No speculation on contingency,
However dim and vague, too vague and dim   100
To yield a justifying cause; and forth,
(Stuffed out with big preamble, holy names,
And adjurations of the God in Heaven,)
We send our mandates for the certain death
Of thousands and ten thousands! Boys and girls,   105
And women, that would groan to see a child
Pull off an insect's wing, all read of war,
The best amusement for our morning meal!
The poor wretch, who has learnt his only prayers
From curses, and who knows scarcely words enough   110
To ask a blessing from his Heavenly Father,
Becomes a fluent phraseman, absolute
And technical in victories and defeats,

And all our dainty terms for fratricide;
Terms which we trundle smoothly o'er our tongues   115
Like mere abstractions, empty sounds to which
We join no feeling and attach no form!
As if the soldier died without a wound;
As if the fibres of this godlike frame
Were gored without a pang; as if the wretch,   120
Who fell in battle, doing bloody deeds,
Passed off to Heaven, translated and not killed;
As though he had no wife to pine for him,
No God to judge him! Therefore, evil days
Are coming on us, O my countrymen!   125
And what if all-avenging Providence,
Strong and retributive, should make us know
The meaning of our words, force us to feel
The desolation and the agony
Of our fierce doings?   130

              Spare us yet awhile,
Father and God! O! spare us yet awhile!
Oh! let not English women drag their flight
Fainting beneath the burthen of their babes,
Of the sweet infants, that but yesterday   135
Laughed at the breast! Sons, brothers, husbands, all
Who ever gazed with fondness on the forms
Which grew up with you round the same fire-side,
And all who ever heard the sabbath-bells
Without the infidel's scorn, make yourselves pure!   140
Stand forth! be men! repel an impious foe,
Impious and false, a light yet cruel race,
Who laugh away all virtue, mingling mirth
With deeds of murder; and still promising
Freedom, themselves too sensual to be free,   145
Poison life's amities, and cheat the heart
Of faith and quiet hope, and all that soothes,
And all that lifts the spirit! Stand we forth;
Render them back upon the insulted ocean,
And let them toss as idly on its waves   150
As the vile sea-weed, which some mountain-blast
Swept from our shores! And oh! may we return
Not with a drunken triumph, but with fear,
Repenting of the wrongs with which we stung
So fierce a foe to frenzy!   155

              I have told,
O Britons! O my brethren! I have told

Most bitter truth, but without bitterness.
Nor deem my zeal or factious or mistimed;
For never can true courage dwell with them,   160
Who, playing tricks with conscience, dare not look
At their own vices. We have been too long
Dupes of a deep delusion! Some, belike,
Groaning with restless enmity, expect
All change from change of constituted power;   165
As if a Government had been a robe,
On which our vice and wretchedness were tagged
Like fancy-points and fringes, with the robe
Pulled off at pleasure. Fondly these attach
A radical causation to a few   170
Poor drudges of chastising Providence,
Who borrow all their hues and qualities
From our own folly and rank wickedness,
Which gave them birth and nursed them.
   Others, meanwhile,
Dote with a mad idolatry; and all   175
Who will not fall before their images,
And yield them worship, they are enemies
Even of their country!

                Such have I been deemed –
But, O dear Britain! O my Mother Isle!   180
Needs must thou prove a name most dear and holy
To me, a son, a brother, and a friend,
A husband, and a father! who revere
All bonds of natural love, and find them all
Within the limits of thy rocky shores.   185
O native Britain! O my Mother Isle!
How shouldst thou prove aught else but dear and holy
To me, who from thy lakes and mountain-hills,
Thy clouds, thy quiet dales, thy rocks and seas,
Have drunk in all my intellectual life,   190
All sweet sensations, all ennobling thoughts,
All adoration of God in nature,
All lovely and all honourable things,
Whatever makes this mortal spirit feel
The joy and greatness of its future being?   195
There lives nor form nor feeling in my soul
Unborrowed from my country! O divine
And beauteous island! thou hast been my sole
And most magnificent temple, in the which
I walk with awe, and sing my stately songs,   200
Loving the God that made me! –

                                    May my fears,
My filial fears, be vain! and may the vaunts
And menace of the vengeful enemy
Pass like the gust, that roared and died away   205
In the distant tree: which heard, and only heard
In this low dell, bowed not the delicate grass.
        But now the gentle dew-fall sends abroad
The fruit-like perfume of the golden furze:
The light has left the summit of the hill,   210
Though still a sunny gleam lies beautiful,
Aslant the ivied beacon. Now farewell,
Farewell, awhile, O soft and silent spot!
On the green sheep-track, up the heathy hill,
Homeward I wind my way; and lo! recalled   215
From bodings that have well-nigh wearied me,
I find myself upon the brow, and pause
Startled! And after lonely sojourning
In such a quiet and surrounded nook,
This burst of prospect, here the shadowy main,   220
Dim tinted, there the mighty majesty
Of that huge amphitheatre of rich
And elmy fields, seems like society –
Conversing with the mind, and giving it
A livelier impulse and a dance of thought!   225
And now, belovéd Stowey! I behold
Thy church-tower, and, methinks, the four huge elms
Clustering, which mark the mansion of my friend;
And close behind them, hidden from my view,
Is my own lowly cottage, where my babe   230
And my babe's mother dwell in peace! With light
And quickened footsteps thitherward I tend,
Remembering thee, O green and silent dell!
And grateful, that by nature's quietness
And solitary musings, all my heart   235
Is softened, and made worthy to indulge
Love, and the thoughts that yearn for human kind.

The Nightingale: A Conversation Poem

No cloud, no relique of the sunken day
Distinguishes the West, no long thin slip
Of sullen light, no obscure trembling hues.
Come, we will rest on this old mossy bridge!
You see the glimmer of the stream beneath,   5
But hear no murmuring: it flows silently.

O'er its soft bed of verdure. All is still.
A balmy night! and though the stars be dim,
Yet let us think upon the vernal showers
That gladden the green earth, and we shall find   10
A pleasure in the dimness of the stars.
And hark! the Nightingale begins its song,
'Most musical, most melancholy' bird!
A melancholy bird? Oh! idle thought!
In Nature there is nothing melancholy.   15
But some night-wandering man whose heart was pierced
With the remembrance of a grievous wrong,
Or slow distemper, or neglected love,
(And so, poor wretch! filled all things with himself,
And made all gentle sounds tell back the tale   20
Of his own sorrow) he, and such as he,
First named these notes a melancholy strain.
And many a poet echoes the conceit;
Poet who hath been building up the rhyme
When he had better far have stretched his limbs   25
Beside a brook in mossy forest-dell,
By sun or moon-light, to the influxes
Of shapes and sounds and shifting elements
Surrendering his whole spirit, of his song
And of his fame forgetful! so his fame   30
Should share in Nature's immortality,
A venerable thing! and so his song
Should make all Nature lovelier, and itself
Be loved like Nature! But 'twill not be so;
And youths and maidens most poetical,   35
Who lose the deepening twilights of the spring
In ball-rooms and hot theatres, they still
Full of meek sympathy must heave their sighs
O'er Philomela's pity-pleading strains.

My Friend, and thou, our Sister! we have learnt   40
A different lore: we may not thus profane
Nature's sweet voices, always full of love
And joyance! 'Tis the merry Nightingale
That crowds and hurries, and precipitates
With fast thick warble his delicious notes,   45
As he were fearful that an April night
Would be too short for him to utter forth
His love-chant, and disburthen his full soul
Of all its music!
                And I know a grove   50
Of large extent, hard by a castle huge,

Which the great lord inhabits not; and so
This grove is wild with tangling underwood,
And the trim walks are broken up, and grass,
Thin grass and king-cups grow within the paths.   55
But never elsewhere in one place I knew
So many nightingales; and far and near,
In wood and thicket, over the wide grove,
They answer and provoke each other's song,
With skirmish and capricious passagings,   60
And murmurs musical and swift jug jug,
And one low piping sound more sweet than all
Stirring the air with such a harmony,
That should you close your eyes, you might almost
Forget it was not day! On moonlight bushes,   65
Whose dewy leaflets are but half-disclosed,
You may perchance behold them on the twigs,
Their bright, bright eyes, their eyes both bright and full,
Glistening, while many a glow-worm in the shade
Lights up her love-torch.   70
                  A most gentle Maid,
Who dwelleth in her hospitable home
Hard by the castle, and at latest eve
(Even like a Lady vowed and dedicate
To something more than Nature in the grove)   75
Glides through the pathways; she knows all their notes,
That gentle Maid! and oft, a moment's space,
What time the moon was lost behind a cloud,
Hath heard a pause of silence; till the moon
Emerging, a hath awakened earth and sky   80
With one sensation, and those wakeful birds
Have all burst forth in choral minstrelsy,
As if some sudden gale had swept at once
A hundred airy harps! And she hath watched
Many a nightingale perch giddily   85
On blossomy twig still swinging from the breeze,
And to that motion tune his wanton song
Like tipsy Joy that reels with tossing head.

Farewell! O Warbler! till tomorrow eve,
And you, my friends! farewell, a short farewell!   90
We have been loitering long and pleasantly,
And now for our dear homes. That strain again!
Full fain it would delay me! My dear babe,
Who, capable of no articulate sound,
Mars all things with his imitative lisp,   95
How he would place his hand beside his ear,

His little hand, the small forefinger up,
And bid us listen! And I deem it wise
To make him Nature's play-mate. He knows well
The evening-star; and once, when he awoke   100
In most distressful mood (some inward pain
Had made up that strange thing, an infant's dream)
I hurried with him to our orchard-plot,
And he beheld the moon, and, hushed at once,
Suspends his sobs, and laughs most silently,   105
While his fair eyes, that swam with undropped tears,
Did glitter in the yellow moon-beam! Well!
It is a father's tale: But if that Heaven
Should give me life, his childhood shall grow up
Familiar with these songs, that with the night   110
He may associate joy. Once more, farewell,
Sweet Nightingale! once more, my friends! farewell.

Notes

1 I am indebted to several discussions of these poems as a group, including: Reeve Parker, *Coleridge's Meditative Art* (Cornell University Press, 1975); Kelvin Everest, *Coleridge's Secret Ministry: The Context of the Conversation Poems, 1795–1798* (Harvester, 1979); and K.M. Wheeler, *The Creative Mind in Coleridge's Poetry* (Heinemann, 1981).
2 Stephen Bygrave, *Coleridge and the Self* (Palgrave, 1986), p. 114.
3 These eight lines – from 'O the one life within us and abroad' to 'Is Music slumbering on her instument' – form a well-known substantial addition to the version of the poem first published in 1796. But they don't add any significantly different content to the poem (since their 'pantheism' is no more extreme than that in the lines about 'all of animated nature') and because they remain anchored in the 'locatory present' (drawing attention, for instance, to the 'warbling breeze' and the 'mute still air') they do not affect the structural model I am putting forward.
4 H. R. Rookmaaker, Jr, *Towards a Romantic Conception of Nature: Coleridge's Poetry up to 1803: A Study in the History of Ideas* (John Benjamins, 1984), p. 39.
5 The moment of transition from the delineated present to the recalled past, or to the transposed scene which is the locus of the central 'deep reverie' in each poem, is most fully depicted in 'Frost at Midnight', as described in detail by Jennifer Ford in *Coleridge on Dreaming: Romanticism, Dreams, and the Medical Imagination* (Cambridge University Press, 1998). She writes: 'Actions are subdued, preparing the reader to enter and descend into the opaque world of consciousness: to be "presageful", to gaze (line 27), to be "lulled . . . to sleep" (line 35), to brood (line 36), to have a book before you that swims. All that occurs within the domain of gazing, lulling,

dreaming and being soothed is unclear and only partially understood'
(p. 90).

6 In his *Dictionary of Narratology* (revised edition, University of Nebraska Press,
2003), Gerald Prince defines focalisation as 'the perspective in terms of which
the narrated situations and events are presented . . . Should what is presented
be limited to the characters' external behaviour (words and actions but not
thoughts and feelings), their appearance, and the setting against which they
come to the fore, external focalisation is said to obtain' (pp. 31–2). This
effectively defines both types of focalisation.

7 The word 'were' is in fact italicised in all versions of the text, but if the
remark 'And we *were* bless'd' responds to the comment 'It is a blessed place'
then we would expect the response 'And it *was* bless'd'. The passer-by
comments on the cottage, but the speaker takes his words as applying to its
inhabitants, as if he had said '*You* are bless'd'. Between the two lines the
text slips from reported to direct speech, reported speech itself being a device
which dissolves one utterance into another. The greatest emphasis in the
poem is on the man's silence (the verbs used of him are 'paus'd', 'look'd',
'gaz'd', 'eyed', 'gaz'd round again', and 'sigh'd'), and his only utterance is
appropriated to validate the speaker's own nostalgically retrospective view
of his situation then.

8 For instance, Michael O'Neill's discussion of 'The Aeolian Harp' (pp. 84–
6 in *Romanticism and the Self-Conscious Poem*) ends with the remark that
Coleridge's 'violation of his own poem, his misrepresentation of it as
"Bubbles that glitter as they rise and break / On vain Philosophy's aye-
babbling spring", has a kind of dialogic authenticity, even if the voice it
ventriloquizes strikes us as shrilly orthodox' (p. 86). All the terms used
here – 'violation of one's own poem', 'dialogism', 'ventriloquy' – are clearly
adjacent to the notion of surrogacy.

9 This emphasis on Coleridge as compulsive 'revisionary' does not, I hope,
make me guilty of what Michael O'Neill calls 'a reductive tendency in
recent accounts of Coleridge' (p. 62). He sees this as especially embodied
in books by Marilyn Butler and Jerome McGann which, he says, implicitly
deny 'the claims on the reader's imagination and intelligence made by
Coleridge's poetry'. In support he cites Thomas McFarland's *William
Wordsworth: Intensity and Achievement* (Oxford University Press, 1992), and
quotes approvingly McFarland's phrase about a prevalent 'inability to con-
front the quality of the poem'. O'Neill and McFarland do, I think, point
to a growing and genuine problem in Romantic studies: many discussions
of the former 'big five' Romantic poets turn out to be arraignments of
various kinds; increasingly Romanticism is discussed only when coupled
with something else – history, gender, or colonialism, for instance. There
is also a very marked shift away from poetry among Romanticists, or at best
a growing preference for poets whose talents are self-evidently minor (I have
written about the 'depoeticisation' of the period in *Cambridge Quarterly*,
vol. XXVI, no. 3 (1997), pp. 205–18).

4

Contextualising Hemans's shipwrecks

This chapter exemplifies (in Rob Pope's terms) a version of 'inferred intertextuality'. The chapter looks at two poems by Felicia Hemans, one very well known, one less so, and considers them as examples of the celebration of the 'heroic sublime' in accounts of maritime disaster. These poems are contextualised in terms of representational practices seen in paintings, in memoirs, and in the national hagiography of a naval hero. The juxtapositions involved in this approach are in some ways like those of New Historicism, but the aim is not historical reconstruction but the construction of a valid critical context for reading the work of this now controversial poet.

The Felicia Hemans file at the Liverpool Records Office contains a pamphlet entitled 'The Liverpool Homes of Mrs Hemans', which was published in Liverpool in 1897. It identifies a house in Duke Street in the city centre as the one in which she was born (in 1793). It also describes another house, on Wavertree Road, a few miles from the centre of the city, in which she lived for a time during the latter part of her adult life. The pamphlet laments the fact that Liverpool fails to honour its past writers and artists and suggests that a start be made by marking these houses with a suitably inscribed plaque. A plaque was indeed placed on the Duke Street house, although it is not there now (early 2006) and the house itself is in a dilapidated condition. The Wavertree Road cottage, presumably, never received its plaque, and in any case it was demolished in the 1920s, the site now being occupied by a garage forecourt. These two houses can be taken as emblematic of the fluctuations in Hemans's standing; the grandeur of the big Duke Street town house suggests her immense status as a poet in the nineteenth century, while the demolished Wavertree cottage reminds us of the complete collapse of her reputation in the twentieth century. The Duke Street house is ambiguously poised at present, but looks likely to be part of the refurbishment of the area, which it is hoped will restore the district to something of its former status. This too seems emblematic, for Hemans has acquired enthusiastic new academic supporters in Romantic studies during the past twenty years. Indeed, she has become something of a 'site of struggle' within the discipline, and, if Romanticism is your field, then your attitude towards her will reveal a good deal about whether you are a 'New Romanticist' or a more traditional 'Big Five' Romanticist.[1] But how good a poet is Hemans? How important is it to ask that question, and how should her work be read now? In other words, in what professional context can we best read Felicia Hemans, a poet whose reputation has been enormously volatile and whose 'after-life' has been especially eventful?

Hemans's reputation

It is difficult today to appreciate the extent of Hemans's cult-like contemporary fame, and her detractors have often suggested that there was something artificially manufactured about it, as if it were merely the product of her skilful manipulation (and construction) of the peculiarities of the literary tastes of her day. She published her first book of poetry in 1808, at the age of fourteen, the poems having been written when the author was between the ages of eight and thirteen. The list of subscribers began with the Prince of Wales, and she went on to become one of the most widely published poets of the nineteenth century. At eighteen she married a Captain Hemans, and they had five sons in five years, but he then left her and went off to live in Italy, on the grounds that they had nothing in common (apart from the five sons, presumably).[2] The success of her poetry brought her great celebrity, especially in America, where her works were constantly reprinted, and she was able to support her large family on the proceeds – invited to contribute to the *Edinburgh Review*, she specified anonymity and added 'I have never been accustomed to receive less than ten guineas a sheet' (Trinder, *Mrs Hemans*, p. 41). In the history of women's poetry in particular she has always been widely recognised as an important figure, and the Victorian poets Christina Rossetti and Elizabeth Barrett Browning saw themselves as the successors of the two pre-eminently successful women poets of the previous generation, Felicia Hemans and Letitia Elizabeth Landon.

In the twentieth century, however, Hemans's serious poetic reputation suffered a total collapse. Until recently she was remembered, if at all, as the author of the much-parodied Victorian parlour piece 'Casabianca' ('The boy stood on the burning deck'), and of the poem

'The stately homes of England', made into a facetious song for a Noel Coward musical in the 1930s. But the collapse of her reputation is no surprise, really, since the same thing happened to nearly every aspect of Victorian culture – music, painting, architecture, and literature. Hence, dismissive asides about Hemans become commonplace in literary histories. Even George Saintsbury's *A History of Nineteenth Century Literature: 1780–1895* (1896), which has room for almost everybody, has very little room for her. He quaintly assures us that her character was blameless, in spite of the fact that she spent most of her married life apart from her husband, 'through no known fault of her own'. Her verse has 'a certain ingenuous tenderness', and though it is 'impossible to allow her genius, she need not be spoken of with any elaborate disrespect' (p. 112). Oliver Elton's *Survey of English Literature* (1912) showers her in gender-stereotyping: she 'had an abundance of eager poetic emotion, a passion for the obviously romantic, an enthusiasm for foreign literature, and languages, and an endless flow of facile and not discreditable verse' (pp. 265–6). Like Saintsbury, he likes 'England's Dead', and some of her shorter poems. Sometimes in these, he says, 'her genuine exaltation of soul and temper, usually squandered and wasted, concentrates itself into fit and rememberable words' (p. 266). In 1938, in *The Victorians and After, 1830–1914* (1938), Edith Batho and Bonamy Dobrée are also suspicious of a craft learned too well, of her fluency and fecundity as a poet: her work is 'characteristic of the rather unregulated sensibility and enthusiasm of the minor literature of the thirties and forties. She had a genuine poetic gift . . . but a dangerous facility' (p. 224). Even by 1960s things had little changed: Ian Jack in *English Literature, 1815–1832* (1963) writes (pp. 168–9) that:

> The general level of her work is high, but unfortunately it almost always stops short of memorable poetry. Many of the better things . . . might be the work of a poetical committee. For her, we feel, poetry was a feminine accomplishment more difficult than piano-playing and embroidery but no less respectable. She has a definite affinity with Scott in her fluency, her love of the picturesque, and her refusal to confront conventional morality. What we miss in her work is poetic individuality.

The revival of Hemans's fame in the past two decades has been the result of the major historicist 'turn' in the study of British Romanticism beginning around the start of the 1980s, and seen initially in the work of major figures like Marilyn Butler and Jerome McGann.[3] The historicist emphasis began to move attention away from the former exclusive focus on the work of the 'Big Five' poets, looking increasingly at prose writing, at the work of women poets, and at the

whole cultural context of Romantic writing. A key moment was the
Modern Language Association Convention in December 1985, which
included 'the first sessions devoted entirely to the problem of the English
Romantic poets and women'. A foundational collection of essays
emerged from this conference, *Romanticism and Feminism* (1988) edited
by Anne K. Mellor, and a few years later Mellor brought out a related
monograph, *Romanticism and Gender* (1993). Hemans is increasingly
anthologised in collections which provide material for the undergraduate study of this kind of 'New Romanticism'[4] and more recently a paper-
back edition of a major collection of her work has appeared in a modern
edited edition rather than a facsimile reprint.[5] Academics, generally speaking, have much less influence on the contents of the canon than their
pronouncements on the matter would imply, but they do, of course,
determine the contents of the syllabus, and there can be no doubt that
Hemans is now back on it.

Yet now that she is being championed by university academics,
Hemans again confronts us with the problem of whether she is merely
the incidental beneficiary of a change in taste, academic taste this time,
and especially of a widespread desire to democratise and feminise the
Romantic period, so that, instead of giving almost exclusive attention
to an elite male core, we want to include women poets, 'labouring-
class' poets, and popular poets. Identifying one's own motives for
wanting to study and teach Hemans then becomes strangely fraught
and problematical (do I simply want to show, by writing on Hemans,
that I am not an 'old school' elitist?) and she seems unique as a poet
in thus being at the 'cutting edge' of the continental drift of the syllabus, poised at the point of dangerous friction, where the tectonic plates
of old and new Romanticisms grind uncomfortably against each
other. There is, I think, an element of self-doubt and self-interrogation
within many of Hemans's New Romanticist supporters, which is nicely
dramatised by Jerome McGann in the last chapter of his book *The Poetics
of Sensibility* (1986), which stages an internal debate over Hemans
between three aspects of himself under the title 'Literary History,
Romanticism and Felicia Hemans: A Conversation between A. Mack,
J. J. Rome, and G. Mannejc'. The debate is conducted in the high-baroque
style of recent American rhetorical criticism (of which McGann and
Stanley Fish were the major figures), so that pronouncements abound
like 'Her poetry is not clichéd and sentimental, as many have charged,
it is a prolepsis of the ideas of cliché and sentimentality' (p. 189). All
the same, this internal debate has moments of brilliance and is strik-
ingly analogous to the one which has been conducted within the academic community at large, as instanced by the e-mail list discussion on

Hemans on the web site of the North American Society for the Study of Romanticism (NASSR) which took place in the summer of 1997.[6]

Generally, British Romanticists have tended to favour Hemans less than their American counterparts (with notable exceptions like Isobel Armstrong and Jennifer Breen) as exemplified by some testy exchanges of the mid-1990s. In the May/June 1995 issue of the poetry journal *PN Review* Donald Davie criticises Felicia Hemans in the context of a discussion about the canon and the debates surrounding it. He resents the presence of twelve poems by Hemans in Jerome McGann's *New Oxford Book of Romantic Period Verse* (1993) – a key moment in her contemporary rehabilitation – and quotes her poem 'The Stately Homes of England' as evidence of the poet's dishonesty. 'We fault the poem', he says, 'because it is not truthful: not only we with the benefit of hindsight can see this, *but Felicia Hemans as she wrote the poem must have known it* . . . the vision of hierarchical stability purveyed by her poem was *a lie*.'[7] So what are her poems doing in the anthology? Well, says Davie, 'They are co-opted by the timid male anthologist merely to placate a vocal lobby. The augmented presence of women poets in the anthologies should be seen for what it mostly is, a manifestation of male panic' (p. 14). Much could be said in response to this, but I will say simply that accusing the poet of lying is a Platonic ploy which had better be used on all poets if it is to be used on any (for example, on Gray and his Elegy – he must have known that this vision of the countryside as a place of rural contentment was a lie – or on Tennyson's *Idylls* – he must have known that this vision of knightly chivalry was a lie, and so on, right through the canon).

Later the same year the *TLS* carried a 'Commentary' piece about Hemans by Peter Cochran entitled 'Fatal Fluency, Fruitless Dower: The Eminently Marketable Felicia Hemans'. He reminds us that she was 'the most successful English-Language poet of the nineteenth century and, commercially, the most successful woman poet ever' (*Times Literary Supplement*, 21 July 1995, p. 13) and that she was admired by the greatest women writers of her day, including George Eliot, Charlotte Brontë, and Elizabeth Gaskell. Tennyson's mother, he adds, used to read Hemans's verse to him when he was a child, and the influence was certainly significant. But Cochran clearly regards Hemans as a relentlessly commercial author, able to churn out poetic blockbusters on any topic that allowed her to create a central tableau of the suffering woman. Her work was based on book research rather than personal experience and on highly wrought dramatic situations – an American settler family burying a dead infant in the wilderness, a mother failing to recognise her returned crusader son, so greatly transformed is he by suffering. The uncomfortable pattern suggested by these British comments is of female and feminist-inclining scholars supporting Hemans's belated 'canonisation' (or, at least, her admission onto the Romantic syllabus), and of male scholars voicing scepticism or cynicism about this process, and by implication, thereby defending 'higher' literary-critical values.

For the individual academic, the issue of the ultimate poetic quality of the work can also be somewhat fraught. To argue against Hemans on such grounds is likely to be read as an act of dissent from *the whole* agenda of 'New Romanticism', which for a young scholar could well have negative career consequences. A way round the dilemma is to avoid the question of intrinsic poetic merit altogether and argue instead that Hemans merits attention because of her literary-historical importance as a key bridging figure between the Romantic and Victorian sensibilities, and as a poet with a claim to be the inventor of that key Victorian poetic form, the dramatic monologue. This potentially extends the common ground between new and old Romanticists, for there is more likely to be a degree of consensus on Hemans's importance as an innovator, than on the matter of her individual worth relative to that of the Big Five. Her 1828 collection *Records of Woman* (edited by Paula R. Feldman, 1999) uses 'fiction or quasi-historical narrative to explore the values that matter to her as a woman writer'. The poems are interior monologues of women characters (examples being 'Arabella Stuart', 'Gertrude, or Fidelity till Death', 'The Switzer's Wife', 'Properzia Rossi', and 'Joan of Arc, in Rhiems'), women who, whatever the source of their fame, long ardently for the requited love that fame has not brought them. Reading poems like those just mentioned makes it immediately apparent why Hemans was so enormously popular in her day. She combines an often-flawless Tennysonian mellifluousness with a real dramatic sense. Thus, she anticipated Tennyson and Browning in their use of the dramatic monologue, combining Tennyson's ability to create atmosphere with Browning's novelistic psychological portraiture. Paradoxically, her dramatic monologues are really extended soliloquies, or thought sequences, which do not suggest a real dramatic situation, as in Browning, with actually spoken words and silent auditors, but rather evoke a conjectural space which opens an essentially private, meditative reflection to the scrutiny of a *readership*, rather than an *audience*. In other words, they are more interior monologue than dramatic monologue, which is to say that they are better described as *novelistic* monologues than dramatic ones. It might therefore be claimed that they bridge the gap between the Romantic 'conversation poem' and the later Victorian form. As this suggests, Hemans could usefully be seen as a transitional poet, combining Romantic and Victorian qualities, and hence becoming a potentially important figure in this period of literary history. The writer of the facsimile introduction brings out the affinity between 'Arabella Stuart' and the conversation poem, for 'in its turns and counter-turns it reminds us of . . . the original version of Coleridge's "Dejection, an Ode"'. Arabella Stuart, the 'speaker' in the poem, is in captivity, separated, for reasons of state, from her bridegroom, William Seymour. Hemans's introductory note characteristically remarks that she is thus 'shut out from that domestic happiness which her heart appears to have so fervently desired', and there seems to be a vicarious identification of the poet with this persona. The argument for a limited affinity between Coleridge and Hemans here would be that, while the male poet can speak of his feelings directly – because the poetic licence issued to male poets has a clause allowing them to do this (though Coleridge's poem was, of course, rigorously self-censored) – the female poet is not expected to indulge in this kind of self-display, and hence requires the 'screen' provided by the persona and the monologue device. This apart, both poets voice their feelings in a long, loose poem concerned with shifts and nuances of unresolved inner tension. This argument has, though, a kind of gender-determinism, which (crudely speaking) ascribes the woman poet's artistic choices to 'social' factors. In other words, it makes her utilisation of a dramatic persona into a necessity – she had no other available way of expressing her feelings. It also leaves unexplained the *choice* of the dramatic 'screen' by male writers who could have spoken 'directly' had they so wished. Hence, the difference between the 'interior monologic' poems of Hemans and the Coleridgean 'conversation poem' remains crucial, for one poet makes the breakthrough to a meditative, non-lyric poem of personal and psychological focus with autobiographical detail, while the other operates within a very different mode of the imaginative poetic novelisation of characters from history or legend. Hemans, then, is more a prolegomenon to the age of the novel than an outgrowth of Romanticism, that is to say, she is 'really' a historical 'novelist', ultimately more akin to Scott than to Coleridge. Thus, it is certainly possible, in various ways, to claim for Hemans a considerable hybrid or transitional significance.

Hemans and poetic quality

But we should not let ourselves evade that key and uncomfortable question of the ultimate poetic quality of Hemans's work, a point which cannot be decided at this level of remoteness from detailed textual explication. Until recently, detailed critique of Hemans's work was hardly anywhere to be found, but the publication of Isobel Armstrong's *Victorian Poetry: Poetry, Poetics, and Politics* (1993) altered matters, for in her chapter on women poets she discusses Hemans in general, and in particular her poems 'Arabella Stuart' and 'Casabianca'. The context for this discussion is a broad general claim about women's poetry which is made near the start of the chapter: Armstrong claims a characteristic 'doubleness' in women's poetry, which comes from its ostensible adoption of an affective mode, often simple, often pious, often conventional. But those conventions are subjected to investigation, questioned or used for unexpected purposes. The simpler the surface of the poem she claims, in a bold and stark assertion, the more likely it is that a second and more difficult poem will exist beneath it (p. 324). The claim here is that what is simple, pious, or conventional in women's poetry is often only ostensibly so. In fact, beneath apparent simplicity the conventions are being 'interrogated', and, indeed, the greater the ostensible simplicity the more difficult the poem really is. These are perhaps surprising claims to make of women's poetry as a whole. To accept them is really to issue women's poetry in general not just with a poetic licence but also with a blank intellectual cheque, so that (one might argue) no *individual* woman poet can actually benefit, since the claims are made not about some women poets, or women poets some of the time, but, simply, about 'women poets'.

A more cautious reformulation of this claim would suggest that all women poets, no matter how apparently conformist, will have *some* poems which reveal ambivalence, doubts, and so on, about the attitudes and conventions which their work primarily expresses. This, I think, is a plausible claim to make about Hemans. Seeking out these crucial poems, distinguishing them from the rest, and revealing their contradictions and intricacies is a fascinating and worthwhile critical exercise, and these 'rogue' poems have all the more impact because of their contrast with the surrounding *oeuvre*. In effect, one might say, in spite of the broad-scale declaration, it is implicitly this more limited brief which Armstrong pursues in her long chapter on women's poetry, with considerable success.

So, for instance, she looks, in her treatment of 'Arabella Stuart', for the 'doubleness' she has said is central to women's poetry. At the start of the poem the speaker, in captivity, describes a dream:

> 'Twas but a dream! I saw the stag leap free,
> Under the boughs where early birds were singing;
> I stood o'ershadowed by the greenwood tree,
> And heard, it seemed, a sudden bugle ringing
> Far through a royal forest.

The pathos, of course, is that dreaming of a stag's miraculous escape from the hunters, and then awakening, renews the pain of captivity – there will be no miraculous escapes for her. But Armstrong provides the doubleness by converting the dream to a memory ('In the extremity of the memory it is precisely important that the lover was *there*', p. 330), while at the same time blurring the distinction between the two:

> The diction is used to render the vestigial, uncertain and discontinuous retrieval by memory of an event which even then may have been a dream and 'seemed' (there is a double 'seeming', the event and the memory of it) like a masque. (p. 330)

But the cost of achieving doubleness is having to contradict what the poem explicitly tells us ('"Twas but a dream'), always a procedure best avoided in criticism. The 'doubling' effect, if it is in the poem, provides the kind of complexity which close reading has traditionally thrived upon, but, again, one may wonder whether the tactic is really sound, since the poetic effect Hemans achieves seems (as often) essentially a mono-dimensional one, the strength of which derives precisely from its simplicity. Armstrong risks sacrificing the strength in order to claim a certain kind of complexity.

She then moves on to 'Casabianca' (see the appendix to this chapter), her link being that 'Like that woman in "Arabella Stuart" who "stood" transfixed under the greenwood tree, the boy in "Casabianca" "stood" on the burning deck, and in both cases the word seems to denote positioning outside the control of the character' (p. 330). The boy, then, remains at his post under fire 'on the burning deck' because he has not been released by his father's telling him his duty is now discharged. He asks repeatedly 'Say, Father, say / If yet my task is done?' but receives no answer from below decks because his father has been killed or rendered unconscious in the battle. So the boy remains on the blazing ship and is blown up when the vessel explodes. The situation is, as Armstrong calls it, an 'Oedipal fiasco' and 'a deeply affective lament', but her emphasis is surprising. She repeatedly stresses the notion of an obedience which is ruthlessly demanded by an implacable paternal/patriarchal power, and blindly given by a helpless child-victim. Hence, in the space of a paragraph, 'The boy is subject to commands'; he shows 'absolute obedience to the father's orders', or 'simple obedience', and eventually he is blown to pieces, 'through the act of blind obedience' in response to 'patriarchal imperatives', so that 'the absoluteness of the patriarchal imperative' is made apparent. Thus, the boy perishes because of 'the patriarchal imperatives of heroism', and the poem suggests 'the way masculinity is founded . . . this is a law to the death, killing a child on a burning deck' (pp. 330–1).

I have several reservations about all this. Firstly, the boy's obedience is anything but 'blind'. He can see that the situation is hopeless – he can already feel the heat of the flames, and far from 'responding unquestioningly', as the critic maintains, he asks three increasingly desperate questions, beginning with 'Say, Father, say / If yet my task is done?' This is a rather different figure from the automaton suggested by the frequent references to 'blind obedience'. Secondly, the whole pathos of the poem lies in the fact that, far from insisting on 'a law to the death' which would condemn his child to die for no useful purpose whatever, the father would surely have told the boy to flee if he had heard his voice, for, whatever their failings, 'patriarchal imperatives' never enjoined futile acts of suicide. Finally, Armstrong's conclusion, that the poem 'takes its revenge on war even as it sees that war takes revenge on itself' (which I take to be a British example of the McGannian style of 'rhetorical criticism') is perhaps an implausible way to interpret this account of the death of someone the poem calls 'A creature of heroic blood'. The poem admires the boy's heroism (it is one of a great many of Hemans's poems which present a tableau of heroic behaviour), and the emphasis on the non-stoical side of the boy's attitude increases our sense of how young he is and how futile it is that he should go on standing there and die for nothing. It is so far from being a coherent or typical warlike act that it makes little sense to construe the piece as an anti-war poem. The anti-war reading (the notion that the poem shows war's revenge on itself) is also, perhaps, a surprising one to attribute to the work of a poet whom Shelley admired for everything but her Christianity and her approval of what he called 'fatal sanguinary war'.[8] But Armstrong's general proposition about women poets does require such a reading: since the poem (for her) *seems* to celebrate the heroic aspect of war, it must be seen as, in some way, attacking rather than celebrating it, even if only in the form of 'war's revenge on itself'.

Extending the 'intertextual domain'

However, I want to suggest that a better way of reading the poem is to place it within an extended 'intertextual domain', one in which both its conventional and its unconventional aspects can be seen more clearly. For Hemans's treatment of the incident shown in her most famous poem is consonant with a narrative and pictorial style which remained the norm for the depiction of such incidents right into the twentieth century. Hemans's dramatisation and pictorialisation of the incident is the product of a received set of conventions for the representation of the boyish 'heroic sublime'. Yet Hemans does not simply accept these conventions slavishly but humanises her hero by making him anything but a silent, passive accepter of his fate. On the contrary, he questions it, and clearly seeks to escape it if he possibly can, and all the pathos and force of the poem lies in this manner of depiction. If the boy were merely standing unprotestingly waiting for the ship to explode, the poem would be a piece of inert and sickly hagiography. The effect of including his protests (and it is quite overt, not a matter of ironic or 'subversive' undertones) is rather like that achieved by religious poets such as Herbert and Hopkins when they include in their poems their protestations about God's unreasonable demands upon them (and, again, this is a matter of the poet's own foregrounding, not something implied or ironic which would need to be teased out by critical ingenuity). All the same, the conventions with which Hemans works are actually there, and impose limitations of some sort on what can be depicted.

Understanding what these conventions are, how this 'climate of representation' or 'discourse' (Foucault) of the heroic sublime actually worked may be achieved by considering the representation of comparable incidents of 'heroic' young deaths at sea. Effectively, this is to extend the 'intertextual domain' of the poem into a much wider context of visual and historical representation. A brief description of two examples may therefore be helpful. The first concerns the notorious mid-nineteenth-century shipwreck, on 27 September 1854, of the Atlantic liner *Arctic*, owned by the Collins Line of New York, which sank in fog off Cape Race after colliding with the French steamer *Vesta*. Some three hundred people died, including Collins's own wife, son, and daughter. Cartoons of the day had depicted Edward Collins as the embodiment of Yankee energy and determination, taking on the maritime might of John Bull and contesting British dominance of the lucrative transatlantic passenger and immigrant trade. The disaster was seen as the consequence of the ruthless of pursuit of fast crossings, with ships in busy sea-lanes travelling at high speed through fog. The hero of the *Arctic* episode was the young Stewart Holland, who remained on deck firing the distress cannon until both he and the ship disappeared beneath the waves. A contemporary lithograph (Figure 2) shows the youth standing on the deck in a pose of saintly calm, hand on breast, as the waves crash over the side of the ship. The iconography of the image derives partly from that of 'holy pictures' of saints made for devotional purposes, in which any trace of inner struggle is removed. Like the 'Casabianca' episode, the incident itself has a stark

Figure 2 A contemporary lithograph of the sinking of the Collins Line
steamer *Arctic* on 27 September 1854, showing the young Stewart Holland
standing on deck firing the distress cannon as the ship went down.
Reproduced by permission of the Arader Galleries, New York.

iconicity; the names *Arctic* and *Vesta* suggest an elemental clash, as if
of a masculine and a feminine principle, but the patriarchal imperatives are actually two-sided, in the sense that there is both the ruthless
drive of Collins himself, the owner of the steamship company, but also
the chivalric code of the sea, which involves giving succour to the weak,
even at risk to oneself. This is seen in the behaviour of the *Arctic*'s
captain, whose ship was far larger than the *Vesta*, so that he assumed
that the smaller ship must have sustained the greater damage, and lost
valuable time by attempting to assist it. Like Hemans's boy on the
burning deck, Holland stands rooted on the deck of the doomed ship,

but there is also a crucial difference: though the action of firing the cannon may seem futile, it is a *rational* act, predicated on the slight possibility that the sound may be heard and rescue arrive at the last moment. In other words, it is not simply the kind of pointless act of suicide that Armstrong's reading of Hemans's poem seems to see as required by patriarchal imperatives of obedience to authority. Holland's act, then, noble and saintly though it is, has a purpose, but the 'standing' in the poem is an act which has no rational purpose and could contribute nothing to saving the ship or winning the battle. In short, the boy in the poem isn't *doing* anything on the deck except standing on it, whereas Holland stood on the deck for a purpose. The Holland episode is reminiscent of the poem in its details, but also reminds us that the patriarchal code was double-sided, and did not enjoin useless death or suffering. Holland would not be a hero if he had simply stood fixated on the deck for no good reason as the ship went down.

The second example, though more distant in time from Hemans, is a closer parallel to the events depicted in 'Casabianca', for in this example we again have a battle, an actual burning deck, and a boy standing on it. The boy is Jack Cornwell VC, a sixteen-year-old 'Sight Setter' or 'Gun Layer' on the British cruiser *HMS Chester* at the Battle of Jutland in 1916. Cornwell's job was to stand by the gun, listening in his earphones for instructions from the Gunnery Officer high up in the control tower and relay these to the gun crew. Having gone ahead of the fleet in fog to investigate the sound of distant gunfire, his ship came out of the mist at 29 knots and encountered four German cruisers:

> *HMS Chester* fought gallantly but was no match for the combined firepower of four enemy cruisers, and subsequently took severe punishment. In all, she was hit seventeen times by major calibre shells. Four of these impacted around the gun turret that was Jack's position. The ship was reduced to a shambles, only one gun being operational. All around Jack, men were laid dying and horribly mutilated by shrapnel, he himself had felt the red hot shard of steel penetrate his chest. With grim determination he stood fast to his post, patiently awaiting orders from the control tower, as the cauldron exploded around him. Jack did not know it, but he was mortally wounded. He remained standing alone at his station, until Admiral Hood's Dreadnoughts appeared, their heavy guns allowing *Chester* to disengage. Medics then were able to go to Jack's aid and take him below.[9]

Cornwell died of his wounds in hospital in Grimsby and became a national hero. He was represented in popular iconography in a manner, again, which is distinctly reminiscent of the way saintly figures are presented in devotional imagery, except that instead of a halo, denoting

Figure 3 Contemporary image of Jack Cornwell, the boy who stood
on the burning deck of the cruiser *HMS Chester* at the Battle of
Jutland in 1916, and won a posthumous V.C. The image is
downloaded from website http://www.ravenspurn.co.uk/jut1.html
which gives an account of Cornwell's exploits.

an elevated state of religious fervour, the image is surrounded with the
victor's laurels (Figure 3), denoting his attainment of the status I have
been calling the heroic sublime. The overall outcome of Jutland was
ambiguous, and is still disputed: British losses in both ships and men
were higher than those of Germany, but it was a battle the British could
win simply by not losing: the British Admiral Jellicoe, as Churchill said,
was the only man who could have lost the war in a single afternoon,
for, if the British battle fleet had been destroyed, a German naval block-
ade of Britain would have made eventual surrender inevitable. As it
was, the German High Seas fleet never emerged from port again, so
the tactical objective was secured. But none of this was easy to explain
to a British public expecting a Nelsonian triumph, so the celebration
in newspapers of deeds like Cornwell's was doubtless a useful boost to
patriotic morale.

At first sight, the similarities with the 'Casabianca' situation are very
striking, for here the act of valour does not at first seem to involve any
act, any actual firing of the cannon, but just standing passively awaiting an instruction, like the boy in the poem. This seems at first to contradict the earlier remark that the act of valour has to be a rational act,

not just a pointless suicidal gesture. But Cornwell's standing on the burning deck does have the purpose of restoring the gun to action when the instructions are received, however unlikely this might seem in view of the devastation caused by the shelling.[10] Once again, the point is precisely that pointless mere endurance, with no discernible object, is *not* required by the patriarchal code, so that, for example, the disabled *HMS Chester* was not required to remain at its station till it was pounded to pieces, but was relieved by the supporting ships so that it could disengage and return to port. This is equivalent to that 'other' side of the patriarchal code, which, my contention is, all these incidents also manifest along with the 'severe' side – as seen in the *Arctic*'s captain trying to save others when his own plight is more severe, and the father who would have told the son to flee, had he been able to hear the cry.

In all three instances, too, emblematic overtones are strongly suggestive giving them what might be called (a bit awkwardly) cultural depth and resonance. For instance, all three incidents are pervaded by a sense of uncertainty, obscurity, and doubt, which is physically realised. The Battle of the Nile, for instance (the setting for the 'Casabianca' incident), was a nocturnal affair which began at 6.30 in the evening, after days of each fleet trying to locate the other and second-guess its intentions; Jutland was very similar, a close engagement in mist and encroaching darkness after days of confused mutual pursuit; and a literal fog surrounded the sinking of the *Arctic*. In all three incidents the class overtones are also very suggestive: the boy in 'Casabianca' absorbs the imperatives of an aristocratic code of conduct; Holland remains to the last the faithful servant of the wealthy ship-owner (who went on undaunted by the *Arctic* catastrophe to build and lose more ships, until his inevitable bankruptcy), and Cornwell, the son of an East End tram driver, was a delivery boy for the Brooke Bond Tea company whose brief life ended with a state funeral. The 'familial' element in all three incidents is also striking: 'Casabianca' is an evident family drama in which the son seeks the father's approval, or fears his disapproval, as Armstrong shows; Holland has an element of this, and also seems the would-be-protective surrogate *alter ego* of the absent father (Collins himself was not aboard, kept in New York by business while his family visited Europe – a scenario familiar from the 'international' tales of Henry James), and Cornwell, setting out from King's Cross Station for the Rosyth Naval Base in Scotland, told his mother, 'Mam, it's what I joined up for, I have to go – it is my duty', which is, as it were, the moment when he chooses the Navy as his new 'family', with its new ties and obligations (an analogous moment of choice is always a key stage in hagiographic accounts too). The similarity between all three incidents may not be accidental; Hemans's poem was universally known in the English-speaking world, learned by heart and parodied by schoolchildren well beyond the First World War. The promulgation of one incident of the heroic and patriotic sublime has the effect of inspiring the next generation to emulate the events depicted. In his graveside speech at Cornwell's funeral, the naval representative said 'His grave will be the birthplace of heroes, from which will spring an inspiration', which exactly captures the sense of this slightly macabre iterative or fertilising impulse of one incident on another.

One further related image captures the way the representation of the heroic sublime has the effect of generating further acts in the same mode, for the same proleptic 'mirroring' effect is seen in a Victorian painting by Thomas Davidson (fl. 1863–1903) which is in the Picture Gallery of the National Maritime Museum at Greenwich (Figure 4). It is entitled *England's Pride and Glory* and shows a boy looking at a painting

Figure 4 England's Pride and Glory by Thomas Davidson (fl. 1863–1903). This painting, now in the collection of the National Maritime Museum, Greenwich, depicts a scene in the Gallery of the Royal Naval College, where the painting itself was formerly displayed. The NMM's catalogue description reads 'The painting symbolises the inspiration that the memory of Nelson provided for all young men who had ambitions in the service of the Navy'. Reproduced by permission of the National Maritime Museum, London.

of Nelson in the gallery of the Royal Naval College (that is, in the gallery where this picture was itself displayed). The boy is in the uniform of a naval cadet, and his rapt gaze is fixed on the face of Nelson in the portrait: Nelson's gaze is outwards at his destiny, while the mother's gaze is downwards, musingly and sadly, at the boy, her arm on his shoulder, which he seems not to notice, fixed as he is in this 'mirror stage' of self-conception, when his defining vocational aspiration is formed. And where is the viewer's gaze? The source of the side-lighting on the mother's cheek is ambiguous, in that no source for it is shown in the picture, but behind her, filling a quarter of the entire frame, we can see the painting which is adjacent to the Nelson portrait: it is *The Destruction of the* L'Orient by George Arnauld (1763–1841), which shows the decisive moment in the Battle of the Nile when the French flagship blew up, and (as the NMM's catalogue describes it) 'the explosion was immense, and for a while the action ceased, gun crews stunned by what they had heard and saw. With the *L'Orient* and her admiral went the rest of the French ships' eagerness to fight and the remaining ships which had not already been taken, surrendered to the British fleet.' The 'admiral', of course, is Casabianca, and this is the moment of the death of the boy on the burning deck. The light of the explosion seems to come out of the picture-in-the-picture, and is proleptic, perhaps, of the boy-in-the-picture's eventual end, probably on one or other of the many burning decks of Jutland. Again, in the painting, the interweaving of the familial story with a larger national story is very striking, for the *grand narrative* of the imperial design is interwoven with the *petit narrative* of family suffering and bereavement, exactly as in Hemans's famous poem 'The Graves of a Houschold'. In 'Casabianca' itself, however, she boldly eliminates the national *grand narrative* entirely, and foregrounds the familial tragedy ('But the noblest thing that perished there / Was that young, faithful heart') even though the moment of the explosion of the enemy flagship marks the culmination of Nelson's patriotic triumph. The final illustration (Figure 5) shows the frontispiece to W.M. Rossetti's 1873 edition of Hemans's works, with the boy standing on a deck and looking naively and innocently confident, on a deck that seems blood-stained rather than burning. The close presence of the flames, however, is vividly conveyed by the strong side-lighting from the left, which is reminiscent of that in Davidson's picture of the Victorian cadet, just as the Hemans boy seems uncannily like the doomed Stewart Holland of the *Arctic*.

Thus, Hemans's poem achieves its fullest resonance when we explore a distinct realm of 'deep' context in which (I would argue) it properly belongs, and the process also highlights its transgressive or anomalous

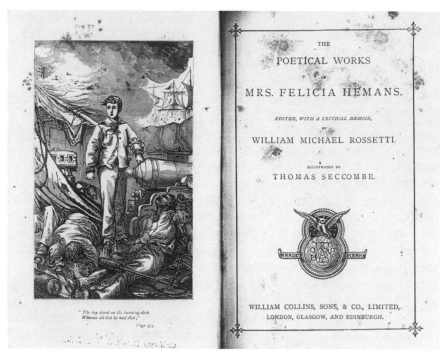

Figure 5 Title page and frontispiece to W.M. Rossetti's 1873 edition
of Hemans's *Works*, showing Thomas Seccombe's illustration of the
boy on the burning deck. (I am grateful to Nanora Sweet for
providing me with this image.)

aspects within this tradition of representation, notably the fact that
it does not show the hero as unwaveringly accepting it as his duty
to stand on the deck till the end (like the depictions of Holland and
Cornwell), but rather as voicing increasingly frantic requests for re-
lease. As already suggested, that is the element in which lies the strange
force of the poem. Furthermore, the reading suggested here does not
require us to see any 'irony' in the poem, nor do we have to make the
further implausible supposition that this 'irony' escaped all previous
readers over a period of a hundred and fifty years until the present-
day 'New Romanticists'. The target of my own irony here is the recent
new edition of *Records of Woman* (ed. Paula R. Feldman, 1999), which
refers to the poem as 'recited by generations of school children over
the following century. Ironically, it calls into question what it most seems
to extol: obedience to patriarchal authority' (p. xviii). This makes the
gratuitous assumption that generations of schoolteachers must have been
very bad literary critics. The real error, in my view, is the one made

by university academics, not schoolteachers, in imagining that the poem 'seems to extol' obedience to patriarchal authority, when there are (again, ironically) no grounds for making such an assumption.

Can Hemans be read today without appeal to 'irony'?

Yet, to come back to it, the challenge of close reading some of Hemans's work can no longer be procrastinated. Close reading is never a sufficient procedure in literary discussion – as we have learned and accepted in our post-Formalist times – but it is always a necessary one. I will therefore take a poem in which Hemans portrays a female version of the heroic sublime in the context of disaster at sea. In her poem 'The Wreck', then (see the appendix to this chapter), we have another image of the heroic sublime, though this poem too has its 'transgressive' element. It shows maternal devotion to duty in a disaster at sea, and is one of Hemans's icons of idealised maternity, but of a distinctly discomfiting kind. The poem tells of a shipwreck, in a fairly generalised way, before homing in for a close-up of three corpses washed ashore, these being the bodies of a crew member and those of a mother and her baby. I will read it in a loosely deconstructive style, claiming an element in the poem which undercuts the values it ostensibly professes, which is very much the contemporary way of reading Hemans. The skill of the poem lies partly in the gradual 'homing in' on the three corpses, culminating in the thrill of the anticipated close-up, a process of suspenseful protraction which is reminiscent of the technique used in horror films. The poem opens with the firing of yet another cannon.

In the first stanza the storm and the shipwreck are heard in the distance, as if by a sleeper in a house near the shore, and the wrecked ship is then seen in the light of dawn:

A bark from India's coral strand,
  Before the rushing blast,
Had vailed her topsails to the sand
  And bowed her noble mast.

The second stanza details the devastation of the ship itself and the last line – 'And sadder things than these!' – hints at worse things still to be shown, beginning the 'homing in' process, and whetting the appetite for further horrors, so to speak. The third stanza is moralistic and emblematic: the enterprise on which the ship was engaged when lost was commercial and materialistic, and the wealth which it had been bringing back from India is now spilled along the shore – pearls, rubies, and gold strewn along the wet sand. This is a stylised scenario, of course, and obviously not a realistic picture at all of what ships in general actually brought back from India. Indeed, the 'India' connoted here is not a real (or, at least, a realised) place but a mythical orientalist 'East' whose ultimate provenance is the *Thousand and One Nights.* In fact, the stylisation is so great that one might be tempted to read jewels and gold as primarily emblematic of the surplus value which the imperial enterprise is extracting from the colonies. Could the poem be read, therefore, as a 'subverting' image which expresses a notion of the ultimate futility of the whole imperial enterprise? This, I think, would be to go too far: the analogy to 'Casabianca' is very close: the poet is acutely conscious of the human cost of war and empire, and she often registers this cost with her characteristically plangent note of sombre, mellifluous melancholy. But this may, in the end, be merely the cultural equivalent of a General or a Foreign Minister expressing regret at the casualties incurred in a military action overseas. The poem, then, merely *registers* the human cost of all this commercial and imperial activity to the colonisers themselves, in terms of family loss and bereavement. All the same, a more conventional poem would have stopped short of the point which Hemans reaches in this one, which is a close-up of the resulting corpses, for, again, the last line of the stanza tells us, there are even sadder things to see.

In the fourth stanza we begin to see what the whole poem has been inexorably drawing us toward, for also on the shore is the corpse of a crew member, which is studied in some detail, so that the facial expression is carefully noted and carefully read. What the speaker reads in the face, however, is actually difficult for *us* to read. The 'strife' may indicate that the man struggled against his fate, which might be seen as evidence of manly resolve and courage, or else as resistance to God's will. Alternatively, the 'strife' may simply indicate a painful death agony, which *rigor mortis* has frozen on to the now rigid features of the face. This sight, though sufficiently harrowing, one might have thought, is not enough to move the speaker to tears. The speaker's emotions are frozen like the corpse of the male victim until a female corpse nearby is seen to be that of a mother. Though the male corpse was that of a strong man, a certain desperate strength is the first characteristic of the female corpse which is emphasised:

> For her pale arms a babe had prest
> 　With such a wreathing grasp,
> Billows had dashed o'er that fond breast,
> 　Yet not undone the clasp.

Further, the mother had attempted to make her whole body into a kind
of protective shield for the child:

> Her very tresses had been flung
>   To wrap the fair child's form,
> Where still their wet long streamers hung,
>   All tangled by the storm.

The reader now expects a view of the mother's face to contrast with
the face of the male victim, but the speaker goes on to break yet another
taboo, and instead describes the face of the dead child. The implication is that the viewer even touches the corpse, to part those long wet
streamers of the mother's protecting hair from the child's face; this is
what is seen:

> And beautiful, 'midst that wild scene,
>   Gleamed up the boy's dead face,
> Like slumber's, trustingly serene,
>   In melancholy grace.

> Deep in her bosom lay his head,
>   With half-shut violet eye –
> *He* had known little of her dread,
>   Naught of her agony!

This sight of the dead child's gleaming wet face and partly closed eyes
takes us far closer to the scene than the title, or the early parts of the
poem, would lead us to expect. 'Gleamed' is grimly physical, suggesting the sea-chilled skin of the corpse, rather than any angelic or
transcendent quality. There is a kind of 'generic violation' here; the
conventional expectations of this kind of poem (that is, those about
battles or disasters) are that they will present the material in a certain
manner, that carnage and death will not be shown in a graphic way
(this, after all, is the convention that the best-known First World War
poets became famous by defying). The conventions violated by the
unflinching gaze on the dead are also gendered; the implied speaker/
witness in the poem is female, and contemporary notions of feminine
delicacy and refinement would entail the idea that only a male viewer
could look steadily at such victims. Hemans, of course, is imagining
the scene – as is usual with her poems, she is neither recounting
experiences of her own nor using an eye-witness account, but she is
re-imagining it, not just passively reproducing a way of seeing and
saying which is already deeply embedded in her culture. The image
she presents is like a sculptural tableau, a reversed secular *Pietà*, in the
sense that the mother died for the son, and not vice versa.

But this is as far as the poem goes (as regards pushing against the received norms of taste and representation are concerned), for it is now as if the speaker's iron nerve falters, and, having moved relentlessly forward to view the full terror and pathos of the scene, it suddenly draws back and begins to read a reassuring message into these relics of maternal heroism: yes, the speaker tells us, the mother was successful in protecting the child from the terror of death:

> *He* had known little of her dread,
>   Naught of her agony!

Of course, this is to claim the privileges of an omniscient, internally focalised narrator, for neither reader nor speaker could be sure of this. It is a *reading* of the features of the dead, and we see retrospectively the purpose of describing the sailor's face earlier in the poem ('Yet, by that rigid lip and brow, / Not without strife he died'), for it establishes as an undisputed norm this confidence in the reading of situation from features. In a similar way, early Victorian criminology produced rogues' galleries of 'criminal types', asserting a correspondence between character and physiognomy.

This last stanza, then, runs against the grain of the poem to make its transcendent affirmation stick, as frequently and interestingly happens at the end of Hemans's poems. At any rate, the withdrawal to a safe distance from this terrible event is now very rapid: the poem contorts itself into a self-contradictory affirmation of human love and a simultaneous insistence that there must be a world elsewhere in which this poor child will be given, literally, a second chance, another throw of the dice, 'another lot', to make up for its catastrophic bad luck in this one. But that straining word 'Surely', which introduces the sentiment, seems to signal that this may be just wishful thinking – 'Surely', surely, is not far removed from 'if only':

> Surely thou hast another lot,
>   There is some home for thee,
> Where thou shalt rest, remembering not
>   The moaning of the sea!

There seems, then, to be a tacit and contradictory admission here that the mother may not after all have been entirely successful at shielding the child from trauma, since the moaning of the sea is something which would need to be erased from the child's memory in any future life.

'The Wreck' will bear direct comparison with Hemans's better-known 'The Image in Lava', which presents another mother/child *Pietà*, this poem (says Hemans's note) being about 'the impression of a woman's form, with an infant clasped to the bosom, found at the uncovering of

Herculaneum' (actually Pompeii). 'The Wreck' is undoubtedly the better piece, much starker and more unflinching in the images it presents, less trite in its juxtapositions (the 'Lava' poem, inevitably, contrasts the empires which have passed away with the surviving image of fidelity left by the protecting mother). The diction in the 'Lava' piece is particularly tired, archaic, and contorted, suffocating the victims a second time in a blanket of verbiage:

> Haply of that fond bosom
>   On ashes here impress'd
> Thou wert the only treasure, child!
>   Whereon a hope might rest.

According to Isobel Armstrong, this supposition is an error, as 'two little girls ran beside her, holding on to her garments'.[11] It isn't known (says Armstrong) where Hemans saw the image, or read a description of it, and it isn't that distance from the material reality of the object which is the problem – Seamus Heaney, for instance, had never seen the exhumed bog people when he wrote powerful poetry about them, and his 'The Tollund Man' begins 'Some day I will go to Aarhus / To see his peat-brown head'. The problem, really, is to do with carrying on writing when the poetic imagination isn't really fired at all but just wants to be, or simply wants to get a point across. The 'Lava' poem ends like 'The Wreck', though, wanting to believe that 'Love, human love!' 'Outlives the cities of renown / Wherein the mighty trust!' And the poem concludes 'It must, it *must* be so!'

What I have mainly been doing here is reading 'The Wreck' 'deconstructively' somewhat against what I assume to be its own grain. I am conscious that this may not be different in kind from asserting that the poem 'calls into question what it most seems to extol', and aware, therefore, of the precariousness of the critical manoeuvre. Rhetorical criticism, of course, would have no difficulty in finding a formula which would distinguish the one from the other. Ultimately, my own sense of the distinction is that I am not claiming any inadvertent 'irony' on the part of the poet, or suggesting that the poem in some way seems to know more than the poet. Simply, to use the word 'surely' in the way Hemans does in the poem *admits* the possibility of a doubt, however shocking that thought might be: thus, a locution like 'Surely he can't have forgotten what day it is' is a short step from the appalled realisation that that is exactly what has happened. The 'fault lines' in the Wreck poem (like the word 'surely', or the suggestion in the 'remembering not' phrase that the child's death might not have been so serene after all) are used to open up the grain and read the poem against itself, that is, against the primary current of its sense. But this does not necessarily involve accepting a concept of the poem in which the poem's own 'itself' does not include, or half admit, these doubts. Can we be sure, as critics, that, if we had instead been reading Shelley, for instance, we would not have proceeded differently, constructing the poem's 'itself' as *including* the doubts, and thereby constituting a structure which is pervasively ambivalent? This is, I would suggest, a question of fundamental importance for Romanticism. We are helped in answering it when we follow both the 'close-reading' and deconstructive tracks used here on 'The Wreck' and the 'inferred intertextuality' procedures used earlier on 'Casabianca'. The real challenge is to find a way of using both on the same poem.

So does the intertextualising approach used in this chapter constitute a form of 'deep' context? Well, there is a unique closeness of fit between the content of Hemans's 'Casiabianca' and the cases of the real-life boys on burning or sinking decks which have been examined, and the moral dilemmas and challenges which their conduct provokes are the same as those in the poem. The same visual and historical texts could not be used for any other poem, and the juxtaposition between 'Casabianca' and 'The Wreck' gives further nuance, depicting another parent who is unable to save a child from shipwreck and death. The 'institutional' contextualisation (via the on-going narrative of Hemans's eventful reception history) is a way of reading which will be taken further in the next chapter, but with a different nineteenth-century poet.

Appendix: 'Casabianca' and 'The Wreck'

Casabianca*

The boy stood on the burning deck
  Whence all but he had fled;
The flame that lit the battle's wreck
  Shone round him o'er the dead.

Yet beautiful and bright he stood,
  As born to rule the storm;
A creature of heroic blood,
  A proud, though child-like form.

The flames roll'd on – he would not go
  Without his Father's word;
That Father, faint in death below,
  His voice no longer heard.

He call'd aloud: – 'Say, Father, say
  If yet my task is done?'
He knew not that the chieftain lay
  Unconscious of his son.

'Speak, Father!' once again he cried,
  'If I may yet be gone!'
And but the booming shots replied,
  And fast the flames roll'd on.

Upon his brow he felt their breath,
  And in his waving hair,
And look'd from that lone post of death,
  In still, yet brave despair.

And shouted but once more aloud,
  'My Father! must I stay?'
While o'er him fast, through sail and shroud,
  The wreathing fires made way.

They wrapt the ship in splendour wild,
  They caught the flag on high,
And stream'd above the gallant child,
  Like banners in the sky.

There came a burst of thunder sound –
  The boy – oh! where was he?
Ask of the winds that far around
  With fragments strew'd the sea! –

With mast, and helm, and pennon fair,
  That well had borne their part –
But the noblest thing which perish'd there
  Was that young faithful heart.

* Young Casabianca, a boy about thirteen years old, son of the admiral
of the *Orient*, remained at his post (in the Battle of the Nile), after the
ship had taken fire, and all the guns had been abandoned; and perished
in the explosion of the vessel, when the flames had reached the powder.

The Wreck

All night the booming minute-gun
  Had pealed along the deep,
And mournfully the rising sun
  Looked o'er the tide-worn steep.
A bark from India's coral strand,
  Before the rushing blast,
Had vailed her topsails to the sand,
  And bowed her noble mast.

The Queenly ship! – brave hearts had striven,
  And true ones died with her! –
We saw her mighty cable riven,
  Like floating gossamer.
We saw her proud flag struck that morn,
  A star once o'er the seas –
Her anchor gone, her deck uptorn –
  And sadder things than these!

We saw her treasures cast away, –
  The rocks with pearls were sown,
And strangely sad, the ruby's ray
  Flashed out o'er fretted stone.
And gold was strewn the wet sands o'er,
  Like ashes by a breeze;
And gorgeous robes – but oh! that shore
  Had sadder things than these!

We saw the strong man still and low,
  A crushed reed thrown aside;
Yet, by that rigid lip and brow,
  Not without strife he died.
And near him on the seaweed lay –
  Till then we had not wept –
But well our gushing hearts might say,
  That there a *mother* slept!

For her pale arms a babe had prest,
  With such a wreathing grasp,
Billows had dashed o'er that fond breast,
  Yet not undone the clasp.
Her very tresses had been flung
  To wrap the fair child's form,
Where still their wet long streamers hung,
  All tangled by the storm.

And beautiful, 'midst that wild scene,
  Gleamed up the boy's dead face,
Like slumber's, trustingly serene,
  In melancholy grace.
Deep in her bosom lay his head,
  With half-shut violet eye –
He had known little of her dread,
  Naught of her agony!

Oh! human love, whose yearning heart
  Through all things vainly true,

So stamps upon thy mortal part
  Its passionate adieu –
Surely thou hast another lot,
  There is some home for thee,
Where thou shalt rest, remembering not
  The moaning of the sea!

Notes

1 A rudimentary summary of the main characteristics of what I call the 'New Romanticism' would include as salient features that (1) the period is stretched chronologically in both directions from the traditional 1790–1820s timescale, (2) it places more emphasis than used to be the case on prose writers, (3) it brings the Gothic from the margins to the centre, (4) it places much emphasis on the 'public domain' in which Romantic works appeared, (5) it is much interested in women writers, (6) and generally in matters of gender, class, and postcolonialism. By contrast, 'Old Romanticism' studied a much more compressed and strictly literary period, sharply concentrated on the 'Big Five' male poets (Wordsworth, Coleridge, Keats, Shelley, and Byron) and their political and aesthetic ideals.

2 For biographical details see Peter W. Trinder, *Mrs Hemans* (University of Wales Press, 1984).

3 For a convenient bibliographical summary of the main relevant publications see chapter 9, 'Women Poets of the Romantic Period' by Jennifer Breen, pp. 181–91 in *Literature of the Romantic Period: A Bibliographical Guide*, ed. Michael O'Neill (Oxford University Press, 1998).

4 For example, Jennifer Breen's *Women Romantic Poets 1785–1832* (Everyman, 1994) and Andrew Ashfield's *Romantic Women Poets, 1788–1848* (Manchester University Press, 1998).

5 *Records of Woman, With Other Poems, Felicia Hemans*, ed. Paula R. Feldman (University Press of Kentucky, 1999).

6 This material can be accessed at http://listserv.wvu.edu/archives/nassr-l.html (Last accessed on 22 April 2005).

7 'The Canon: Values & Heritage', *PN Review*, 103, May–June 1995, p. 14. The first set of italics in the quotation is mine.

8 Letter of March 1811, in the Bodleian, cited in the introduction to the facsimile edition of *Records of Woman*.

9 For a full account of the battle see Donald MacIntyre's *Jutland* (Evans Bros, 1957).

10 The description of Cornwell's conduct in MacIntyre reads: 'He himself received a wound that he must have suspected was mortal. But steadfastly he remained at his post, passing orders and adjusting the gun sights, until at last the gun fell silent, the last of the crew hit. In a lull of the fight, he

was found there, his telephone earpieces clamped to his head, standing erect awaiting orders, dying as he stood' (p. 120).

11 See footnote 3 to Isobel Armstrong's 'Natural and National Monuments – Felicia Hemans's "The Image in Lava": A Note', Chapter 12, pp. 212–30 in *Felicia Hemans: Reimagining Poetry in the Nineteenth Century*, ed. Nanora Sweet and Julie Melnyk (Palgrave, 2001).

5

'Seeing the spot': Hopkins, Liverpool, and context

In a piece originally published in the *TLS* (19 March 1971, pp. 331–2) the Jesuit Alfred Thomas relates his discovery that the 'Felix Randal' of Hopkins's great sonnet was a man called Felix Spencer, a blacksmith ('farrier' on his death certificate) who died of pleurisy at 17 Birchfield Street, Liverpool, having been given the Last Rites by Fr Gerard Manley Hopkins. The poem records, among other things, one of the priest's greatest satisfactions of his ministry – the young man, broken by sickness and cursing his fate, was given the Sacraments and found peace as a result of his ministrations, as Hopkins tells himself in the poem, as if in awe of the powers he possesses as a consequence of his office – 'My tongue had taught thee comfort, touch had quenched thy tears'. So in recalling the death when writing the poem a few days after it occurred, Hopkins can say, with quiet conviction, 'Ah well, God rest him all road ever he offended!', even slipping into a version of a Liverpool dialect expression (that locution 'all road ever'), suggesting a rare moment of empathy and at-homeness with the place. Alfred Thomas, then, finds the context which uniquely fits the poem, putting in the leg-work, identifying the street and photographing it for the article, and having the luck to be on the spot – in the nick of time – when the original nineteenth-century houses were still standing. He reproduces the relevant entry by Hopkins in the parish register, and a copy of the death certificate itself. It is a perfect investigation, an open-and-shut case, and it prompted me to try something similar, though with less clear-cut success, as will be seen. But I did find a kind of negative counterpart to the 'happy' case of Felix Randal/Spencer, in one of the other streets in Hopkins's parish 'patch', and I make that the end-point of a more circuitous essay than Alfred Thomas's precision piece.

In this chapter, then, I explore a more speculative and open-ended 'take' on context: the artist Paul Klee famously described the process of composition as 'taking a line for a walk', and here I take a line (of argument) for a walk (literally, at a later point in the chapter), unsure of where 'exactly' it is headed. But the aim is to raise issues of contextuality in as stark a form as possible, in relation to the work of Gerard Manley Hopkins. The method used is based on two cognate principles: the first is the Ignatian procedure usually known as 'composition of place', that is, the imaginative visualisation of 'the place where what we are about to meditate on occurs', as set out in the *Spiritual Exercises* of Ignatius Loyola.[1] This 'pre-meditation' practice of 'seeing the spot' became a common element in English religious poems,[2] but it is, of course, part of a progressive structure, being one of a series of steps towards an ultimate contemplative goal. I am using it here, however, more self-sufficiently, and not just as a mere preliminary, in the hope that the sustained envisaging of the specific urban setting by which Hopkins's sensibility was so indelibly marked can help us to enter his writing. The kind of deep localised scrutiny which is the essence of composition of place is also the basis of the literary-critical practice of 'close reading', and in that procedure the intensely localised focus on a single word or phrase at first seems to blot out all the rest, but then reaches (or can reach) a certain point of intensity at which it passes through a kind of invisible barrier and seems to subsume the whole text. In the same way, the composition of place seeks to move meditation towards this elusive goal, towards this moment of 'opening out by opening in'. Hopkins, of course, wrote only a small proportion of his poetry in Liverpool, and, in any case, there is little direct discussion of the poetry in the present chapter, but it tries to draw Liverpool, and places like Liverpool, right through his work, pushing it towards that invisible barrier, towards the moment when the part illuminates the whole and redelivers it fresh to the reader.[3] It will be clear from the foregoing that I am intending to extrapolate from that meditative preliminary stage of 'seeing the spot' in a somewhat opportunist way. The essence of 'seeing the spot' lies in its precise *localising* of the attention, rather than the *generalising* implicit in socio-historical contextualisation. It seeks to focus the mind on a deep contextuality, as I have been calling it, rather than the broad kind.

The second underlying principle of this piece is encapsulated by Hopkins himself in a notebook entry which contains the succinct remark 'What you look at closely seems to look closely at you'. This amounts to saying that all knowledge is ultimately in some way *self-* knowledge, a view which is embodied in the notion (once fundamental to ideals of critical practice) of an '*in*sight'. Hence, one of the strands in this enquiry is personal and autobiographical, and the implication of

Hopkins's remark about looking closely is that all enquiries are like this, once a certain closeness of scrutiny is achieved. The usual academic convention is to leave the autobiographical implications of our work implicit. One modest innovation here is not to follow that convention.

'Down these mean streets . . .'

Gerard Manley Hopkins arrived at Liverpool on 30 December 1879[4] to take up his appointment to the Jesuit church of St Francis Xavier's in Salisbury Street. The building of this large 'inner-city' church had been funded by a group of wealthy Catholic lay people, several of them 'old boys' of the Jesuit college at Stonyhurst, to provide a ministry 'in a respectable part of the town where a church would be desirable'.[5] It was four years building, eventually opening in December 1848. In Hopkins's time the church was somewhat different from today: the spire was added to the belfry tower in 1883, two years after he had left, and the imposing Sodality Chapel (which is about a third of the size of the original church) was built on to the main structure in 1887 to increase the church capacity of what became (in terms of population) the largest Catholic parish in England. Together, these external changes give the building its present cathedral-like appearance. The richness and elegance of the interior, with its slender columns of polished Drogheda limestone and its tall arcades, suggest that the church had been intended to minister to a wealthy clientele, and indeed, until the early 1830s, the district had been an area of well-to-do merchants' houses. But the balance had begun to change in the mid-1830s:

> The demand for housing in the district declined rapidly from 1835, with the merchants beginning to move to the outskirts of the town. Building stopped for a number of years, and then lower class housing began to be erected. As the streets were built northward, they showed a visible deterioration until eventually courts, alleys, and early back-to-back housing merged into a terrible slum district.[6]

This new but inferior housing catered for the influx of Irish Catholic immigrants resulting from poverty and famine in Ireland, and the packed squalor of the immediately adjacent streets soon became notorious. The church retained some traces of the former gentility of the district – a proportion of the congregation each week travelled to its services from elsewhere, in or near the city, and, as Christopher Devlin tells us, the packed trams arriving on Sundays at SFX (as it has always been called locally) were a common sight until after the First World War.[7] The provision of services by the Salisbury Street Jesuits in the private chapel of Randall Lightbound at Rose Hill in Lydiate was also a residue of the area's formerly higher status.[8] But for the priests, (including Hopkins – 'I am often here for the night', he tells Bridges, 26 October 1880),[9] these pleasant overnight visits to Lydiate were merely brief interludes, and the core of the parish business lay in the deprived streets in the immediate vicinity of the church.

Hopkins named some of the streets which formed his 'patch' in another postcard to Bridges some weeks after his arrival (15 February). Undertaking to entertain a visiting friend of Bridges', he gave an ironic assurance that his friend would be well looked after:

> I will do all that Jenkinson Street and Gomer Street and Back Queen Ann Street and Torbock Street and Bidder Street and Birchfield, Street and Bickerstaffe Street and the rest of my purlieus will spare of me to entertain him. (*Letters to Bridges*, pp. 99–100)

Of these, Jenkinson, Birchfield, and Bickerstaffe Streets still survive, running contiguously a little west of the church, the first being the short arm of an 'L' shape which these streets make together, the other two forming the long arm, along with Page Street, which Hopkins mentions in his 'Death' sermon, as discussed below. This long arm of the 'L' is intersected by William Henry Street, which Hopkins mentions in the same sermon – the whole little web of streets has the logical compactness of a postman's walk. What Hopkins saw in these streets as he carried out his priestly duties shocked him deeply, so much so that he was sometimes too depressed and exhausted even to keep up the correspondence which was such a vital intellectual lifeline to him. Indeed, the importance to Hopkins of writing and receiving letters, especially while he was at a place he disliked as much as he did Liverpool, is tellingly revealed in the late sonnet 'I wake and feel the fell of dark, not day', where his image of unanswered and unacknowledged prayer is a 'dead letter', sent to a defunct address and returned by the postal authorities, unopened and unread, to the sender ('And my lament / Is cries countless, cries like dead letters sent / To dearest him that lives alas! Away'). On 26 October he writes to Bridges:

> I daresay you have long expected as you have long deserved an answer to your last kind and cheering – let us say number or issue. But I never could write; time and spirits were wanting; one is so fagged, so harried and gallied up and down. And the drunkards go on drinking, the filthy, as the scripture says, are filthy still: human nature is so inveterate. Would that I had seen the last of it. (p. 110)

In a letter to the *TLS* (18 September 1969, pp. 1026–7) Alfred Thomas, SJ, the biographer of Hopkins's Jesuit training, emphasised the bad reputation of the teeming district in the immediate surroundings of the church, quoting from the parish magazine, *The Xaverian*, in 1885 (just a few years after Hopkins left), which records then recent progress in 'cleaning up' the locale, in which 'many dens of iniquity have been closed about Hardwick Street and Iden Street, and even Bidder Street has at last aroused itself to a sense of the foul plague spots that defiled it, and is asserting its right to freedom from such contagion'. Bridges comments on Hopkins's situation with characteristic bluntness, writing later of his friend that 'when sent to Liverpool to do parish work among the Irish, the vice and horrors nearly killed him', and that in such places he 'served without distinction'.[10]

The poet as priest, the priest as poet

The assumption that Hopkins's parish work was undistinguished is one I want to dwell upon for a moment. To ask how good Hopkins was at being a priest is not the same as asking how good T.S. Eliot was at banking or Wallace Stevens at selling insurance, for the professional self and the poetic self in Hopkins's case cannot be sliced neatly apart. Difficulties in making contact with parishioners are cognate with those of making contact with a readership, not least because the problem in both cases is that of finding the right words. Yet his religious superiors might have agreed with Bridges that his service lacked distinction, for, as Anthony Kenny writes, 'The frequent movements [from one post to another in the period 1878 to 1881] suggest what is confirmed by other evidence, that he was not very successful as a curate; he found it difficult to relate to many of his parishioners, and sometimes found his Jesuit colleagues uncongenial'.[11] However, a study of Hopkins's frequent reassignments, by Fr Joseph J. Feeney, SJ (see *The Hopkins Quarterly*, vol. 11 (1984–5), pp. 101–18), concludes that his pattern was like that of many other English Jesuits of his time, so it may be that no inference should be drawn from his early career pattern.[12] The poems of the Liverpool period (such as 'Felix Randal' and 'Spring and Fall'), reveal something of a paradox; an intense concern for individual parishioners that co-exists with a consistent disparagement (in his letters) of Liverpool itself, which he calls a 'horrible place', inimical to the muses.[13] He also reacts very negatively to Liverpool people *en masse*, often noting their coarse and unhealthy features. Thus, he tells Bridges that at the May Day procession 'I remarked *for the thousandth time* with sorrow and loathing the base and bespotted figures and features of the Liverpool crowd' (my italics – he had by then resided in the city for just four months).[14] But Hopkins in Liverpool was a young man of privileged background encountering the full impact and cost of industrialisation for the first time, and his sense of appalled despair is hardly to be wondered at. From Manresa House, shortly after leaving the city, he wrote to Dixon:

> My Liverpool and Glasgow experience laid upon my mind a conviction, a truly crushing conviction, of the misery of town life to the poor and more than to the poor, of the misery of the poor in general, of the degradation even of our race, of the hollowness of this century's civilisation: it made even life a burden to me to have daily thrust upon me the things I saw.[15]

The Jesuit training for priests like himself, most of whom would spend significant periods of their careers at such inner-city parishes, was lengthy and intense, but it was more a training in spirituality than in ministry, spent in a rural or semi-rural collegiate environment (such as St Bueno's, on what he called in 'The Wreck of the *Deutschland*' a 'pastoral forehead in Wales', Stonyhurst College, near, but not in, Blackburn, and Manresa House at Roehampton). More generally, his distaste was the product of the inevitable gap between any form of 'pre-service' training and what is actually encountered when we enter the field of our endeavours – as, for instance, the contrast between the intellectual intensity of graduate study and the demands of administration and teaching, for which it supposedly prepares us. Again, the late sonnets record his sense of the difficulty of making contact and forming links with any community in the lines 'To seem the stranger lies my lot, my life / Among strangers'.

Yet Hopkins did to some extent accommodate himself to his surroundings, and this is very much bound up with the question of how good he was at being a priest. For instance, his well-known letter to the Bishop of Liverpool[16] (requesting permission to conduct a Catholic marriage in slightly unusual circumstances) shows real empathy, pragmatism, and compassion, as well as an ability to remain unshocked by serial and multiple sexual relationships among his parishioners. With the social confidence of his class, and with his Superior's permission, he was able to walk over to the more salubrious district of Rodney Street (birthplace of the recently re-elected Liberal Prime Minister William Gladstone, whose second general election victory in 1880 Hopkins deplored).[17] To get there he crossed half a mile, and a social gulf, from Bidder Street and the rest, to knock on the Bishop's door and explain the case in person – he had found His Lordship 'from home', hence the need to write the letter.[18]

The episode is indicative of a man willing to go to considerable lengths to help a parishioner, and his effectiveness as an obviously concerned local priest doing his rounds is difficult to assess, especially at this distance in time; but such evidence as we have testifies to the profundity of his concern. As is well known, he never became a safe pair of hands with a sermon, and it is hard to imagine him as one of the pulpit stars drawing in those crowded Sunday trams to the region of Salisbury Street. In the Bischoff Papers at Gonzaga University, Spokane, is a notebook of the late Fr Bischoff, in which he records the comment of an old SFX parishioner who had heard Hopkins preach and whom Fr Bischoff interviewed (probably in 1947); the man said that the sermons were too 'vasty' for the congregation.[19] But one of his discourses, the meditation 'On Death', has a curious and indicative aside. He is speaking of how even those who do not die suddenly cannot be sure that they will have the comfort of the last sacraments. The whole discourse is bleak and discomforting – 'Comforter, where, where is your comforting?' his hearers might have asked him, echoing his own later words. But he merely goes on to ask them the further strangely demoralising and discomforting question 'Will you trust a priest?' and the whole performance then seems to go beyond the norms of the anxiety-inducing pulpit rhetoric of anyone delivering a retreat sermon (as famously caricatured by James Joyce in *A Portrait of the Artist as a Young Man*) to what seems more like an empathetic anticipation of the feelings of spiritual abandonment which are presented in his own final sonnets. In imagining this extreme situation (in which the consolations of religion are withheld or unavailable) he is, perhaps, 'schooled at forepangs', to take his own phrase from the sonnet 'No worst, there is none', and anticipating this awful moment in his own future life. As the sermon continues, Hopkins imagines himself to be (or recalls himself once having been) a priest who, for some reason, fails to answer the call of the dying for comfort, and so causes the kind of inner desolation which those late sonnets record:

> May not even a wise and zealous man for once be careless or misjudge and think there is no danger when there is? Few are the parish priests that never, as the saying is, let one slip through their hands.[20]

All this, indicates, surely, some unsureness of touch – Hopkins seems not to know when to stop a line of speculation, and shows a certain lack of professional tact in publicly drawing attention to the unreliability of the professionals on whom his hearers would depend in their time of direst need (it's as if a firefighter were to remind people about to be lowered to the ground from a blazing building that safety harnesses have been known to fail). Of course, not knowing when to stop is also an element in Hopkins's poems, one which readers must often feel to be his predominant characteristic, even as they recognise at the same time qualities of elusive excellence, for often the verse is pitched to a level of sustained intensity which is almost unbearable, so that his auditors begin mentally (as he noticed his colleagues once doing as he delivered a practice sermon) to squirm and roll about with suppressed embarrassment. A parenthesised note to himself then suggests that he might at this point in the sermon cite some actual examples (another bad idea), but the examples (two, at least, of the three) are evidently from his Liverpool parish experience:

> Here one may tell the story of the woman that died calling on St Winifred to curse Fr – for not coming; also, of the woman in Page Street, Liverpool, when the bell was not answered, no one knows why; and of my man in Wm. Henry Street.[21]

Getting the last sacraments, it seems, could be something of a lottery. The bell of the presbytery might not be answered, or the priest might simply arrive too late, as perhaps in the case of Hopkins himself and 'my man in Wm. Henry Street'. Of the three, the 'St Winifred' example is presumably an incident remembered from his time in training (1874–7) at St Bueno's College in North Wales, near St Winifred's shrine at Holywell, which had been administered by the Jesuits since 1873. The other two are from his painful Liverpool sojourn, though the inclusion of the name 'Liverpool' would seem to indicate that the sermon was composed after the Liverpool period. This irruption of 'loco-specific' detail like street names curiously breaks the generic conventions which are usually followed in this kind of discourse. It is as if the drab realities of his professional territory, the dreary pavements he had tramped so often (Page Street, William Henry Street, and the rest) irrupts into the sermon, just as local idiom and speech patterns occasionally break into the poetry.[22]

   The anxiety evident in this passage is clearly an expression of Hopkins's own deep-rooted phobias about having to withstand a trial of faith with nothing to rely on but his own inner resources. That is the inevitable other side of the high pitch of ecstatic belief which is a frequent note in the poetry. The cases listed in the sermon, where no comfort was available, suggest that the happy outcome described in 'Felix Randal' had its darker counterpart, where the comfort never came, or never came in time, and the matter stays on the priest's conscience. That anxiety produces both this curious passage in the sermon, and (far more significantly) the late sonnets, so that again there is a powerful generative co-textuality linking the two. But it is also indicative of a priest acutely conscious of his parishioners' dependence upon him at times of extremity, and it seems unlikely that they perceived him as serving them 'without distinction'. Furthermore, in the letter to Baillie already mentioned in which, he says, he had written a great deal about Liverpool, and then destroyed it as being too negative, he also writes of his strong sense of rapport with the 'Lancastrians', in contrast to the Oxford townspeople among whom he had spent eight months of 1879 at a Jesuit parish there. 'With the Lancastrians', he says, 'I felt as if [I] had been born to deal with them.' And he goes on, 'Now these Lancashire people of low degree or not of high degree are those who most have seemed to me to welcome me and make much of me' (to Baillie, 22 May 1880). Hopkins is, presumably, making a distinction – as is common – between Lancashire and Liverpool, even though the latter is actually in the former. Though writing from his presbytery address, 8 Salisbury Street, Liverpool, he uses the past tense of the Lancastrians – 'I *felt* as if [I] had been born to deal with them' (my italics), referring back to his few months at St Joseph's, Bedford Leigh, near Manchester, between the ending of his Oxford appointment in August 1879 and the move to Liverpool at the end of December. He preferred Glaswegians to Liverpudlians, for 'though always very drunken and at present very Fenian, they are warm-hearted and give a far heartier welcome than those of Liverpool'.[23] To repeat, these remarks seem to show that Hopkins was able, on occasion, to establish a real rapport with the kind of people among whom his mission lay, even if less so than usual at Liverpool. It might help us to be surer of these things if we knew something about people like 'my man in Wm. Henry Street'. Yet at this distance in time, how much of the past at this level is recoverable, or, at least, usefully recoverable? Perhaps we need to 'see the spot' again.

To go to St Francis Xavier's today is to feel that Hopkins is both very near and very distant. The church – still a place of worship – and the adjoining college building (the premises of SFX Grammar School for over a hundred years, from 1856 until its move to a new building on the outskirts of the city in 1961) are now part of the 'Hope at Everton' campus of Liverpool Hope University. The first phase of this development opened in 1999, including the Gerard Manley Hopkins Hall of Residence for students. This is the kind of inner-city 'enterprise' partnership which can transform the urban atmosphere in a dramatic way, and there is a powerful sense in the district of decline arrested and reversed. Along Shaw Street, adjacent to SFX Church, and opposite the vast and gaunt façade of the former Liverpool Collegiate School (being made to pay dearly for its preservation by conversion of the building into 'luxury' flats) is a long terrace of tall and once elegant Georgian town houses now awaiting renovation. But on turning the corner into William Henry Street and viewing these from the rear, it can be seen that during the nineteenth century, as the area declined, the capacity of these houses was doubled by the addition of colossal and mean-looking back extensions, reaching the full height of the house, and with meagre fenestration, which must have had the effect of reducing in a drastic way the light and air available to the crowded tenement rooms inside. Hence, if the elegant façade of the terrace, with its delicate wrought-iron balconies and the classical orders flanking the front doors, is a monument to civilisation, then the rear is certainly a monument to barbarism, to an unfettered, *laissez-faire* form of capitalism which exploits the powerless. In other words, the kind of thing which drove Hopkins to write of how his Liverpool experience imbued him with the 'crushing conviction of the misery of town life to the poor', as quoted earlier.

William Henry Street itself, however, is no longer what it was, for the houses now to be seen there are mainly new 'maisonettes' and bungalows with pleasant front gardens: one end of the street points to the city-centre office buildings and the river beyond, and the other runs uphill slightly, towards the steep escarpment of Everton Brow, whose pastoral name was for so long at odds with the bricky reality of its now (amazingly) green hillside. The fields beneath (in William Blake's words of such urban places), which 'lay sleeping' under the cobbles and the tarmac for two hundred years, have now awoken and re-emerged. Turning left out of William Henry Street and back into Salisbury Street itself, we can see that, though the church survives, it does not survive intact, for the presbytery in which Hopkins and the other priests lived has been demolished, as has the external cloister which once joined it to the church. The secluded 'domestic chapel' above the sacristy, which he and the other priests used for private prayer, still survives, but it is now inaccessible, as the demolition of the presbytery also removed the staircase which led up to it. One might imagine it lying undisturbed and awaiting its eventual re-opening, a kind of Catholic 'Rodinsky's Room'.[24] However, no records or documents from Hopkins's time remain in the church. In the dark period of the 1970s and 1980s, when virtually the whole of this church was threatened with demolition, for the second time since the end of the war, old records and documents were packed into tea chests and dispersed or destroyed.[25]

'Every day I write the book'

Yet, fortunately, not entirely. Some of the parish records were deposited by the Rev. H. Craig at the Liverpool Record Office (now in the William

Brown Library in the city centre) in 1975, and further material, which had been at the Friary, Bute Street, Liverpool, was added in 1983. The deposited material[26] comprises nine volumes of baptismal registers, covering the period 1848–1923; three volumes of marriage registers, covering 1850–1921; a volume of death registers, covering 1891–1907 and 1942–69; and a single volume recording confirmations from 1849 to 1852. The relevant baptismal volume is that for 1875–85. What can it tell us of Hopkins and his Liverpool ministry?

The volume records the 'bureaucratic' side of one aspect of the professional life of a man now known to the world chiefly as a poet, but, to repeat, they are more significant in status than would be the discovery of (say) documents signed by T.S. Eliot during his nine-year stint in the offices of Lloyds Bank in London in the 1920s, because what made Hopkins a priest also made him a poet. To open the 1875–85 Baptisms volume and begin to look at the entries signed by Hopkins is to enter the past, and the realities of his day-to-day work, more vividly than even contemporary photographs can enable us to do. The book contains the details of 153 baptisms performed by him, the first entry being for 15 January 1880 (a fortnight after his arrival) and the last for 30 June 1881 (a week before his departure). His last letter to Bridges from Liverpool is dated 28 June, with a postscript added on 3 July to say that 'I cannot go to town before Tuesday at the earliest'.[27] It is both poignant and symptomatic that Hopkins here uses the expression 'to go to town' in its 'educated/national' sense of going to London, rather than in its local sense of going to visit Liverpool city centre, thus indicating both his imminent departure from the city, and (as always) a certain mental holding aloof from it. It was always for him a city at least as foreign as Dublin was later to prove.

Is there, then, anything significant to be learned from studying this material? Tom Dunne, in compiling his indispensable Hopkins bibliography, seems to believe not, for the entry on parish record books reads in full:

> GMH's autograph entries exist in the parish records of ST ALOYSIUS' CHURCH, OXFORD, and ST. FRANCIS XAVIER'S CHURCH, LIVERPOOL. These entries are merely records of baptisms, marriages, visits to the sick, and other church business.[28]

Yet there are various ways of answering the question about the usefulness or otherwise of such material. One way would be to adopt the forensic principle that the whole picture has to be construed from the available evidence, however minimal that evidence may be. It would always be nice to have more evidence, but when no more is to hand you must increase your intensity of scrutiny of what *is* available. Let us make some observations, then, about the run of Hopkins's entries in the volume. Firstly, it is noticeable that he seems to make more frequent slips and deletions than his colleagues do. Occasionally the deletions seem to indicate something of his social attitudes, as when (12 February 1881) the Irish family name 'Reilli' – a spelling indicative of what he would disapprove of as Fenian convictions – had originally been entered in its more common Anglicised form as 'Riley'. More frequently, they are simple slips of the pen, of the kind likely to be made by somebody who feels rushed or in some way ill at ease. Of course, he is not the only SFX priest to make errors – a colleague was responsible for the bizarre jump in the enumeration of the entries, whereby No. 1099 is followed by No. 2000, an error which adds nine hundred non-existent souls to the tally of the church-faithful, and seems to have gone unnoticed until pointed out by a modern hand in felt-tip pen. All the same, Hopkins's slips do seem surprisingly frequent.

Secondly, the style of his handwriting is different from that of his colleagues, most of whom use the distinctly Victorian-looking 'copper plate' style which (to modern eyes) is high on aesthetic qualities and low on readability, especially when single words occur in isolation. For instance, the name index to the volume, which is contained in a separate ledger-book and looks to have been made when the baptism book was full in 1885 (a great labour to produce, but it would enable the religious credentials of applicants for Confirmation or Marriage to be checked quickly) is quite difficult to use because it consists, of course, of nothing but a list of surnames in copper plate script. By contrast, Hopkins's handwriting is more angular, less immediately pleasing to look at, but much easier to read, and as a physical medium it has a more modern look than the entries made by his professional colleagues, just as (to be fanciful) his poetry has a more 'up-to-date' feel than that of his poetic colleagues, though it too characteristically lacks the aesthetic surface smoothness of more routine contemporary verse in the manner he called 'Parnassian'.

Thirdly, Hopkins's signature is usually followed by full details of his status, suggesting a kind of pedantic scrupulosity, whereas his colleagues mostly just put their names, followed sometimes by 'S.J.'. The entries in the book are in Latin, of course, so Hopkins usually writes 'Gerardo M. Hopkins', followed in the early entries by the formula '*miss. coad. ap.*'. This is sometimes preceded by 'S.J.' and is quite often laboriously written out in full as '*missionario coadutore apostolico*'. Only late on in his period at Liverpool – round February 1881 – does he begin to omit

all this and just add 'S.J.' to his name, but there are some throwbacks
to adding the full formula, or an abbreviation of it, as if his conscience
were upbraiding him for laziness.

A fourth point of interest (and this bears upon the question of the
kind of ministry Hopkins conducted) concerns the fact that endorse-
ments for various kinds of special baptismal circumstance are more
frequent in Hopkins's entries than in those of his colleagues. For instance, the formula 'sub conditione' or 'sub conditionate' is fairly frequent,
indicating a non-infant baptism administered to a convert on a kind
of spiritual 'belt-and-braces' principle, the sacrament being operative
only if any previous baptism were to be invalid. (This ingenious
formulation of the Catholic canon-lawyers avoided any public proclamation of the invalidity of the baptismal rites of other Christian
denominations, while at the same time proceeding as if they were in
fact invalid.) These entries occur with birth dates, indicating a child
or adult convert; examples are (with the surname and date of the
baptism, followed by the date of birth in brackets): Abbey, 15 January
1880 (1851); Maguire, 28 February (1815); Evans, 5 March (1853);
Carter, 26 April (1869); Carter, 20 May (1865); Fagan, 5 May 1881
(1876). On 3 September 1880 Hopkins baptised three pre-teenage girls,
all from different families, but with the same sponsor or godparent –
a Mary Helen Burns – the three being Carrey (1869), Badley (1868),
and Fox (1870), for the first of whom the full endorsement reads 'sub
conditione tamquam a ministro acatholico baptizata' ('conditionally, had
also been baptized by a non-Catholic minister'). All these cases would,
presumably, be converts from Anglicanism, and we can surmise either
that Hopkins, given his own religious history, would tend to attract
or encourage these or else that his colleagues would regard him, for
the same reason, as the 'specialist' in this area and would refer such
cases to him. The other possibility, which cannot be ruled out, is
simply that all the priests had more or less equal numbers of such cases
and that Hopkins was more fastidious than the others about recording the precise details in the book.

Another endorsement which seems to occur more frequently in
Hopkins's entries than in others' is 'in periculo', sometimes given
more fully as 'in periculo mortis constituta/us' indicating an emergency
baptism performed on an infant in danger of death. Sometimes these
cases are designated 'privatim', indicating that the priest had been called
to the house and that the baptism was performed there. Either way,
a further endorsement is added some weeks later if the infant has
recovered and a standard baptismal ceremony has been performed at
the church, this being signified, usually, with the formula 'ceremioniis

postridie suppletis', or some variation or abbreviation of this phrase. In
the absence of such an endorsement it seems likely that the child did
indeed die: occasionally, this is made explicit, as with Murphy, 25 March
1881, when the ceremony was performed *'in periculo morti'* (*sic*) then
'brevi post mortuus est' ('the child died shortly afterwards'). One can
imagine the suffering represented by each of these terse entries; here
is the inevitable harvest of places like those cramped and airless back-
room tenements along Shaw Street. With people living in crowded and
unsanitary conditions, and with no means of controlling their own
fertility or providing adequately for their large families, high rates of
infant mortality were sure to follow, and these child deaths were undoubtedly typical of the sights which impressed Hopkins with (again)
that 'truly crushing conviction, of the misery of town life to the poor,
of the misery of the poor in general'. Hence, there is a clear line of
continuity between the airless tenements on Shaw Street, the entries
in the baptismal register, the despairing remarks in the letters, and the
compassionate tone of Liverpool-period poems like 'Felix Randal' and
'Spring and Fall'. Such continuity is an example of another way in which
what I called earlier a 'deep' contextuality can be constructed.

Of course, a preponderance of Irish names is very marked throughout the Hopkins entries (MacCartney, Maguire, O'Connell, Higgins,
Duffy, MacKeon, Quinn, Murphy, Docherty, Magee, and so on), but
there is also a sprinkling of Italian names (Buoni, Persichini, Muti),
representing earlier patterns of migration. Many of the names which
fit in neither category would represent internal migration from rural
Lancashire by people in search of labouring work in the city, sometimes with a transitional period of summer work in the fields and
winter labour in the city. Overall, the pattern of Hopkins's entries does
seem to endorse the impression created by the letter to the Bishop of
a priest of scrupulous temperament, willing to go the extra distance
to meet the needs of those in complicated situations, and probably unable
to protect his own sensibilities with the professional detachment that
even priests require.

The further question remains as to whether there might exist a 'data-
trail' which could tell us more about elusive figures like 'my man from
Wm. Henry Street', the figure who seems to crystallise Hopkins's sense
of his professional failings and inadequacy, for, when summoned to
administer comfort and the Last Rites to this dying man, Hopkins, for
reasons unknown, arrives too late, and the case remains on his conscience. This case, then, is like the dark opposite of the one described
in 'Felix Randal', and, since several examples are mentioned in the
memo for the 'Death' sermon, it might even seem that Felix was more

the exception than the rule, not in the sense that the priest arrived in time, but that the comforting manifestly brought comfort, and that the crisis was not faced in isolation.

The process of doing the tracking of the man from William Henry Street would, however, present us with a problem not unlike that encountered by Hopkins himself in the 'Death' sermon, which is that of knowing where to stop. What, we might need to ask, would a literary critic usefully be doing, deciphering and transcribing the copper plate scrawl of Census returns from the screen of the microfilm reader? Certainly the route whose first stop is the Census returns seems to take us out of the realm of deep context, and into a more diffuse kind of socio-historical contextualising. So, while it is conceivable that the identity of the man from William Henry Street might still be traceable, it is hard to conceive it capable of materially shifting the picture which is deducible from the remark itself.

In reaction, therefore, to this road not taken we might see the man from William Henry Street as an emblem of the necessary limits of our attainable contextual knowledge, a reminder of how much it is ultimately impossible (or not useful) to know. This is to infer, from the context in which he cites them in his sermon on death, that the three people Hopkins mentions in his aside are emblematic of a goal which eludes the seeker, the goal in his own case being that of priestly perfection. But the emblem has both a *recto* and a *verso*: the *recto* is that the three figures signify the impossibility of ever entirely fulfilling the high priestly ideal by serving always with distinction, for the speaker reminds himself that 'even the wise and zealous . . . may for once be careless or misjudge'. Whatever our profession, we all must from time to time 'as the saying is, let one slip through [our] hands'. Thus, we have the woman who invokes the aid of a saint to curse a priest, thereby paradoxically testifying to the survival of her faith (and her spirit, in the fullest sense of that word) in extremity, and so teaching the priest the limits of his own indispensability. The *verso* of the emblem presents a reflexive version of the same (or similar) issues, this being the point at which the story turns to (or on) the reader, the '*hypocrite lecteur*', and says '*De te fabula*' – 'The story is about yourself'. This is the point, in other words, where what we have been looking at closely begins to look closely at us. So we may see the emblem as also pointing to the unattainability of our own professional ideal, that is, the ideal of finding the perfect balance between the older textual and theoretical approaches to our discipline, on the one hand, and the newer historicist and contextual ones, on the other. There is, too, it might be added, the significance of the woman in Page Street, that street where

we academics would all like to live all the time, on perpetual sabbatical with our books, in the blessed peace of the scholar at the desk,
which (says F. Scott Fitzgerald) is the only rival on earth to heavenly
peace. But like that of Hopkins the poet, our lives cannot really be
that way, and we must also deal with the other side of our professional
lives, the side equivalent to his baptismal registers, which for us is
represented by module evaluation sheets, degree-scheme documents,
and the like.

   In putting forward this final line of speculation, and speaking about
Hopkins's 'man from Wm. Henry Street' as a double-sided emblem,
I am influenced by a classic work of deconstructive criticism and theory
published in 1979 (deconstruction's *annus mirabilis*), namely Frank
Kermode's book *The Genesis of Secrecy: On the Interpretation of Narrative* (Harvard University Press). Kermode's focus in this book is partly
on a range of oddly inexplicable figures who crop up briefly in narratives, and seem like an irritating grain of sand caught in the smooth
machinery of our usual interpretive methods. His examples include the
unexplained 'man in the mackintosh' who appears among the mour-
ners at Paddy Dignam's funeral in James Joyce's *Ulysses*, and the young
man 'with nothing but a linen cloth about his body' who appears briefly
in Mark's passion narrative, slipping out of the cloth and running away
when the authorities try to seize him. The oddity of these figures lies
in the suddenness of their appearance, and the apparently redundant
specificity of the detail which surrounds them (the emphasis on cloth-
ing in Kermode's two cases). They are just a momentary flash in the
narrative – 'Now where did he pop up from?' people say of the man
in the mackintosh in *Ulysses*, and Kermode uses the phrase about
popping up to convey the sense of the reader's bewilderment concerning
them. He also notes the sense that a readerly contract is being broken
in some way when they do crop up, for we expect a story to *unfold* in
an orderly manner and anticipate that the given details will have some
evident interpretive significance. He notes the wider sense of narrative
disjuncture and textual incongruity provoked by these figures, remarking that 'Everyone notes how different [they] are from what precedes
them; they have a quality not to be found in their prologues' (p. 113).
This same sense of narrative or discursive disjunction is felt in the
details we have been discussing from Hopkins's 'Death' sermon, which
proceeds along its familiar track of devotional generality until it is
suddenly interrupted by these three real people popping up, along with
the redundant specificity of their very postal addresses.

   Kermode's wise counsel is that the challenge to the reader is not to
discover the *truth* of the text – he doesn't try to find out who the young

man in the linen garment really was, turning back, as we did, from that seductive highroad to a more diffuse kind of context. Instead, he says, our job is to discover the *meaning* in the text. He attributes this distinction (between truth and meaning) to Spinoza's *Tractatus Theologico-Politicus*, but it has, of course, long been important to literary studies, and Kermode sees it corroborated by Jean Starobinski in the injunction that in interpretation we must not ignore what is written in favour of what is written about. Kermode, then, cautions us against the glide of our best attention from word to world, from text to context. Manifestly, there is a constant oscillation of the literary-critical metronome between these two poles: in W.K. Wimsatt's heyday in the early 1960s, and again in 1979, attention was at the 'word' end of the spectrum; by the 1990s, and still today, it was at the 'world' end, and younger literary critics all now seem to want ('deep down', if I can say that) to write either history or social critique. Curiously (and this is my problem), there doesn't really seem, in practice, to be a sustainable mid-point between 'word' and 'world' as focal ideals, and the professional aspiration of a balance between the two still seems dauntingly unattainable.

Like one of Kermode's incongruous narrative intruders I want, finally, to make a brief irruption into my own narrative. When members of my family first came to Liverpool in the mid nineteenth century they were part of that Irish post-Famine influx of immigrants that St Francis Xavier's church began to cater for as it slipped downmarket during the nineteenth century. In fact, they too lived in William Henry Street, and among the baptismal entries in the volume discussed earlier is that of my paternal grandfather, on 23 November 1879, a month before Hopkins's arrival at the church.[29] So as I walk down William Henry Street, retracing Hopkins's footsteps along the streets which made up his 'purlieus', I am also tracing my own story. I look back up that street to the newly greened slopes of Everton Brow, now gleaming, almost, in the August sunshine, but don't much like seeing the greenery there. It doesn't, in my eyes, make for that poised balance of culture and nature, urban and rural, that Hopkins celebrated in 'Duns Scotus's Oxford' as his 'Towery city and branchy between towers'. This is in fact the only time in the poetry that Hopkins uses the word 'city', and the part of Oxford whose presence he regretted and wished away is the 'base and brickish skirt', the kind of district in which he was condemned to labour in Glasgow and Liverpool, as well as in Oxford itself.[30] Retrospectively, in the SFX district of Liverpool, that wishing away of the brickiness is now posthumously fulfilled, and the greenery of 'neighbour-nature' is reinstated. But the rural vision (in that poem) of 'folk, flocks, and flowers' somewhat sentimentalises a Catholic, pre-urban, pre-industrial England, where, for Hopkins, the visible hills are the shoulder of God ('the azurous hung hills are his world-wielding shoulder', as he says in 'Hurrahing in Harvest'). Clearly, the Everton Brow I remember, with its rows of brick terraces, could not be thought of as the shoulder of God, or not, at least, by Hopkins. Yet I miss precisely the 'base and brackish skirt' it used to be clothed in. I look at it as the contemporary Dundee poet W. N. Herbert looks at his now de-industrialised native city and thinks 'I remember when all these fields were factories'.[31] Everton Brow can never recapture the innocence of 'rural rural keeping', and these green slopes, far from re-establishing the 'Sweet especial rural scene' ('Binsey Poplars') which existed before they were covered by their bricky skirt, are actually the by-product of the brutal deracination of people by compulsory-purchase orders, and their enforced diaspora to high-rise blocks on the outskirts of the city. This was the process which threatened in the 1970s to reduce SFX Church, and the whole district, to rubble. So the newly greened urban hill is a sad thing, a token of loss and absence, a reminder of the Hibernian 'middle passage' in the post-Famine period, and of how the powerless are always moved about, regardless of their own feelings on the matter, in the wake of economic forces. To be shifted in this way, like pawns on somebody else's chessboard, remained the lot of the descendants of Hopkins's parishioners (as it was – but on a vocational/voluntary basis – of Hopkins himself). This compulsory dispersal is the typical story of postwar, working-class, urban Britain, quite different, of course, from the voluntary, individual, outward migrations of those whose upbringing and education had provided them with the new possibility of choosing their place of abode. Acquiring the skills needed to analyse 'The Windhover' in ways acceptable to the dominant interpretative communities seldom confers riches, but it does provide a pretty effective immunity against being forcibly decanted, as 'overspill population', to places we would rather not live in. In this kind of investigation, then, the usual forms of academic detachment become difficult to maintain, and we become the object of our own quest. Or as Hopkins so beautifully said, 'What you look hard at seems to look hard at you'.[32] It is perhaps a way of saying that the happy case of Felix has its opposite – the man from Wm. Henry Street who remained uncomforted. It lay on Hopkins's conscience because he empathised with that man and later faced what he imagined his lonely ordeal might have been, in the religious crisis recorded in his so-called 'Terrible Sonnets'.

Notes

1 *The Spiritual Exercises of St Ignatius Loyola*, ed. Robert Backhouse (Hodder and Stoughton, 1989), p. 15, The First Exercise, First Prelude.

2 See Louis L. Martz, *The Poetry of Meditation: A Study in English Religious Literature of the Seventeenth Century* (Yale University Press, 1954), Chapter 1.1. 'Spiritual Exercises: Composition of Place', pp. 25–32.

3 Hopkins, of course, had a special interest in the composition of place, and read a paper on the topic at the St Bueno's 'Essay Society', 28 April 1877: the Society's records note that the culminating point of the argument was that 'Its true object is to make the Exercitant present in spirit at the scenes, persons, etc. so that they may really act on him, and he on them' (Alfred Thomas, SJ, *Hopkins the Jesuit: The Years of Training*, 1969 (Oxford University Press), pp. 173, n.3, and 178, n.3). The phrase 'and he on them' implies a reciprocity of effect which is suggestive in the present context.

4 Letter to Baillie, 22 May 1880, *Further Letters of Gerard Manley Hopkins*, ed. Claude Colleer Abbott, 1956 (Oxford University Press), p. 245.

5 Details from John Kennedy's booklet *St Francis Xavier's, Liverpool, 1848–1998*.

6 Freddy O'Connor, *Liverpool: Our City, Our Heritage* (Printfine Ltd, Liverpool, 1990), p. 123.

7 See Paddy Kitchen, *Gerard Manley Hopkins: A Life* (Carcanet, 1978), p. 196.

8 The family included Thomas Lightbound, first president of the Society of St Francis Xavier, the core of which was the Stonyhurst College 'old boy' network. This was the group of Catholic lay people which had bought the land and provided the money to build the church.

9 *Letters to Robert Bridges*, p. 110.

10 *Letters to Robert Bridges*, p. 99, footnote 1.

11 *God and Two Poets: Arthur Hugh Clough and Gerard Manley Hopkins* (Sidgwick & Jackson, 1988), p. 10.

12 I am grateful to Fr Feeney for drawing my attention to this piece.

13 *Letters to Robert Bridges*, p. 126.

14 *Letters to Robert Bridges*, p. 127.

15 *The Correspondence of Gerard Manley Hopkins and Richard Watson Dixon*, ed. Claude Colleer Abbott (Oxford University Press, revised edition, 1955), p. 97.

16 Reprinted in the *TLS*, 4 September 1969, pp. 1026–7.

17 *Further Letters*, p. 157.

18 The bishop was Bernard O'Reilly, third bishop of Liverpool, who was far from being the genteel 'Barchester' stereotype of a bishop. He had been a curate and parish priest among the poor of the south end of Liverpool. He was also the founder of the diocesan seminary at Upholland, Lancashire, and is buried in the simple cemetery there, rather than with

his successors in the greater pomp of the Cathedral crypt. I remember the cemetery as a modestly hedged-off area near the cricket field.

19 I am indebted to Fr Joseph J. Feeney, SJ, for this information.

20 *The Sermons and Devotional Writings of Gerard Manley Hopkins*, ed. Christopher Devlin, 1959 (Oxford University Press), p. 247.

21 Devlin's note (*Sermons and Devotional Writings*, pp. 315–16) describes the general character of William Henry Street but does not speculate on the identity of the person concerned.

22 The best-known example occurs in the Liverpool-period poem 'Felix Randal', where the beautiful line 'Ah well, God rest him all road ever he offended!' could easily have been spoken by one of his Liverpool parishioners.

23 Letter to Baillie, 6 May 1882, *Further Letters*, p. 248.

24 The story of the room above the synagogue in Whitechapel, abandoned by Hebrew scholar David Rodinsky in the 1960s, and left forgotten and unentered for eleven years, is told by Rachael Lichtenstein and Iain Sinclair in *Rodinsky's Room* (Granta, 1999).

25 For many of these details about the church and its contents I am indebted to Brother Ken Vance, SJ, the Parish Administrator.

26 'Records of Roman Catholic Churches Held at the Liverpool Record Office', 282 SFX.

27 *Letters to Robert Bridges*, p. 134.

28 Tom Dunne, *Gerard Manley Hopkins: A Comprehensive Bibliography*, 1976 (Oxford University Press), p. 361.

29 Recently I learned that my father, Frank Barry, was christened Francis Xavier Barry, presumably in reference to the parish the family moved away from as it established roots in the city.

30 Hopkins and Matthew Arnold are unique as Victorian, Oxford-educated poets whose professional lives (as priest and schools inspector, respectively) were largely conducted in industrial towns and cities which never appear directly in their poetry, and which most people of their social class never entered. The only city which they do feature directly in their work is Oxford, in both cases in a 'ruralised' form which was already becoming anachronistic.

31 This kind of 'reversed' urban nostalgia occurs in Herbert's poem 'Port Selda', and refers to a recently cleared and 'ruralised' district of his native city (rather like the Everton Brow district discussed here).

32 *Gerard Manley Hopkins*, ed. Catherine Phillips, Oxford Authors, 1995 (Oxford University Press), p. 204 (journal entry for 13 March 1871).

6

Picturing the context:
contemporary poetry and ekphrasis

During the 1990s there was a revival of critical interest in ekphrastic poetry, that is, poetry which speaks to or of an art-object, such as a painting, a statue, or a photograph.[1] Indeed. a commentator in *Poetry Review* has stated recently that 'photographic ekphrasis' has 'become a set-piece of most collections',[2] and my interest in the form here is that such poems have an unusually determinate context, one which is, by definition or '*ex officio*', deep. The word 'ekphrasis' itself has complicated associations, connoting (in rhetoric) a plain or formal description, declaration or proposition. But the Greek roots, '*ek*' and '*phrasis*' in combination, simply mean 'speaking out' or 'out-speaking', which can also bear the connotation that what the poem speaks of lies unambiguously 'outside' the poem, rather than within the poet's imagination, even though it is not in the 'real' world, but in the parallel universe of art. When first encountered, ekphrasis seems to designate a fairly simple situation, since the poem's referent is so much more contained and defined than is usually the case in poetry. However, even a rudimentary consideration of the kinds of ekphrastic poem which might conceivably be written quickly reveals a range of finely graded alternatives.

A typology of ekphrasis

The critic John Hollander, who has been a major theorist of contemporary ekphrasis, makes a fundamental sub-division of ekphrasis into 'actual' ekphrasis, in which a genuine art-work is being described or addressed (the usual example is Auden's 'Musée des Beaux Arts') and 'notional' ekphrasis, in which, he says, the 'object' is a 'purely fictional painting or sculpture that is indeed brought into being by the poetic language itself' (the classic example is Browning's 'My Last Duchess').

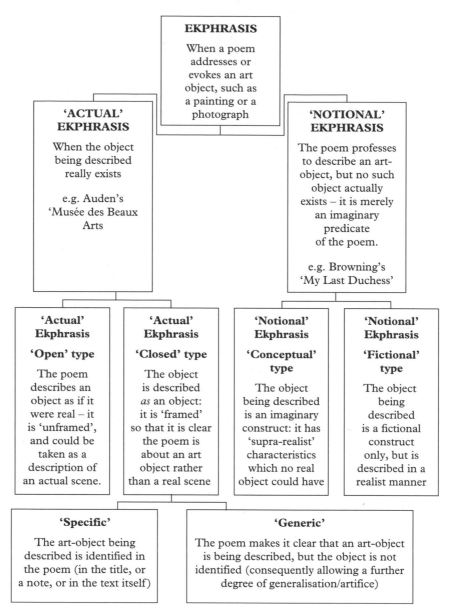

Figure 6 Varieties of ekphrasis.

I suggest a further sub-division of both these sub-categories, and for ease of reference the proposed schematisation is shown in Figure 6. Actual ekphrasis (poems about real pictures or real photographs) can usefully be sub-divided into 'closed' and 'open' variants. In the closed type, such as Auden's 'Musée', the poem makes it explicit that it is speaking not about a real witnessed event but about a scene which is viewed in a painting. Thus the poem says 'In Brueghel's *Icarus*, for instance', and this phrase 'closes' the ekphrasis by identifying the painting which the poem discusses. In the 'open' type, by contrast, the object of the ekphrasis is presented 'unframed', and so could be taken as a description of (say) an actual scene, rather than a pictorial representation of that scene. For example, Blake's 'Tyger' is an 'open' ekphrasis, often read as if it were describing an actual tiger in the jungle, but it actually represents both Blake's own engraving and also paintings he had seen at Burlington House. Clearly, in the open kind of ekphrasis, the ekphrastic element tends to be merely implicit, since, in effect, the act of making it explicit 'closes' the ekphrasis. In practice, the most interesting examples of ekphrasis are often neither absolutely open nor absolutely closed, but, so to speak, 'ajar', as discussed later.

On the 'notional' side of the ekphrastic divide (containing poems which are about imagined or projected paintings or photographs), a sub-division is also useful, this time into 'fictional' and 'conceptual' variants. In the former, the art-object addressed by the poem is a fictional construct which doesn't actually exist, like the painting in Browning's 'My Last Duchess', for instance, but that imagined painting is presented in entirely 'realist' terms – it has (for instance) a fictional artist and a fictional provenance, and it doesn't do anything which paintings don't usually do, which is to say that it just hangs on the wall and people look at it, and sometimes talk about it and what it depicts. But the conceptual variant is markedly different: again, of course, the object is imaginary, but in this case it also has 'supra-realist' characteristics which no real art object could have. An example is Auden's 'The Shield of Achilles', where the envisaged shield is 'filmic' – scenes are played out on it, and it has a 'sound-track'. So it is a *conceptual* object, one which not only *doesn't* but also *couldn't* exist. Across the more basic divide between actual and notional ekphrasis, we can perhaps sense interesting affinities of attitude and effect between 'open actual' ekphrasis (where a painting is being described, but implicitly) on one side of the main divide, and 'fictional notional' ekphrasis on the other (where an imagined painting is being described, but in a realistic way) – for this is where the most interesting ekphrastic poems tend to be situated.

Another crucial aspect of ekphrasis concerns the manner in which the object is addressed. The issue here is how the words of the poem stand in relation to the art-object depicted in the poem, and there are four basic possibilities (plus variations and combinations which I will ignore for the time being). The four basic positions can be summarised as follows

Firstly, the poem can speak *to* the object, as Keats does in 'Ode on a Grecian Urn' – 'Thou still unravish'd bride of quietness', he begins, knowing, of course, that he is speaking to an inanimate object which isn't going to answer back, though its silence may seem pregnant and in the end will 'tease us out of thought'.

Secondly, the poet can speak, not to the object itself, but to the person depicted in the painting or photograph, as if that person were actually present, though there are always complications. Thus, in Matt Simpson's poem 'We meet at last' (discussed later), a photograph of a woman is described, and the poem begins 'This is what / you look like then?'

A *third* option is that the poem speaks *about* the painting or photograph, rather than *to* it, as Auden does in 'Musée', chatting to the reader about the kind of images we see in Old Master paintings ('About suffering they were never wrong, the Old Masters'). Here, the situation is again deceptively simple: Auden tells us that he is talking about a painting ('in Brueghel's *Icarus*'), and the situation is the most usual one in poetry – the poet is musing, and the reader is a kind of privileged inner auditor who over-hears the poet's interior monologue.

A *fourth* option is that the poet, again, talks *about* the painting, not *to* it, this time, or *of* it, but addressing words to hearers who are within the poem, and part of its dramatic situation, as in Browning's 'My Last Duchess', which begins 'That's my last duchess hanging on the wall', and is addressed to an individual who is being shown the painting which is the subject of the poem.

The potential for overlap or 'glide' between two and four will be evident, and it can be said without qualification that nothing is more characteristic of ekphrastic poetry than instability within the basic identifiable types – indeed, 'glide' across the identifiable sub-categories is what most accounts for the fascination of the ekphrastic sub-genre.

Further varieties of ekphrastic poetry

All the foregoing applies to what might be called the 'classic' type of ekphrastic poem, the kind in which a poem responds to a single art-object. The norm is that the art-object is singular and precedes the poem. Expressing it this way immediately draws attention to a wide range of potential variants: some of these can be briefly listed and exemplified as follows, but (with one exception) these additional types are not further discussed here

Composite ekphrasis occurs when the poem comments on more than one painting. Yeats's 'The Municipal Gallery Revisited' is the perfect example. The poem cites successively a whole series of pictures in the gallery, thematised round the ideas of nationhood and friendship, with the poet as the hub of the circle of pictures cited, who thus self-flatteringly becomes the hub of modern Irish culture and history:

> Around me the images of thirty years:
> An ambush; pilgrims at the water-side;
> Casement upon trial, half hidden by the bars,
> Guarded; Griffith staring in hysterical pride;
> Kevin O'Higgins' countenance that wears
> A gentle questioning look that cannot hide
> A soul incapable of remorse or rest;
> A revolutionary soldier kneeling to be blessed;
> An Abbot or Archbishop with an upraised hand
> Blessing the Tricolour.

Here each line cites one or more paintings, giving us a rapid 'slide-slow' of key images, providing an over-arching parabola of recent Irish history in a uniquely economical way.

Reverse ekphrasis occurs when the painting is a response to the poem, rather than the other way round. An example of a reverse-ekphrastic pairing of poem and picture is William Carlos Williams's poem 'The Great Figure', about the apotheosis of the figure five (as seen painted in gold on the side of 'a red fire truck'), and Charles Demuth's 1928 responding picture 'I Saw the Figure Five in Gold'. Various verbal acts of homage to Williams are incorporated in the picture – such as the word 'Bill' at the top, and the letters 'WCW' centralised like a signature at the bottom. So ekphrastic traffic isn't just one way.

Multiple reverse ekphrasis occurs when several paintings all respond to the same poem. For instance, there are many Victorian paintings and drawings illustrating Tennyson's poem 'The Lady of Shalott': but just as the ekphrastic poem never just inertly describes a painting, so in reverse ekphrasis the paintings are not just illustrations – often they are interpolations or, at least, interpretations: thus, John Waterhouse's picture adds overt Christianisation to the poem – the lady's boat has candles and a crucifix prominently placed: Atkinson Grimshaw's version of the same scene makes it into a Viking Valhalla, with his character-istic burning sky and water, and a Viking dragon at the prow of the boat, and so on. The cross-textual, multi-media web which results is complicated – several pictures concern the ending of the poem, which is radically different in the 1832 and 1842 versions, and the story overlaps a great deal with Tennyson's own re telling of it in his 1859

Idylls of the King, when the Lady of Shalott becomes Elaine of Astalot, who is rejected by Launcelot and ends up afloat in a boat, just like the Lady of Shalott. Thus, a complex of multi-media co-textuality is evident in such instances.

Double ekphrasis is another complex trope which results when one ekphrastic piece evokes or builds upon an earlier one: thus Auden's modern poem 'The Shield of Achilles' is a reprise or remake of the description of the shield of Achilles in Book 18 of the *Iliad*, the most famous example of ekphrasis in classical literature. In such cases the earlier text might be called the 'pre-text', and the later one the 're-text'.

Oblique ekphrasis describes the situation in the kind of poem which has an ekphrastic element or motif, but is not primarily an ekphrastic piece, but merely uses ekphrasis as one element in a range of strategies or devices – an example is discussed later in this chapter.

Ekphrasis, finally, may even be taken as gesturally emblematic of the condition of all poetry, for poetry is only able to engage the 'real' through conventional modes of perception and representation which (as we used to say) 'always already' exist. Thus, (for example) the landscape depicted in poetry is always embedded in a 'discourse' – it may be part of a moralised Bunyanesque terrain which is to be read allegorically; it may conform to eighteenth-century conventions of the picturesque (as if viewed through a verbal Claude glass); it may be imbued with the moral and aesthetic thematisations characteristic of Romanticism; or it may be seen as the locus of a vanishing 'organic community', as in twentieth-century Georgianism – and so on. Hence, ekphrastic poetry seems to embody an acknowledgement of the unbridgeable hermeneutic gap between poetry and the real, which is what makes it so fascinating. Writing a poem about (say) a photograph seems to involve tacitly accepting that poetry can deal only with *representations* of reality, never with reality itself. There is no easy contact between the world of the poem, and the 'extra-literary' world beyond, and the two can only communicate with each other through the intervening medium of the ekphrastic object. A metaphor may clarify what is meant here: it's rather as when two parties in a dispute are too much at odds to negotiate face-to-face, and instead have to do so through an intermediary. The ekphrastic object is the intermediary, whose very presence is a reminder of the gulf between the two sides.

Ekphrasis exemplified: Matt Simpson, Tony Curtis, Margaret Atwood

To illustrate how even the most apparently straightforward examples of ekphrasis are full of hidden complexities, I will take the 'straightest' kind of ekphrasis I have been able to find, which is a poem by the contemporary poet Matt Simpson. The poem is called 'We Meet at Last', and it occurs in his collection *Cutting the Clouds Towards*, 1998).[3] Perhaps, however, the impression of straightforwardness will disappear as soon as the theme of the collection is described: Simpson is a poet and academic whose father was a merchant seaman, and his father's voyages had taken him to Tasmania, including Hobart, its capital, and 'When he mentioned Hobart there was always a twinkle in my father's eye that suggested some kind of romantic experience'. In 1995 Simpson was himself invited to undertake a period as writer-in-residence in Tasmania, and the poems in the volume are the result of this experience. Before leaving the UK, he had come across a book called *My Home in Tasmania*, the journal of the nineteenth-century writer and artist Louisa Anne Meredith, who had emigrated to Australia from Birmingham. Simpson had read the journal and written a sequence of poems relating to Meredith before visiting Tasmania. The poem 'We Meet at Last' is written in response to a photograph of her which (most unusually for an ekphrastic poem) is printed on the facing page (Figure 7):

Figure 7 Louisa Anne Meredith, reproduced from Matt Simpson's *Cutting the Clouds Towards*, by permission of the Allport Library and Museum of Fine Arts, State Library of Tasmania.

We Meet at Last

This is what
you look like then?

An obvious
charmer still,

hand on shoulder
fingering curls.

We meet at Warrandyte,
the good professor's house

where distant bell birds ping
and magpies chortle in

the pepper trees.
I mean I get to see

a frontispiece. The *carte
de visite* photographer

has gone for that soft-focus
pre-Raphaelite look

the men all like:
that studied ambivalence,

noli me tangere yet
console me in my hour of need.

I know – for I have miles
of retrospect –

that your if-only eyes
are artist's eyes,

the company you yearn for
is angels different from

the ones aloft: you want
luminaries of the brush and pen.

And there are fraught times ahead,
counting the lost, the dead,

the Swan River flood,
terror-stricken horses straining necks,

and only just,
above the battering water line.

If we consider this poem as a purely textual object (that is, ignoring
the fact that the photograph is printed alongside it) it seems that the

'glide' is from 'open' to 'closed' ekphrasis, for the first eleven lines could well be describing the speaker's inner reactions on actually meeting Meredith, rather than just seeing her photograph. The ekphrasis, though, is abruptly closed by line twelve ('I mean I get to see / a frontispiece'), so this is really less of a glide than a sudden shift of gear which switches the poem into a different dimension. The anaphoric 'This' at the start of the poem gestures out (the literal 'ek-phrasis') to the addressee, who is present, we at first think, though later we realise that only her picture is: Browning's 'Last Duchess' begins with a similar anaphoric gesture ('That's my last duchess . . .') but immediately indicates that only the picture is present ('. . . painted on the wall'), so perhaps the gesture should strictly be described as 'deictic' (literally 'pointing'), rather than 'anaphoric'. Simpson's poem shifts out of its apparently simple ekphrasis in words like 'still' (in 'An obvious / charmer still'), which ought to have a deictic 'fixing' effect, setting Meredith within her own time and place (so that 'still' would mean 'at the time the photograph was taken', with the implicit addition 'even though then middle-aged') – the caption to the photograph reads 'Louisa Anne Meredith (née Twamley) in middle age'. But the meaning is also something like 'even now', indicating her posthumous effect on the writer, and highlighting the artistic effect of the photograph which is made to look like a painting, with its 'soft-focus / pre-Raphaelite look' and the *vignette* style that melts the image into its background. Of course, Meredith is 'appropriated by the male gaze'; the look is mannered and composed, and is read as discreetly flirtatious, but in reality, the poet implies, she is flirting with art ('I know . . . that your if-only eyes / are artist's eyes'), and that is her ultimate longing ('you want / luminaries of the brush and pen'); in this desire she will be frustrated by the cares and troubles of daily life, which prevent her from fulfilling this aspect of her nature. Hence, although the poem sets itself up as a description of a romantic encounter ('We meet at last'), this is actually a kind of 'spiritual' relationship, counterpart of the father's imagined romantic liaison. It trumps the father's assumed romantic involvement with a woman from Tasmania by setting up a 'meeting' in a past which would be remote even to him ('I have miles / of retrospect'), putting in a back-dated counter-claim for the worth and reality of his craft as a poet against his father's trade as a sailor. The ekphrastic poem, with its adjacent photograph, is heavily 'framed' by these Oedipal and broader thematic issues. Its role as part of a sequence, and the place of this book in the *oeuvre* as a whole, complicate the apparently straightforward ekphrastic process.

'Apparently straightforward'? Well, let's look again: the poet *seems* to be speaking to the woman herself. He says 'you', and the poem begins

'This is what / you look like then?', as if the poet were speaking directly
to her, not 'This is what / *she* looks like' (or 'looked like'), which would
indicate that he is speaking *about* rather than *to* Louisa Anne Meredith.
Actually, though, the phrase used isn't *quite* what could be said directly
to the person in question: *firstly*, wouldn't 'this' be 'that' if the person
were actually present in front of him ('So *that's* what you look like!').
Secondly, the next couplet ('An obvious / charmer still') is *thinkable* at
the moment of first meeting, but surely not *sayable* (the 'still', for instance,
is a reference to the subject's no longer being young, and 'charmer'
registers the presence of a possible degree of artifice and calculation).
The phrase is sayable to another person, someone who can see either
the woman in reality, or her picture, but not to the woman herself.
Thirdly, 'Hand on shoulder / fingering curls' is not sayable at all,
either to the woman herself, or to a fellow-observer, and it is really
'thinkable' only when performed 'musingly' or 'inwardly'. Hence, even
the most apparently simple ekphrastic situation quickly develops com-
plicating overtones.

The middle section of the poem (from 'We meet at Warrandyte' to
'*in my hour of need*') describes the circumstances of the 'meeting', namely
that the poet is shown the picture, which is the frontispiece of one of
her books, at the house of the professor who was the poet's host during part of a reading tour in Tasmania. The remainder of the poem
is chiefly what might be called 'retrospective foreknowledge' – the poet
knows what happened to Meredith later in her life, for as he says 'I
have miles / of retrospect', and he uses this to 'ironise' the image and
give it a depth of pathos. And finally, he introduces the 'thematising'
element of the isolation of the writer, in this case an intellectual
whose life has taken her far away from the circles in which she might
have hoped to find kindred spirits who would be on the same wave-
length as herself. To sum up the operative elements we have identified
in this poem: *firstly*, there is the direct address to the subject of the
photograph herself, but combined with elements which subtly suggest
that the woman is both met and (as it were) 'viewed' at the same time.
Secondly, the circumstances in which the picture is looked at are
brought in, so that the speaker's circumstances and that of the subject
of the portrait are in some way intermingled. *Thirdly*, the element
of what the poet knows which is *un*known to the subject is brought
in, greatly increasing the 'depth' of the poem. Here, then, is actual
closed specific ekphrasis in practice, showing that the process is much
less stable than the technical description might suggest. Shadowing
the closed ekphrasis is a process whereby the meeting is imagined as
real ('We meet at last'), and there is a kind of 'flicker' between the open

and closed variants throughout the poem. This, too, is characteristic of the Ekphrastic sub-genre. Printing the photograph alongside the poem, nevertheless, gives the maximum possible degree of 'closedness' in the sense described earlier, so Simpson's poem makes a logical starting point.

Another contemporary poet who frequently writes in ekphrastic mode is Tony Curtis, and a striking example appeared in a recent issue of the Oxford poetry magazine *Thumbscrew* (No. 15 (Winter/Spring 2000), page 61).[4] The poem is called 'Lottie Stafford's Neck', and the painting described in it is *The Wash House* – a key work in the history of Irish art – by the Irish artist Sir William Orpen (1878–1931), the most successful portrait painter of the Edwardian period (Figure 8):

Lottie Stafford's Neck

Morning sunlight catching
the heat of her like sex.
The way the light glazes her neck
at that moment she turns,
her hands gripping the washing tub,
as Jenny comes down the stairs with
the bedding across her shoulders
in a fluster of gossip.

That shining, taut slope of skin
Sir William caught with his brushes,
a scene from the mind,
the life of service he imagined.
Hours in his studio after work
her neck craned and stiffening
while the gas-light came and went
with the breeze of the evening.

To be finished on her Sunday off,
when she straightened from the pose
and walked around to his side.
And afterwards she drank his tea,
put on her coat and went back to the big house,
her room in the attic.
Or sipped tea
and did not put on her coat.

The painting is not precisely identified as such in the poem, though the poem makes it clear that *a* painting is being described. On the other hand, the mention of the model Lottie Stafford in the title, and the name 'Sir William' in the second stanza do give strong pointers as to

Figure 8 The Wash House by Sir William Orpen. Reproduced by permission of the National Gallery of Ireland.

which painting this is, so this is clearly actual ekphrasis. Lottie Stafford, the model for the painting, was 'a washerwoman living in the slum cottages of Paradise Walk' (in Chelsea, near Sir William's London home) who was 'much in demand as a model, though she declined to pose in the nude . . . she was a goddess, a Juno figure, robust, laughing, subtle and enormously warm'.[5]

Curtis's first stanza is a straight ekphrastic 'transcription' of the painting, but is it 'open' or 'closed'? When first encountered, it is probably read as 'open' – we take this as a scene actually observed, since non-painterly elements, like heat and movement, are emphasised. But the second stanza makes it clear that what is being described is a painting, so what was at first read as 'open' is reread retrospectively as 'closed', so perhaps the true description would be that the first stanza is in ekphrastic terms neither 'open' nor 'closed' but 'ajar'.

The second stanza, however, seems to 'glide' from actual to notional ekphrasis, as the poet asserts that what Sir William 'caught with his brushes' is 'a scene from the mind, / the life of service he imagined'. So the artist, says the poet, can (or does) only paint scenes from the mind, as if notional ekphrasis were really the only possible kind. The poem draws attention to the unnatural element in this supremely naturalistic painting, a work whose *vérité* quality was (and is) its most striking feature – it's a 'spontaneous' gesture which is held still for several hours so that Sir William can 'capture' it.

The third stanza seems to leave the painting behind and enters a world which is frankly fictive: this is more like an incident from a novel. The speculative feel of this is very striking: *what*, exactly, is finished on her Sunday off? What does she drink tea after? The poem's movement into fictionalisation here parallels the poet's function and that of the artist: Sir William doesn't paint what he *sees*, rather he projects a scene from the mind: in the same way, the poet doesn't just write what he knows about Lottie Stafford, but sets out a fictional version of her. The fictional Lottie of the poem is 'in service'; she is a servant with a Sunday off, living in an attic room at the 'Big House'. An Irish setting seems to be implied, so that she seems implicitly to embody the 'servitude' of Ireland in Edwardian times (a figure analogous in function to the old woman at the start of Joyce's *Ulysses*, or the woman described in Eavan Boland's poem 'The Achill Woman'): Sir William seems to represent the Anglo-Irish Ascendancy and is depicted as using her for his own ends (there are hints in the poem of her sexual availability, for instance). This fictionalised version of the model seems to diverge quite knowingly from the known facts about the woman represented in the picture. In fact, Lottie Stafford was a Cockney, living near Sir William's London residence. She wasn't a live-in servant but a washerwoman, not 'in-service', in other words, with the serf-like status that implies, but a freelance, who also worked as an artist's model, and set her own terms – she wouldn't pose in the nude, as we saw. She is remembered as someone 'with a . . . great capacity for capping any story, never at a loss for words', and seems to have had none of that deference towards authority figures which the phrase 'the life of service' implies. Does it matter that the poet has 'thematised' a real person in this way, making her, in fact, into rather a cliché? The facts (in so far as they can be known) have been made to collude with the *poet's* imagination ('the life of service he imagined'), and with his thematic preoccupations. If, as readers, we find something slightly disturbing about this, and wonder whether we should let it pass without comment, the poet simply flashes his poetic licence, confident that it will disarm all criticism. But there is, surely, an ethical issue here concerning how the negotiation between poetry and the real is conducted, an issue which ekphrastic poetry always seems to intensify. When a poet begins to write ekphrastically there is a kind of implicit 'compact' with the reader that this time, at least, there will be no tricks with 'the real', and the poems often begin with the kind of apparently straight description of the visual image which we see in Curtis's first stanza. But pretty soon readers realise that poets in ekphrastic mode tend to be using the method as a cloak for something which is, if anything, going to be even more tricksy than usual.

The 'tricksiness' of ekphrastic poetry is equally apparent in another outstanding contemporary example, Margaret Atwood's poem 'This is a Photograph of Me', an example of 'notional' ekphrasis, since it emerges unambiguously as the poem goes on that the photograph it purports to describe could not exist:

This is a Photograph of Me

It was taken some time ago.
At first it seems to be
a smeared
print: blurred lines and grey flecks
blended with the paper;

then, as you scan
it, you see in the left-hand corner
a thing that is like a branch: part of a tree
(balsam or spruce) emerging
and, to the right, halfway up
what ought to be a gentle
slope, a small frame house

In the background there is a lake,
and beyond that, some low hills.

(The photograph was taken
the day after I drowned.

I am in the lake, in the center
of the picture, just under the surface.

It is difficult to say where
precisely, or to say
how large or small I am:
the effect of water
on light is a distortion

but if you look long enough,
eventually
you will be able to see me.)

This is the first poem in *The Circle Game*, Atwood's first major book
of poetry,[6] and it is often seen by critics as a variant of literary Gothic;

> [The poem] asks us to look beneath the surface of both the charming
> snapshot and the lake at something less visible but more significant – the
> 'drowned' narrator. Is she metaphorically 'drowned' – denied, sup-
> pressed, repressed? Is she herself a metaphor for the natural forces which
> the circle gamesters seek to obliterate? Like many Gothic novels before
> it, the poem leaves us guessing at a mystery.[7]

The title declares the ekphrastic basis, and this is reinforced throughout the first half (that is, up to the parenthesis), as the description
incorporates terms like 'left-hand corner', 'to the right', and 'background'.
All these terms keep the viewer's attention on the process of representation itself, preventing us from simply entering the depicted scene
and taking it as real. But the parenthetical second half of the poem
makes it clear that this cannot be any real photograph, so that we have
to retrospectively reread as notional what had at first seemed actual
ekphrasis (again, the need to reread sections of the poem retrospectively reoriented seems to me a common one with ekphrastic writing).
Further, we realise, too, that it can only be the conceptual kind of notional
ekphrasis, for this 'photograph' is like no other – it has metaphysical
capabilities, such as the ability to make the dead speak.

Just as Sir William painted 'a scene from the mind', so here the image
has to be 'developed' by the viewer, and the process is exactly like
what happens when a photographic print is being developed: in the
developing-tray at first, it's just 'blurred lines and gray flecks', then 'as
you scan', you begin to see objects – 'part of a tree . . . emerging', and
so on. The first glance at the developing picture in the darkroom
shows vague, emerging marks on the photographic paper which cannot
easily be recuperated or narrativised – they are just a kind of visual

equivalent of 'white noise'. Then the marks pass from semiotic 'blur' to the hard precision of the 'imaginary', as interpretable shapes are gradually perceived (a decoding process surely very familiar – in its verbal equivalent – to the habitual poetry reader, and mimed here in the first half of the poem). In other words, the ekphrastic element of the poem here reflects to the reader the (often laborious) process of making sense of the words in poetry. (A previous reader has written 'Lake = culture?' against the poem in the library copy I am using.) Always, the danger is that of a 'premature recuperation' which prefers to rush into simplified sense, rather than undergo longer durance in the intolerable 'blur' of none-sense. I am not (so help me) assuming that this poem's true subject is the writing or reading of poems (an assumption which is nearly always trivialising, and never as clever as it takes itself to be). I am simply stressing that, as the poem says, we may have to look a long time before we (eventually) see what is really there. In the Curtis poem, it was argued, we can choose our own ending (the one where Lottie puts on her coat and goes home, or the one where she doesn't put on her coat, and presumably doesn't go home). In Atwood's poem, by contrast, the ending of the story is given, and we have to work out what happened *before* the end, but it's difficult to do that, partly because of the shifting about of the physical elements referred to in the poem, which thus constitutes a foregrounding of the fictive, just like Curtis's double ending. Hence, one moment the lake is in the background, the next it's 'in the centre of the picture': one moment the speaker tells you exactly where she is ('I am in the lake, in the center / of the picture, just under the surface') next moment she says 'It is difficult to say where / precisely'. The items in the poem, then, seem to have a counter-Aristotelian dimension, for certain things are both the case and not the case at the same time.

I have two further specific comments on Atwood's poem. Firstly, I notice how it takes the reader's response and incorporates it into the poem, miming the hermeneutic procedures of an idealised reader who is attuned to the voice which emanates mysteriously from within it. Thus, the poem says (speaking for the projected reader/viewer of the poem/photograph, for these are words which can make sense of nobody else) 'At first it seems to be . . . // then, as you scan / it, you see', etc. These ekphrastic poem-pictures may remind us of how the ancient and Classical definitions of poetry always seem to teeter on the edge of identifying poems with pictures, and vice versa. Thus, in the *Ars Poetica* Horace famously says '*ut pictura poesis*' – a poem is like a picture – which seems to make a very natural elision between the picture in the mind and the picture before the eye. Simonides, too, according to Plutarch, says that 'a painting is a silent poem: a poem is a speaking picture'. In Atwood's poem the projected locus of the discourse (by which I mean, literally, the expected speech situation in which sentences like those in the poem might be expected to occur) is that of photographs being handed round for friends and family to look at. In this situation people say things like 'Here's one of me at Monte Carlo; it was taken the day we went to the Casino.' That is, unmistakably, the linguistic register of the title and opening of the poem: 'This is a photograph of me; It was taken some time ago.' The poem then breaks free of its chronotopic 'anchorage' or 'embedding' in this specific and recognisable situation and 'goes walkabout', beginning to shift into what I would call a 'chronotopic out-take', in which time and place start to blur, and then blur some more. Thus, at first the locutionary patterns (of lexis and syntax) which are typical of the identified chronotope seem to persist: we can still recognise, in other words, the situation of the family snapshot session in the sentence 'At first it seems to be / a smeared / print', which echoes the form of a remark like 'At first you can't see Uncle Bill, but if you look at the shadow of the pillar you notice . . .'. But the language then begins to accumulate features which would be distinctly anomalous in this situation; for instance, the precision with which the tree is identified sounds forensic, almost, rather than chatty – 'part of a tree / (balsam or spruce)' – and there is a curious hint at some traumatic repressed narrative in the lines 'halfway up / what ought to be a gentle / slope'. What is happening at this point in the poem is like the fading of one scene into another in a film, as gradually elements associated with the comfortable family situation are 'faded out', and those associated with some more sinister scene are 'faded in'. Thus, the poem begins to slip into a kind of open fictive space, in which the utterance, and the event it tries to give voice to, cannot be precisely situated at all. On the surface, the posited picture is pretty well empty and featureless (a lake, a slope, a house, some hills), but it hints at an underlying, repressed violence (that slope maybe ought to be gentle, but it isn't). The voice then speaks from out of the parenthesis of death, in a chronotopic out-take suspended somewhere both beyond the poem and beyond our familiar day-to-day reality. It speaks from 'just under the surface', a liminal underworld where things are distorted by the effect of water on light (*not* the effect of light on water, notice – the viewpoint is *under* the water). The voice may be imagined as speaking the unspoken, perhaps referring to domestic abuse, suffering, and violence, but it is a voice which never has been, and never can be, heard, for no voice can ever say 'The photograph was taken / the day after I drowned'. The notional ekphrasis on which the poem is based (this writing about a photograph which isn't there) facilitates the achievement of its uncanny and liminal feel. The effect is palpable, but very hard to characterise, and the speaker in the poem gives up the attempt to describe, and uses a final echo of the photo-session discourse which again pre-empts the reader's response – 'if you look long enough, / eventually / you will be able to see me'. And, if we think long enough, eventually, we might be able to understand the effect of this kind of ekphrasis, this strange process of writing about a painting or photograph which not only *doesn't* exist, but *couldn't*. Surely one would only do that if it seemed to offer the possibility of some kind of breakthrough in the on-going negotiations between poetry and the real. How, then, does Atwood's poem relate to external reality? In the *Tractatus* Wittgenstein says '*That* is how a picture relates to reality – it reaches right out to it'. We might reverse this proposition and say '*That* is how a poem relates to reality – it reaches right *into* it'. In other words, the poem is always 'at work' on its reality, projecting it, developing it, fictionalising it (and constructing it, even, as we always used to say). A certain sceptical quizzicality about poetic procedures is both embodied in and provoked by the ekphrastic process, which may account for its current popularity.

Oblique ekphrasis

This final type of ekphrasis occurs, as suggested earlier, when a poem which is not primarily ekphrastic nevertheless contains ekphrastic elements. Craig Raine is a contemporary British poet associated with the tendency in 1980s poetry known as 'Martianism', which takes its name from the title poem of his book *A Martian Sends a Postcard Home* (1979). 'Martianism' in poetry refers to the use of elaborate visual metaphors, whereby everyday objects are 'defamiliarised'. Raine's poem 'The Butcher' (from *The Onion, Memory*, 1978) also has an element of 'open ekphrasis', since the art object obliquely alluded to (a photograph in this case, Figure 9) is not explicitly identified:

The Butcher

'And even St George – if Gibbon is corect –
wore a top hat once; he was an army contractor
and supplied indifferent bacon'
                                        – E. M. Forster: *Abinger Harvest*

Surrounded by sausages, the butcher stands
smoking a pencil like Isambard Kingdom Brunel . . .

Figure 9 Isambard Kingdom Brunel.

He duels with himself and woos his women customers,
offering them thin coiled coral necklaces of mince,

heart lamé-ed from the fridge, a leg of pork 5
like a nasty bouquet, pound notes printed with blood.

He knows all about nudity – the slap and trickle
of blood, chickens stripped to their aertex vests.

He rips the gauze from dead balletic pigs,
and makes the bacon slicer swish its legs.   10

How the customers laugh! His striped apron
gets as dirty as the mattress in a brothel . . .

At 10, he drinks his tea with the spoon held back,
and the *Great Eastern* goes straight to the bottom.

The poem has a number of 'levels': firstly, it's a description of a butcher serving his customers, but represented (via the familiar Martianesque visual puns) as a cartoon-like romantic courtship: he offers them flowers (the leg of pork), a pearl necklace (the coils of mince), and finally his heart (the animal's heart from the fridge). Secondly, there is an underlying stratum of explicit eroticisation with sadistic undertones, as a series of sexual innuendoes are applied to the butcher's trade – the 'slap and trickle' of blood for 'slap and tickle', the chickens are 'stripped', and 'the bacon slicer swishes its legs', suggesting the swish of silk stockings, and the dirty striped apron linked with the mattress in a brothel. The ekphrastic element works along with these, for the picture evoked is the familiar Victorian photograph of the great engineer Isambard Kingdom Brunel, taken by the *Times* photographer Robert Howlett, which shows Brunel in 1857 at the height of his fame, standing in front of the huge drag-chains of his monster steamship the *Great Eastern*. He is wearing a top hat which looks about a foot high, and standing in a confident, macho pose, with a cigar in his mouth, legs slightly apart, and hands in his pockets. He is not smiling at the camera but looking sternly and levelly past the viewer, as if still preoccupied with his calculations. Everything about the picture contributes to an image of archetypal, confident, uncompromising masculinity.

Raine's poem takes up the notion of macho masculinity which is suggested by this photograph, and uses it as part of a characterisation of another traditionally manly trade: the 'top hat' is mentioned in the epigraph to the poem, and the initial scene of the butcher standing confidently behind his counter is directly paralleled to this photograph: thus, the butcher stands in front of strings of suspended sausages, just as Brunel stands in front of the suspended drag-chains: the butcher has a pencil in the side of his mouth, just as Brunel has a cigar in his. At the end of the poem all this confident masculinity seems to be defeated: the reference to the *Great Eastern* sinking reminds us that Brunel's ship was actually a failure; it took several months to get it into the water as its colossal 20,000-ton bulk stuck fast in the mud of the Thames. The strain ruined Brunel's health, and he had a stroke and died the year after the picture was taken. So the ekphrastic parallel with the Brunel photograph perhaps reminds us of the vulnerability of this kind of macho masculinity. In 'oblique ekphrasis', then, the allusions to the art object are merely one element in a poem which has other resources, and the art object itself is not explicitly identified. The butcher is placed within a whole series of representations of macho masculinity; the first item is the Brunel of the photograph, the second (in lines 4 to 6) is the dashing wooer in a Victorian melodrama, fighting duels, and offering bouquets on bended knee, and the third (in lines 8 to 12) is a showman in a risqué and ribald music-hall entertainment. Finally, in the last couplet, the Brunel motif is reintroduced to round off the poem with a kind of deflation of all these almost comically self-confident images of masculinity.

The ekphrastic pairing of poem and art object results in a unique form of 'site-specific', built-in contextuality or co-textuality, each example a one-off, non-generalisable partnership. The 'centripetal' pull of this kind of contextuality is perhaps the most forceful kind of all, and the fascination of the genre is that what ought to be a gentle, un-problematical kind of critical slope nearly always turns out to be nothing of the sort. Ekphrastic contextuality, then, has a uniquely solid claim to be considered 'deep': it is always uniquely dovetailed with a single poem, and is, by its very nature, non-transferable.

Notes

1 For influential discussion of ekphrasis see especially: Murray Krieger's *Ekphrasis: The Illusion of the Natural Sign* (Baltimore: Johns Hopkins University Press, 1992); John Hollander's *The Gazer's Spirit: Poems Speaking to Silent Works of Art* (University of Chicago Press, 1995); also Jay David Bolter's 'Ekphrasis, Virtual Reality, and the Future of Writing', in Geoffrey Nunberg, and Umberto Eco (eds), *The Future of the Book* (University of California Press, 1996).

2 Justin Quinn, 'Glyn Maxwell's Decade', *Poetry Review*, vol. 91, no. 1 (spring 2001), p. 16). See also a useful short piece on ekphrasis in *New Welsh Review*, summer 2006.

3 Liverpool University Press.

4 The poetry of Tony Curtis (b. 1946) first appeared in book form in *Three Young Anglo-Welsh Poets* (Welsh Arts Council, 1974), and subsequently in several individual collections from Poetry Wales Press and Seren. His poem 'The Death of Richard Beattie-Seaman in the Belgian Grand Prix, 1939' won the National Poetry Competition in 1994. The genesis of this poem (which has ekphrastic elements relating to contemporary photographs) is described in detail in chapter 2 of his textbook *How to Study Modern Poetry* (Macmillan, 1990). Other ekphrastic work by this poet includes the sequence

'Five Andrew Wyeth Poems', pp. 118–22 in *Tony Curtis: Selected Poems* (Poetry Wales Press, 1986) and the collection *The Arches*, by Tony Curtis and John Digby (Seren, 1998) which contains twenty-five surreal collages by Digby and twenty-five accompanying poems by Curtis, plus separate accounts of the project by writer and artist.

5 These quotations, and all the cited information about Lottie Stafford, are from the standard biography of Orpen, Bruce Arnold, *Orpen: Mirror to an Age* (Cape, 1981).

6 Originally published by Contact Press, Toronto, 1966.

7 Frank Davey, *Margaret Atwood: A Feminist Poetics* (Talon Books, Vancouver, 1984), p. 99.

7

Beyond 'secret narrative': crime-fiction verse narratives by women

This chapter considers poetic narrative sequences by contemporary women poets – Val Warner, Deryn Rees-Jones, Gwyneth Lewis, and Fiona Sampson – all of which use the conventions, atmosphere, and content of the crime-fiction thriller. This (I believe) newly discovered sub-genre – the women's crime-fiction poetic sequence – is contrasted with and distinguished from the adjacent male sub-genre of 'secret narrative' and a tentative explanation of the difference between the two sub-genres is offered. The crime fictioneers are intimately concerned with contemporary social processes and forms of feeling, challenging social norms (such as gender or professional norms) and exploring the interrelationship between those norms and the intimate, personal self.

Val Warner's *Tooting Idyll*

In particular, then, I am interested in experiments with narrative, and I want to differentiate these from the 1980s vogue for 'fractured' or 'tricksy' narrative of the kind typified by Andrew Motion's 'oblique and tight-lipped narratives that for a time looked like the beginning of a new school' (as the British Council's website page on Motion puts it), a style of poetry represented by many of the pieces in Motion's collection *Secret Narratives* (1983). Elsewhere I have described this style as producing 'obliquely told, often fragmented and unanchored narratives, emotive but obscure in character, often with highly coloured colonial or historical settings'.[1] But, as the British Council site notes of Motion's work (but the shift was more general too), 'gradually, these narratives ceded to more autobiographical material'.[2] This trajectory (from, let's say, fractured, conceptual, speculative biography to autobiography) presents no problem for the male poet: after all, the Romantic revolution occurred when Wordsworth and Coleridge began to see the minutiae of their own lives as perfectly valid poetic material, and male poets ever since have seen no reason to disagree with them. But, for the woman poet, the same option is not quite open: Felicia Hemans, as we saw in an earlier chapter, wrote elaborate, constructed 'biographies' of historical figures, and hardly anything at all directly about her own life until a sequence of poems about her final illness. The reason for avoiding the overtly biographical, for avoiding writing which is (in Harriet Tarlo's phrase) '*obviously* and *accessibly* about women's lives', is that such writing, in the case of women, is likely to be deemed parochial, limited in reach, unambitious, and of interest 'only' to other women.[3]

Yet, narrative role-play of the 'secret narrative' kind does not seem to have attracted many women writers, and for Andrew Duncan (http://www.pinko.org/1.html) it represents yet another form of the triumph of conservatism in contemporary British poetry, an importation of a cinematic genre which had already pretty well exhausted itself. He writes:

> It has been claimed that Hitchcock, in making *The Birds* (1963), was influenced by the Continental mystery film, a genre to whose rules he was, for commercial reasons, conforming. *The Birds* is perhaps a reply to *L'Avventura* [Antonioni, 1960], *La Dolce Vita* [Fellini, 1960], and *L'année Dernière à Marienbad* [Resnais, 1962]. The vogue for these films lasted till at least *Blow-Up* (1967). They were the supreme intelligent, fashionable, art film hits of their day; too popular not to have spawned many tedious imitations, but doing so only by being classics of cinema. My taste is perfectly conventional in admiring them; what is more in doubt is the artistic interest of reviving the enigma narrative, the incomplete story, so many years later.

But there does exist a significant cluster of examples of something rather different from those male 'enigma narratives' which were a kind of extended form of 'Martian' metaphorical play. That something takes the form of innovatory verse-narratives by women poets, often written as crime narratives or imagined 'crime-scapes' that involve the empathetic presentation of real life. An example of this crime-narrative sub-genre in embryonic form would be the final piece, 'The Underground Baby Poem', in Jackie Kay's first collection, *The Adoption Papers* (1991). Another, much longer, example is the material which makes up Val Warner's 1998 Carcanet collection *Tooting Idyll*.

Warner's collection consists of two sequences, the first called (like the book as a whole) 'Tooting Idyll', and the second 'Mary Chay'. 'Tooting Idyll' comprises three reflective monologues, all centred on the same house in Tooting Bec, in south London, but each being a different story. In the first, set in June 1939, the house is occupied by two male lovers, one about to become a soldier, the other (the 'speaker') a conscientious objector. In the second, set in June 1984, the same house is occupied by a man and a woman of left-wing convictions with an adopted child and another adoption in progress. In the third, the perspective is that of 'a cross-dressing female friend after the VE Day [Victory in Europe] fiftieth anniversary commemoration of 1995', as the jacket blurb describes it. The second part of the book is the sequence (which, like the first, is about seventy pages long) 'Mary Chay', which is also in three parts, but in this case the three parts are continuous sections of the same story. The story is described in the blurb as 'a murder in Victoria [London] in 1994, seen from many viewpoints and deploying a variety of forms'. The brief entry on Warner in the 'BrandNewWriters' website usefully inserts the word 'imaginary' into this description before the word 'murder', for the murder of Mary Chay is not a real event, in spite of its powerful *vérité* atmosphere, but draws upon features of a number of actual murders widely reported in the tabloid press in the 1990s. One of the poems quotes a *Sun* headline 'Lesbo thread in Hugh Street strangling', and the 'Mary Chay' of the sequence is friendless and unattached, and visiting a house in Hugh Street, near Victoria Station, a street which *does* exist, and consists mainly of low-rate, discount hotels. Hence, as an *Amazon* reviewer of *Tooting Idyll* says, the book 'establishes Warner as the celebrant of those [whom] society prefers to marginalise' (a comment which may, for all I know, be the only critical remark on this text in existence, other than the ones you are reading now). Readers familiar with Jackie Kay's better-known *The Adoption Papers* will recognise many elements of the Kay mixture, including a first-half sequence which has the same title as the book as a whole, and a concentration on those whose lifestyles, sexual orientation, and family set-ups were widely disapproved of, especially before the 1990s.

But my initial assertion about women's narrative writing of this kind, from the 1990s through to the present, was that it differs from the male-dominated, 1980s mode of 'secret narrative' associated with Motion, Fenton, Muldoon, and others, and I want to try to explain a little further what the difference is. One obvious aspect of the difference is that these narratives are sustained over much greater length, that they are not particularly fragmented, even though (in the case of 'Mary Chay') they do use multiple points of view, and (especially) that they are not 'playful' or whimsical. Perhaps the flavour of the piece can be conveyed by quoting one of the poems of the 'Mary Chay' sequence in full. I will take 'Playing the Part', from near the beginning of the sequence, which, in fact, does use the motif of roles and playing which was so

much favoured by the 'secret narrators' of the 1980s. But it does so
with a difference, since the speaker is the woman police officer who
plays the part of the murder victim in the police re-enactment of the
circumstances of the crime, following the police-procedural orthodoxy
of the day. The victim had bought a novel in Waterstone's, then walked
to the Tube station, wearing the white scarf with which she was shortly
to be strangled:

Playing the Part

Walk out of Waterstone's, still
on stage, a copy of

Carey's *Oscar and Lucinda* under my arm,
like her. Neutral eyes gun for me –
blue-jeans, thick navy jersey, short
fair hair and damned

white scarf, spot on. I'm her
to a T in the November evening's
all-consuming murk, and bloody

ache. How did this one make it
past my professional portcullis? She's under

my skin. Last night, I dreamed this
bleeding walk . . . Turned off

her true route at Old Compton Street
to brush against her in that side-street crowd, walk on
together. Keep to her true route now, straight on down

Charing Cross Road, where they watch me – duck

And weave across Cambridge Circus, anonymous. Silver Moon
Bookshop, where she maybe window-shopped the good

minute that day, shuffling
into dead sisters' shoes, 'other men's flowers' . . .
sucked underground down Leicester Square tube,
with one more safe exit before the last:
WPC playing murderee. Re-

construction of bloody X's
last appearance. But I
don't feel her

. . . like that. And besides, the girl is dead.

At the start the WPC is just acting the role ('on stage'), proud of achieving such a good likeness ('I'm her to a T'), but the 'neutral eyes'

gunning for her (the colleagues' who scrutinise passers-by for signs of recognition) suggest the eyes that were probably already 'gunning for' the victim at this stage in her walk. But the WPC is aware that her pretence of professional detachment won't work, for 'She's under my skin'. The re-enactment was pre-enacted the night before in the WPC's sleep, in which she deviated from the fatal route, as if attempting to save the victim, and walked on protectively with her. As she keeps to the route, in the re-enactment itself, she is conscious of walking 'in dead sister's shoes', but as she reaches the entrance to the Tube station, where the victim seems to be sucked underground to her fate, she detaches herself again and restores the professional defences – 'but I don't feel her // . . . like that. And besides, the girl is dead.'

The kind of resistance to empathy seen in the WPC is repeated in the case of the Waterstone's sales assistant who is asked by the police to try to remember the person to whom the till receipt found on the corpse was issued:

> The cop nagged me to 'put a face
> to the chit.' But we hand out receipts like plane-tree leaves.
> Or a voice to the walking corpse to whom I handed it.
> . . . with *Oscar and Lucinda*?

Here the victim is dehumanised as already dead, as already a 'walking corpse', but the identification with the victim, as in the case of the WPC, asserts itself all the same, as the passage continues:

> If
> I'd delayed a second serving her – even a sneeze's
> blessing – she wouldn't have been walking down Hugh Street then,
> the strangler's eye wouldn't have bull's-eyed her,
> the strangler's foot wouldn't have ghosted along
> behind her – phoney shadow

The voices – or stream of consciousness – of other participants in the events are woven together to form the substance of the sequence: the detective in charge of the case (in 'Dental Records') traces her via a Manchester dentist and identifies her as Mary Chay. Struggling with unfamiliar digital technology, the detective muses on the 'feel' of such cases, on how the sight of the corpse no longer affects him, but the sight of the relatives at the funeral increasingly does, though in the case of Mary Chay's funeral 'only cops and bods like me show'. Mary Chay lives an unattached metropolitan life; nobody has reported her missing (like the unidentified victims of the 1987 King's Cross fire, the last of whom was not identified until 2004). The police appeal for information produces nothing, and the *Sun* sets up a 'Murdered Mary

Hotline' (p. 101) so that anyone with information can call in: the 'dead ash blonde' is thirty, 'workless', and 'from Wembley Park'. So why was she in Hugh Street, Victoria? According to 'yesterday's shock-shock report: / a woman claimed that Mary was // maybe en route to some "soirée" / (that's meeting in plain English) – those / "proselytizing lesbians"' (p. 107). The other clues found on her person, apart from the Waterstone's till receipt, include a sentimental antique French postcard – 'These cards are picked up – jumble sales / or down the Portobello Road', and beneath the original sender's turn-of-the-century greeting she has written 'Ever come up the bright lights? / Jobless, but live in hope. Mary.' But the card was unsent and unaddressed. The 'soirée' in Hugh Street that Mary Chay might have been going to was one of a series for 'women confused about their sexuality', and the organisers contact the police in the aftermath of the murder:

> After the murder down the street,
> *I told the cops* about our *soirées* for fear the victim could be
>
> *en route* to us – sometimes women phoned who never showed.
> Though not that evening . . . We were linked to the strangled
> through fear, alone
>
> (p. 125)

The other characters in the narrative are the detective who solves the crime, the various suspects who are questioned, and the person who committed it. The detective is a middle-aged, Morse-like figure – prone to down-to-earth philosophical musings ('we hardly know / ourselves, let alone // the other . . . story', p. 95), divorced, something of a loner himself, struggling to get up to speed on the new forms of policing – computerised databases, ever more technical forensics, and biological 'finger-printing'. The poem 'Can't' (p. 93), which is focused on this character, begins:

> On the screen, for *Disk Error* read *Middle-aged Policeman Can't Hack It'* Floored, I hunch over this word-processor, little
>
> More than a toy for the absent child?

The computer was bought for the child he doesn't have custody of, and he is under pressure from his ex-wife, who works in tourism – 'You must pin / the Victoria strangling on somebody. Have a care / for the tourist industry.' The narrative jumps from one stream of consciousness to another, following the characters round a well-defined 'beat' in central London, and with underlying themes of same-sex eroticism – rather like the formula of Woolf's *Mrs Dalloway*, which is implicitly referenced in the poem. Likewise, Mary Chay, en route to her sexually ambiguous *soirée*, evokes J. Alfred Prufrock, walking the 'Streets that follow like a tedious argument / Of insidious intent' en route to *his* gathering. There are also references to Joyce's *Ulysses*, for instance in 'White Poppy' (pp. 140–1), where a character who lived in the district twenty years before returns, 'Twice-Ulyssed' (in reference to Ulysses' ten-year *periplum*), to old and lamented haunts, aching with nostalgia, and wanting to 'Canute years, bring back yesterday . . . Yes, yes, as Mollies of the world would say / – not only Dublinesque, feminine, gay'. These 'high modernist' allusions signal the intent and ambition of Warner's text, which uses the event of the murder to track glimpses of many lives which intersect – sometimes briefly – with it. For many, as for this 'revenant' character, the past is inescapable, and he is drawn back to it as a kind of Edenic place ('From where I never leave, I walk away', as the beautiful end-line of this poem puts it); but he is mistaken for the criminal drawn back to the crime-scene, and is 'picked up – briefly – as prime? / Chay death suspect'.

The murder (if I read this dense text correctly) is eventually 'pinned on' the transvestite who first encountered Mary Chay briefly in the Ladies of the Army & Navy department store in Victoria (p. 131): Mary Chay had come in in 'Blue-jeans and jersey, white scarf', and dropped what turned out to be a pendant, which he had picked up and handed back to her, remarking 'pretty pendant'. In 'Bearing Witness' he dresses 'normally' to go to the police ('I've psyched up a *self* (who he?) to drop / be-jeaned, all fine and dandy, round the cop- / shop . . . shopping *moi*, if . . . if a conscience-sop: // "I saw her in the Ladies on the day // she died. Christ, officer . . . "'). In 'In the cells' (p. 142) he muses on culpability, on the notion that 'biology is destiny', which the word 'cells' in the title of the poem also obliquely alludes to: the ultimate logic of the new forensics is that criminality is wired into the genes: the poem reads complete:

You think that I'm a leper . . . that I am
beyond the pale . . . on a lower plane.
I too have felt . . . the sadness of the last

pale rose of summer, some November plot . . .
And then, I've sat beside you on the bus,
the 24, the 29, of course
the Clapham 88. We're all in it
together on 'the omnibus' – if one
or two minus a right-on gene or two . . .
Minus imagination, God help you!
Still, in the long run, everybody's dead.

> The future will acquit me, why not now?
> I said I didn't mean to kill the bitch.
> Not *Killed for Kicks by Part-Time Private Nurse*.
> Mugged. Once, my life would have hung by a thread.

The 'thread' which life hangs from is also the DNA thread, the 'accident' of lacking imagination, the absence of a 'right-on gene or two'. His conviction, when convicted, that the future will acquit him refers, not to some future reinvestigation of this particular crime but to an envisaged redrawing of moral and ethical boundaries which will redefine the notion of criminal and personal responsibility. This reading centralises the poems in the sequence which meditate on the forensic process, such as 'Forensic' (p. 90) and 'Forensic God' (p. 79), which sees forensic science as a new divine force, in which it becomes literally true, as is said hyperbolically in the Bible, that in the eyes of god 'Every hair of your head is numbered', every event, no matter how tiny, is quantified, in Hamlet's sense that 'there is a special providence in the fall of a sparrow':

> In the laboratory,
> the comparison microscope waits
> to enlarge on your in-truth-never-guilt-
> but-inadequacy, by weighing a numbered hair
> of your head, lighter than sparrow-
>
> fall.

Examining the human hair from the crime-scene, the forensic scientist touches the human essence, the knowledge of good and evil: 'Expanded beyond belief, this hair's the trunk // of the tree of the knowledge of good and evil – according to the current myth'. Once, crime was explained by 'the expansive hold-all of original sin', now the explanations are 'at the heart of the hair', where 'the medulla's / within the outer wall of the containing cuticle / and the inner wall of the cortex'. The astonishing quality and seriousness of 'Mary Chay' is obvious on every page, and it is an indictment of the profession that work of such quality and intensity can pass virtually unnoticed.

Deryn Rees-Jones's *Quiver*

This emphasis on pondering and probing the genetic determinants of behaviour is seen also in another example of the poetic crime-narrative genre, Deryn Rees-Jones's *Quiver* (Seren, 2004), which, like Warner's 'Mary Chay' sequence, has a precise 'loco-specific' setting – contemporary Liverpool in this case. But the narrative viewpoint is more 'anchored', since the perceiving persona is Fay Thomas, a 'poet with writer's block', who becomes a murder suspect when, while running 'one morning in a local cemetery, she finds the body of Mara (her husband's former lover)' who has been 'pierced with an arrow like a fallen bird'. Subsequently she is questioned by the police, sees Mara in the street and goes to a rendezvous with her, tracks the movements of her geneticist husband, and at the climax of the events, as she and her husband dine in Chinatown as the start of the Year of the Horse is being celebrated, an attempt is made on their lives, as the police had predicted, and the solution of the mystery is revealed. Fay's poems, interspersed with the narrative, grow in confidence, she realises she is pregnant, re-establishes her relationship with her husband, and the book ends with the intensely lyrical 'Afterthought *for my daughter*', which echoes the tone and intensity of such classic instances of poems for baby daughters as Yeats's 'A Prayer for My Daughter' and Eavan Boland's 'Night Feed'. Other writers are more explicitly evoked, such as Paul Muldoon in 'Clone' (p. 65). The other running motif is the myth of Actaeon, retold in the title poem 'Quiver' (originally published separately in *Poetry Review*), in which the hunter Actaeon, of course, sees Artemis/Diana bathing and is turned into a stag by her and killed by his own hounds: the Titian painting *The Death of Actaeon* (in the National Gallery) shows Artemis shooting an arrow at the partly metamorphosed Actaeon as he is pulled down by the hounds.

'Quiver' is very self-consciously reflexive in its manner of telling (as Janet Phillips points out in her very useful review of the book in *Poetry Review*, vol. 94, no. 3 (autumn 2004), on which I have drawn in attempting to work out the complexities of the poem): a whole series of different starting points are proposed in the first twenty lines or so ('Let's start with the stag . . . Let's start, simply, with this tale of transformation . . . Let's start with the head at the feet of the huntsman . . . Let's start with what he once was'), but nearly all of them concern Actaeon, whose actions seem to require little explanation, rather than Artemis. The teller seems to acknowledge the evasiveness of these multiple starting strategies by admitting, twice, that the *real* start is obviously Artemis: 'That's where the story starts, / with the divine inviolate, / that's where the story starts / in the terrible comedy of shame.' But 'Artemis, single-minded, / casting about red-cheeked, / groping for her bow and arrow / refusing to be naked for this man' threatens to turn the piece into a predictable anti-'male gaze' diatribe, with an indignant feminist heroine refusing to submit to it. But the savage indignation of Artemis is ironised by the doubling figure of 'the goddess's companion'; 'Faith, let's call her that', who had 'watched him watching them

/ as they undressed', and lays on a collusive striptease, 'slipped off her dress, / this time without caution, / holding her arms above her head / prolonging the moment of her nudity'. This 'other' Artemis represents the doubling motif which is a constant in the poem, and acts out a reciprocated eroticism which is self-defining for both (for viewer and viewed – 'what she wanted / was to look at the man without fear or shame / with an image of herself with which to begin').

But the story then reverts to its feminist ground motif, naming the hounds which pursue Actaeon (as Ovid does in *Metamorphosis*, Janet Phillips reminds us), 'Those hounds, imagined now as what? / An ever-changing line of mothers, daughters, long-lived women?' Again, the irony is played up, as poor Actaeon is ripped to pieces by the feminist tradition in full historical cry, including: a contingent of wronged tragic heroines ('Antigone, Clytemnestra, Penelope and Joan'); a troup of suffragette pioneers ('Millicent, Sylvia / Christabel, Emily' – that is, Millicent Garrett Fawcett, president of the Women's Suffrage societies in the 1890s, and the Pankhurst sisters Sylvia and Christabel, with their mother Emily or Emmeline); a contingent of feminist writers, including first generation ('Angel Virginia [Woolf], No-nonsense Simone [de Beauvoir]'), and second generation ('Glorious Gloria [Steinham], Unblushing Germaine [Greer]'), and the 'French' variety ('Fierce Luce [Irigaray], Brave Julia [Kristeva], la belle Hélène [Cixous]'). Along with them, a little incongruously, perhaps, is a contingent of virgin-martyrs, '[Saint] Catherine with her crown of thorns, / Little Saint Bride with her cow-print jacket, / [Saint] Agnes the borzoi, the windhound Poor Clare': these female saints are famous for their spooky 'spiritual espousals' of an eroticised Christ, for their unstoppable tears, or for their twelve-year-old martyrdoms, but anyway, they have summoned up the energy to join in the chase, although their motivation isn't explained, and they are placed just in the van of a platoon of writers ('Sappho, Felicia [Hemans], Aphra [Benn], Christina [Rossetti]' and 'so many Elizabeths they can't all be named'). The martyrs' behaviour seems to affect the demeanour of Faith, who has 'tears pouring from her virgin cheeks' but is 'still hoping to find herself, anywhere, anyhow'. She contemplates extravagant forms of mourning for Actaeon, much in the spirit of (say) St Catherine's trademark Crown of Thorns – she would 'wear his head like a headdress of candles / so that wax and blood was intermingled / would drip to her shoulders in rosy tears', but instead 'Faith dresses, rolls back her sleeves, / her eyes more knowing than she is telling, as she holds up a mirror to the goddess, / looks at herself, behind her, through it, / and on'. The comic-epic moment, with its Tam O'Shanter-style pursuit (in which Actaeon doesn't have Tam's luck), dramatises the self-contradictions within the self-contradictory Artemis, goddess of 'childbirth and chastity', a brief which seems to combine the roles of gamekeeper and poacher in an uncomfortable way. The moral of it all might be that double standards, in one sense or another, are pretty well a fact of nature, and that a truly adult life involves some kind of coming terms with that fact.

It will be clear from what has been said so far that the hallucinatory or fictive overlay is much stronger in Rees-Jones's sequence than in Warner's: and there is much more evocation of literary antecedents: for instance, in 'White Nights' (p. 58) the insomniac protagonist is interrogated about the number of Raymond Chandler novels she can name, and in 'Good Cop, Bad Cop' (p. 28) the pair 'must practise their clichés till they know them by heart' / say their lines with this look as they play their part'. The city is present, but in a hyped-up, self-consciously *noir*ish way, not a place, really, but a place-in-a-film, even when its streets are named, as in 'Liverpool Blues' (p. 27):

> *The skyline in the moonlight, the river running thin,*
> *my lover weeping lotus blossom for his next of kin.*
> *The stars will tell their stories over Birkenhead and Cam[m]ell Lairds*
>
> *In Berry Street, in Bold Street, in Princes Park and Princess Street*
> *I've seen a girl I never knew and never thought to meet.*
> *The Liver Birds have flown away, the cathedrals' doors are closed.*

The doubling motif in *Quiver* is seen, too, in the pairing of Fay Thomas and her best friend Erica, who is also pregnant, but in an uncomplicated, mumsy, picturesque way, a bringer of cheering 'tea in willow pattern cups', with 'pregnant belly eight months heavy' and 'hair a corona of auburn curls', who sends the blocked and still un-pregnant writer home 'with a kiss: an unreadable smile: // "Pick up your pen and write"'. She sounds like both a Christ-like miracle-healer ('Take up your bed and walk') and a Sidney-like muse ('Fool, said my Muse to me, look in thy heart and write'), part of a Good Muse/ Bad Muse pairing in which she is the more benign Muse counterpart to the dangerous and threatening Mara figure who spreads *angst* and division.

The other pairing is that of Will, the geneticist husband, and Nate Devine, 'a white-haired man with a tongue of glass' who is his boss, and has seductive designs on Fay Thomas, who touches her arm, as does the apparently posthumous Mara, and leads her to an assignation, a visit to where she (the supposedly murdered Mara) is living incognito ('She's sleeping in a storeroom', in 'Chez Nous', p. 48). This curious space has motifs which relate to the Actacon myth 'From a peeling plaster wall / a stag's head looms. / His glass eyes glint. Beneath him, half-asleep, / the hound.' Then she too 'offers me a cup of tea, hands me scissors / and a tarnished mirror', doubling the doubles motif, so that Artemis and Fay in 'Quiver' are paralleled by Mara (whose 'Classical' features are several times alluded to) and Faith. As in many detective stories, the interchangeability of pursuer and pursued is alluded to ('Am I saving her life with stories, or is she saving mine?'), and the scissors are used by Faith to cut Mara's hair (in 'Haircut', p. 50), and the result is (in 'Second Look', p. 51, quoted complete):

> She's taller and broader than I'd thought:
> Like Artemis the hunter god,
>
> Chaste and secure in her life without men.

This is reminiscent of the sturdy Artemis figure in the foreground of Titian's *The Death of Acteon*, short-haired in appearance, though the hair seems to be tied up, rather than cut short. At the climax of the sequence, during the Chinese New Year celebrations, Nate is shot with an arrow by the Mara figure, who is then shot in turn by a police marksman, and dies in Will's arms on the steps of the (Anglican) cathedral after a chase through Chinatown.

So who killed the Mara discovered in the graveyard at the beginning of the poem, and why, and what does it all mean? Well, a single 'closed' answer to any of these questions would tend to reduce the poem's thematic resonance, but, all the same, a 'murder mystery', as the book bills itself, must have a coherent scenario which allows for plausible solutions to that mystery, even if speculative answers in the plural, rather than *the* answer in the singular, are what we are left with. The first possible 'answer', then, is that the murder was committed by Nate, who is killed in revenge by the second Mara at the end. Why did he do it? Well, like Will, he has previously been involved with Mara, both personally and professionally (in 'Good Cop Pays a Visit', p. 77, Fay is asked 'And Mara, how well did she know Nate? / Were they friends or colleagues, would you say? / What would you say to the layman / was the nature of the work?'). The poems 'Beatitude' and 'Geneticist's Dinner' (pp. 38 and 40) make it clear that the nature of the work concerns 'twins and clones', 'the double helix of DNA'. Is Mara, then, a kind of Rosalind Franklin, the scientist at King's College, London, in the 1950s whose contribution to the discovery of DNA was inadequately acknowledged by her colleague Maurice Wilkins, joint Nobel Prize winner with Crick and Watson for the discovery of DNA? Another 'solution scenario' would see Mara 1 and Mara 2 (as it says in 'The Lantern Festival', p. 83) as 'Sisters who for thirty years hadn't / known each other, finding each other / a birth and a death of the self, somehow': in a scenario rather like that of Henry James's tale 'The Jolly Corner', this would see an antagonism between two aspects of the self, so that Mara 1 is killed by arrow-wielding Mara 2. The antagonism between the sisters also recalls Adrienne Rich's emblematic poem 'Transit', in which the skier-speaker in the poem is passed and repassed by a strange yet strangely familiar figure, of whom the comment is made: 'When sisters separate they haunt each other / as she, who I might once have been, haunts me, / or is it I who do the haunting?' This 'doubling' idea echoes the many other examples of pairing of partial opposites in the poem (like that between Artemis and Faith, for instance).

Gwyneth Lewis's *Keeping Mum*

From Warner to Rees-Jones is a movement from a predominantly *vérité* realism to a form in which realism and elements of the hallucinatory, imaginative, inner projection narrative are blended – perhaps it is something like a movement from realism to magic realism. In Gwyneth Lewis's *Keeping Mum*, we move further along the same spectrum, with the magic beginning to predominate over the realism.

Here is an extract from an obituary:

> The West Caucasian language Ubuh . . . died at daybreak, October 8th, 1992, when the last speaker, Tevfik Esenç, passed away. I happened to arrive in his village that very same day, without appointment, to view this famous Last Speaker, only to learn that he had died just a couple of hours earlier. He was buried later the same day.

This quotation, from the linguist Oleg Stig Andersen, comes from the first chapter of David Crystal's book *Language Death* (Cambridge University Press, 2002). According to Crystal, half the world's approximately six thousand languages will become extinct in the next hundred years. In fact, says Crystal, the Ubuh (or Ubykh) language was already dead when Tevfik Esenç died, for a language is dead when there is nobody left to speak it to. Language death can be viewed in various ways; one way is to say that language death is usually suicide, since, if its speakers remain alive, a language dies only when its speakers start using a different one. Another viewpoint is to say that some languages are language killers – English, Spanish, Russian, German and Mandarin being examples. English is the biggest language killer of all, so much so that it may even kill the language killers, so that by 2500 it could be the only language left on earth. Another viewpoint is that languages are usually killed by political or social forces – AIDS, for instance, is killing languages as well as people in parts of Africa.

Gwyneth Lewis's *Keeping Mum* (Bloodaxe, 2003) is a three-part verse sequence, structurally very similar to the others I have been discussing – the three thematically interrelated parts again, one with the same title as the whole book. Again, too, the underlying conventions of the detective thriller and a pervasive *noir* atmosphere are prominent. Lewis's informative preface tells of her 'double life', hitherto alternating a book in Welsh and a book in English, her survival tactic having been to 'keep both sides of my linguistic family apart for as long as possible'. But 'the death of the Welsh language has been predicted for many centuries': now, in spite of devolution, monoglot Welsh-speaking communities are vanishing, and in 1999 she wrote 'a book-length detective story investigating the murder of my mother tongue, calling it *Y Llofrudd Iaith*, 'The Language Murderer'. The original plot was set in a village in West Wales, 'where an old lady, my embodiment of the Welsh language, had been found dead'. But she also wanted to 'explore how we could free ourselves of the idea of a "mother tongue", with all its accompanying psychological baggage, and its infantilising of native speakers'. The first section of *Keeping Mum*, called 'The Language Murderer' and sub-titled 'POLICE FILE', contains as much of the earlier book 'as I was able to translate in a fairly direct fashion. Only a handful of the poems are literal versions.' New poems are also added to that section which are 'translations without an original text – perhaps a useful definition of poetry'. I will discuss this part in more detail shortly. The second section, 'Keeping Mum', is 'a more radical recasting of my original detective story and a meditation on mental illness and language'. So the second part 'translates' the first (in the broadest sense), and 'my translated detective was to be a psychiatrist in a mental hospital, investigating how abuses of language had led to his patients' illness'. Finally, the third section, 'Chaotic Angels', 'looks at communications between different realms of awareness', a scenario perhaps reminiscent of the author's Welsh book/English book alternating pattern. The title of the section represents its fusion (or juxtaposition) of the notion of angels as 'messengers from another realm', and 'the language of modern Chaos Theory', used to 're-imagine angels as part of our everyday lives – at the centre of experiences like depression and bereavement'. So the book as a whole centres on the triad of detective, psychiatrist, angel, a kind of summative résumé of the sources we might look to for recovery, restoration, recuperation, or, failing all those, just understanding. The book shares the interest in crime and genetics – that issue of whether crime is in the genes, or in social conditions, or in whatever we mean by 'the self', which is also seen in *Quiver* and in 'Mary Clay'.

'The Language Murderer' is a sequence of eleven poems, beginning with 'A Poet's Confession', which starts with the line 'I did it. I killed my mother tongue.' So this is an unusual whodunit, one which starts by telling you who did it, and at the end of the short poem the killer says she is 'keeping mum' till her lawyer arrives. Since she breaks her silence from the next poem onwards ('What's in a name?') we can assume that the remaining ten are spoken in the lawyer's presence. This second poem (given its title) challenges Shakespeare, implicitly asserting that a language is a way of seeing, not just a way of saying:

Today the wagtail finally forgot
that I once called it *sigl-di-gwt*.

It didn't give a tinker's toss,
kept right on rooting in river moss,

(no longer *mwswgl*) relieved, perhaps,
that someone would be noticing less

about its habits

The next poem, 'Mother Tongue', goes back to childhood to trace the origins of the urge that led to the language murder. It began 'in seventy-three / in the schoolyard' when 'I started to translate', portrayed as an addictive, taboo activity, like furtive smoking, carried out mainly for the illicit thrill – 'For a bit of fun / to begin with – the occasional "fuck" / for the bite of another language's smoke'. But the addiction develops its own momentum – 'Soon I was hooked on whole sentences / behind the shed', and she becomes linguistically promiscuous, going through 'Jeeves & Wooster, Dick Francis, James Bond', then on to 'Simenon / and Flaubert', and ending as a full-blown 'language fetishist' ('The "ch"/ in German was easy, Rilke a buzz' . . . 'Umlauts make me sweat, / so I need a multilingual man / but they're rare in West Wales and tend to be / married already.') According to David Crystal, languages die when their speakers are 'unfaithful' (not his word, but the concept used in this poem) and begin to speak other languages. So the poem ends:

'. . . If only I'd kept
myself much purer, with simple tastes,
the Welsh might be living . . .
            Detective, you speak
Russian, I hear, and Japanese.
Could you whisper some softly?
I'm begging you. Please . . .'

The next five poems detail in different ways a sense of the language as a living force, intimately at home in its rural environment, with its metaphorical play and uncannily precise observation of patterns of light, contours of terrain, habits of livestock, but at the same time making it seem fatally isolated from the contemporary, the urban, and the young. Hence, the ninth poem, 'Her End', which records the discovery of the language body at the crime-scene, comes as no surprise:

> 'The end was dreadful. Inside a dam burst
> And blood was everywhere. Out of her mouth
> Came torrents of words, *da yw dant*
> *i atal tafod, gogoniannau'r Tad*
> in scarlet flowers – *yn Abercuawg*
> *yd ganant gogau* – the blood was black,
> full of filth, a well that amazed
> with its vivid idioms – *bola'n holi ble mae 'ngheg?* –
> and always fertile, *yes no pwdin llo,*
> and psalms were gathering in her viscera
> and gushing out of her, proverbs, coined words,
> the names of plants, seven types of gnat,
> dragonfly, rosemary, mountain ash,
> then disgusting pus, and long-lost terms
> like *gwelltor* and *rhychor*, her vomit a road
> leading away from her, a force
> leaving the fortress of her breath,
> *gwyr a aeth Gatraeth . . .*'[4]

This exuberant poem (in the dictionary sense of 'joyously unrestrained'), which was jointly translated from the original by Richard Poole, is the climax of the section, and the last two poems register the bewildering 'after-life' of the language: in 'Aphasia' world and word have spun out of alignment ('I ask for "hammer" but am given "spade", / feel like some "tea" but order "orangeade" // by mistake. I specify "velvet" but am given "silk" / in a colour I don't even like'), and the end result, as the poem ends by saying, is that 'I'll never know what I really mean'. The last poem, 'Brainstorming', envisages desperate measures, the language murderer as a kind of Tess of the d'Urbervilles on-the-run, making instinctively for a spot steeped in myth and history, that is, for Taliesin's stone in Cardiganshire, named after the sixth-century poet: if you spend the night at the stone, it is said, you will wake up either mad or a poet:

> What if I slept tonight beside Taliesin's stone
> to solve the murder? Would it send me mad,
> or make me a poet? It must be remade

daily, this moorland, as it is destroyed
each time we leave it. See it shake
with wind that knocks the noisy larks

off their high pillars. Even they fall
in silence. I need to know
what survives forgetting.

The linguistic energy is envisaged as a force of 'tumultuous energy' streaming down the mountainside 'into livestock, names, / marriages, murders and on into time'. But it needs to survive its own forgetting, has to move somehow beyond that rural fastness into a new age. A language can avoid death only by being constantly reborn, and, if we try only to remember it, then it will inevitably be forgotten.

Fiona Sampson's *The Distance Between Us*

The last of these verse 'crime' sequences is Fiona Sampson's *The Distance Between Us* (Seren, 2005), a sequence in seven parts which is described on the back cover as a verse novel that 'opens with a love affair in crisis, unfolds through loss, risk and existential challenge, and ends with lovemaking in a domain at once sensual and imagined'. It is, says the blurb, 'a passionate exploration of psychology and sexuality set among the tensions of contemporary European identity'. These general descriptive comments suggest that this is (so to speak) a *nouveau roman* kind of 'verse novel', rather than the 'classic realist' sort, and consequently the narrative drive and cohesion are much less dominant than is the case with the other examples looked at. But it continues the move along the continuum from realism to magic seen in the sequences looked at so far. Thus, in the first section (depicting the 'love affair in crisis') images predominate over events, as in *Mrs Dalloway* or *To the Lighthouse*, but, given the cover's description of the collection, a reader will inevitably seek to 'recuperate' image *as* event, as in case of these lines, for instance:

Under a stinging sky
city clothes are flowers falling.

Are the clothes falling like flowers because the people concerned are taking them off? Are they doing that in order to make love somewhere *al fresco* (beneath those 'stinging skies')? Are they still wearing 'city clothes' because they are indulging in some brief clandestine escape from a city office? If so, who are the people? The poet doesn't answer such questions, but immediately flicks to another image puzzle, with the imperative 'imagine' not 'interpret', or 'empathise' or even just 'watch',

which might be taken as the implicit imperatives which usually govern
novel reading (p. 14):

> Or imagine papers on a daylit table.
> An envelope.
>   The hand
> Sealing its long white lip.
> Imagine the heart's life like this.

The daylit table sounds like an item of home furniture rather than
something in an office, but the long white envelope might seem more
like office than home stationery, even if the contents seem to be personal. But what's in the letter, and whose hand is sealing its long white
lip? Someone is ill and in hospital and needing to be operated on ('My
ignorance won't look you in the eye / at the ordinary name of illness,
/ its polished general ward . . . Who will cut you?'), but who is this person? The conclusion of the first part leaves all such questions open,
deliberately it seems, as a comment is quoted on the back cover to the
effect that 'the most generous thing the poet can do is to give us some
vivid, piercing memories that become our experience'. So the book has
a 'radical ambiguity' which 'invites us to experience the lovers' dilemmas as our own', presumably meaning that the material is deliberately
suspended at a generic rather than a specific level. That is what might
fashionably be called its 'ethical' dimension, the element which lets in
the 'other', the reader (p. 17):

> In the desert, absolute light
> Bleaches every landmark.
> To love is always to lose.
>
> Two figures.
>
> This is the uncertain line of story
> the moving finger.
> It is touch.

'To love is always to lose' is the theme of the story; the story is about
'two figures', and such is the ever 'uncertain line of story', which the
'moving finger' can only write and then move on. The process of bleach-
ing the landmarks is designed to cleanse the story of its specificity
and yet bring it to life, and in terms of narrative and characters it does
this extremely well. The text keeps on telling us to imagine ('Imagine
a woman, / a man / Imagine their losses', p. 14), and the people in the
poem remain on this strange threshold plane of virtuality – 'a woman',
'a man', 'two figures'. To pick up a phrase from part III, what the reader
has to 'imagine' is '*Your Face Here*' (p. 35).

What *is* specific and filled in, however, is setting, a sense of place, or rather places, round Europe, but with that notion of 'place' expanded to include *ambience*, mind-set, something more than mere *mise-en-scène*, perhaps rather *Sitz im Leben*, that is, place, situation, culture, rolled into one and considered as an entity which is more than just context. Thus, the Spanish setting of the first part is a state of mind and being – sombre, darkly religious, deeply passionate, pushing towards extremes of emotion and response, where the touch of lovers, for instance, is likely to be imaged as the touch of Thomas in Christ's wounds ('Can I touch you? / Putting my hand into the wound of presence', p. 16). The atmosphere is suffused with the purple emotions – the liturgical purple – of the *Semana Sancta*, with extremes of suffering and self-doubt, a world, in fact, in which the primary associations of the word 'passion' are with suffering. In this world 'desert', 'mountains', 'noon', and 'night' all seem primarily the locale of spiritual crisis – suffering, temptation, atonement, the dark night of the soul.

The second part seems to trace the 'back story' to the crisis shown in part I, reverting to memory and childhood, that of a concert violinist, with images of a precious atmosphere ('Cool rooms. Light arrowing the rugs', p. 22) and Mother a 'perfect stranger' – '*Keep it up* she murmurs / as if distance mutes her already', p. 22). At the 'Wigmore debut' with 'Mother's ring on a chain around my neck' (p. 24) the sense of self seems to have deepened, the meaning of 'home' has loosened ('Home's somewhere else. / You want to know where? / Try meeting you eye in the mirror', p. 24). A conviction that difference is essence seems to pervade – the distance between performer and audience secures the former in 'the plush interior / of self' (p. 25), protected by 'a cushion of faces / on my lids' (p. 25), making her safe (but too safe) behind the Velvet Shutter.

Part III moves to what seems to be an ambiguously registered assault in a foreign city. The title registers the world of black and white films, with artfully composed shots and carefully delineated emotions, but it's more the postwar Vienna of *The Third Man*, with shadowy figures in doorways, rather than the clipped and well-ordered romantic world of Lean's *Brief Encounter*. The assault is 'staged' and managed, with imagistic throwbacks to the performance world of the previous part – 'The distance between us / might be no more than fifty yards / under the proscenium arch / of a stairwell' (p. 31), and what closes the distance is 'A kitchen knife can cut through distance / closing the gap' (p. 42): 'How bring *He* and *I* / into the same story? // A knife is a short cut' (p. 32). The 'closing' of the two is carefully orchestrated (p. 33).

Hand in his blouson pocket
– call it a saunter –
he passes
the stagey first pass
above the garden wall.

Again the imperatives urge us to keep *making* the text (p. 33) –

Think of body heat.
                         The turn of a wrist.
Think of time revolving
                         like a trick of the moon.

The stagey *film noir* effect ('Moon-blade in his hand', p. 33, 'His breath
on my throat' . . . The blade on my throat', p. 34) continues, with the
emphasis on watching and being watched, and on staging and resta-
ging, as in Warner's Mary Chay sequence. The difference is that, where
that sequence occludes the murder itself, this one details the assault,
and the detail has to seem erotic, and, indeed, is eroticised by the
manner of telling and the manner of framing:

And my little round buttons give one
by one
and he cuts through the bounce of fabric
and I don't feel exposed I don't
feel.

                         as we murmur like lovers
in the deserted stairwell.

Innocence
is believing this doesn't happen
– *Your Face Here* –
                         until afterwards
which is when I'm walking fast
towards the police station

As anticipated before the event is described, the four lit top windows,
which are like theatre boxes for the staged event, do not open when
someone runs along the street shouting, and indeed the other sound
heard is that of 'one window slamming up'.

Part IV works with notions of crucial choices in life, using images
of travelling, forests, and pathways ('I hardly know where to begin //
or end / do you?', p. 39). Notions of potential selves seem to haunt
the actual self ('This is the not-taken / where we are / trees flickering
like candle-flames / the path / open-close of reluctance' (p. 40). There
are images of a train rattling across Europe, of fraught incomprehending

conversation (*'ne razumem* [Serbian, 'I don't understand']. Explain', p. 41), and of car headlights 'making and unmaking darkness' (p. 42). How much can be grasped and 'sorted' the speaker cannot say ('Tilt your head, it's all / in the angle of perception', p. 42), and any 'conclusion', it concludes, will be premature – *'look* / how it closes the space and draws shadows down over it' (p. 42). Part V seems to follow one of these potential or imagined selves, one of the paths not taken, into a much more working-class background than that of the budding virtuoso of part II: this is Hillingdon, a nowhere suburb where people talk different (*'Where'm I from?* / Depends who's asking', p. 46), a world marked out by the 'muddy rec' and packet jelly as a treat ('red jelly in a blue bowl') or 'Friday night chips out of the newspaper'. Dad's made 'some office slapper' pregnant, and goes 'round the girlfriend's' when he can't stand the stress: the role model is *EastEnders* – a world of *'Rick's Motors'*, dodgy deals, and people saying *'Lov-er-ly!'* to express strong approval and *'Appy Days, Bruv'* when they've had 'a pint or ten'. This is a consciously restaged life, linking up with the staging and 'performativity' imagery elsewhere in the sequence, a life viewed retrospectively by a bright academic-to-be who will leave it all behind and ponders 'our intimate self / *phenomenon* to *noumenon*' (p. 47), a thinker who thinks the thought 'You tell your life / or it tells you' (p. 51). Eventually, married and tenured, he muses: 'On days rain sheers the campus windows / I find myself / shape shifting / between the pen holder / and framed photo of the girls' (p. 47). In seminar he (it seems to be 'he' at this point) looks at his own reflected face 'over the vista of lawns and lighted windows', and gives the seminar a kind of closure:

> What
> Gives us form? The stories we tell,
> The voice we tell them in
> I reassure students

This is half-way through part V, and at the end the speaker comes back to the same moment, as if not quite sure he's got it right ('How much of our identity is just story?' the cover blurb asks):

> Of course all of this is story:
> Clothes-horses, soccer, wide-screen TV.
> Of course everything in my life's *in vitro*, inseparable, filmic.
>
> *Tell us a story, Jackanory.*
>
> Tell me
>   what you'd like to hear

Beyond the picture window
Faculty buildings graze

among trees

and out of a listening dark
I gather my face.

Again, the 'narrative foretold' of the book jacket pressures us to recuperate all this – might this be another participant of the 'love affair
in crisis'?

The window motif is taken up in the entry poem ('Brief History')
of part IV, a cameo of a 'broken bird' which flies into a window pane
and is killed ('Pull a flick-flack stretch of wing and let it go', p. 55).
The main body of this section images the love affair in a foreign city
('before the circling of mouths // kissing their zero sums . . . lips closing on skin / juice springing across the tongue' (p. 57), and then a reluctant separation, which reintroduces other recurrent images (such as trains
and window panes) – 'A train's long regression: / flatlands sunlight cows
/ the hand / moving away slowly, / the relinquished hand / sliding on
glass / . . . the length of a concrete platform' (p. 58). The last part enters
the aftermath where the love affair is relived in dreaming ('sleep
voyages', p. 61), in remembering ('the sexed, secret, lived-in face / opening into sense / opening in light / in darkness', p. 63) in imagining
('Slowly, slowly / what is inward turns outward towards us', p. 64),
and in forgetting ('*Where / are you?*', p. 66). The aftermath takes them
on into further life ('the long indifferent corridor', as it is called in the
last line of the poem), into a rushing force like gravity, or the pull of
a vacuum ('into the collapsing in-roaring room'), 'pulling truth out of
ourselves out of reach / into pain', like the G-forces of the accelera-
tion into whatever is beyond. This, then, is an extremely ambitious
sequence, much inflected by poetries very different from the often low-
key, counter-metaphysical impulses shared by so many British poets.
Though this final sequence in some ways seems to echo the fragmented,
teasing aspects of 'secret narrative', its autobiographical core and
sustained, extended focus set it aside from that, but at the same time
it is in no sense confined to what is (in Tarlo's phrase again) 'obviously
and accessibly about women's lives'.

The manner of reading these four sequences as a continuum of
practice within a field of inferred contextuality enables a mutual contextualising which relates them not to history but to aspects of the development of contemporary poetry in general, and of women's poetry
in particular. While many poets seem to move into novel writing in
mid-career, these poets move instead towards 'novelisation', breaking

out from the bounds of the short lyric to a territory and a set of techniques which have enormous potential. Whereas male poets seeking the same kind of breakout often resort to translating Ovid, Homer, or epic-scale Anglo-Saxon poetry, these writers have remained with contemporary material but (refreshingly) have risked moving beyond mere accessibility. The result is some of the most ambitious and achieved work on the contemporary British poetry scene.

Notes

1 *Contemporary British Poetry and the City*, footnote 7, p. 135.
2 http://www.contemporarywriters.com/authors/?p=auth76.
3 'Provisional Pleasures: The Challenge of Contemporary Experimental Women Poets', *Feminist Review*, no. 62 (summer 1999), pp. 94–112).
4 *Da yw dant i atal tafod*: A tooth is a good barrier for the tongue; *gogoniannau'r Tad*: the Father's glories; *yn Abercuawg yd ganant gogau*: cuckoos sing in Abercuawg (from a ninth-century poem); *bola'n holi ble mae 'ngheg*: my stomach asking where my mouth is; *yes no pwdin llo*: yes, no, calf's pudding (a nonsensical phrase); *gwelltor* and *rhychor*: the left- and right-hand oxen in a ploughing pair; *gwyr a aeth Gatraeth*; men went to Catraeth (from Aneirin's sixth-century poem, *Y Gododdin* (from Lewis's footnote to the poem).

8

Just the facts: content is context

In its issue of 7 February 2002 the *London Review of Books* published a poem by Mick Imlah called 'Maritime'. It's about the 1930s and the liner *Queen Mary*, and the first stanza is an evocation of the launch of the *Queen Mary* by Queen Mary in 1934:

> With a few soft words Her Majesty
> Christened the liner built as '504':
> 'I name this ship – myself. God bless . . .'

But the *Queen Mary* was *not* 'built as "504"'. It was universally known till launched as 'Number 534' (its number in the builder's order-book). Of course, '504' might have been just a misprint, but, if it was, the poet would surely have noticed it, and the paper didn't print a correction in any subsequent issue. Is the mistake not really a mistake at all, then, because it occurred in a poem rather than an article? Should the matter be brushed aside disdainfully by the poet, with a flash of his poetic licence? If this kind of thing is (or isn't) a mistake when it occurs in a poem, then what are the implications for the whole issue of literature and context? I will leave this example open for the moment and discuss the matter of poetry and facts in broader terms before coming back to it.

The 'literature and fact' debate

The classic and indispensable essay on this issue is 'Literature and the Matter of Fact' by Christopher Ricks, pp. 280–310, in his book *Essays in Appreciation* (1998). Ricks cites the case of Yeats's early poem 'The Indian to His Love' of 1886, which has the line 'The peahens dance on the smooth lawn'. In response to the objection that peahens do not dance, Yeats 'turned not to natural history but to literature': peahens, he said, 'dance throughout the whole of Indian poetry . . . As to the poultry yards, with them I have no concern.' This rush for the Parnassian high ground lacks conviction, and it is difficult to imagine that Wordsworth would have been guilty of such panicky over-reaction if a reader had made the equally fatuous 'objection' to his 'Daffodils' poem that daffodils do not dance and cannot feel glee (but Yeats, of course, was only twenty-one when he made his remarks, and bristling with the pedantic touchiness of youth). But the peahens 'error' isn't an error of fact at all – it's actually a difference of opinion over the appropriateness of a figurative or metaphorical use of language; we may or may not think it appropriate to refer in a poem to peahens 'dancing' (whether or not we are familiar with 'the whole of Indian poetry'), but the poet is entitled to disagree, and going on about 'poultry yards' merely waves the poetic licence about rather unnecessarily.

Such issues of facts and literature are taken up in an able and thought-provoking extension of the debate by Peter Robinson in his essay 'Matters of Fact and Value' (chapter 4 in his *Poetry, Poets, Readers: Making Things Happen*, 2002). He quotes Ricks's key question (p. 89):

> Ricks's engaged and engaging essay examines the question: 'Are works of literature affected if the facts they proffer as facts are not facts, and demonstrably so?' His position is that works of literature are always damaged by factual error, but the extent of the damage and how fatal it may be to the work are matters of critical appreciation: 'The principle is obdurate, though the application of it will always ask tact and a recognition of how complicated and elusive a literary understanding can be'.

Although Peter Robinson does not directly oppose Ricks's broad stance in favour of factual accuracy in literature, he does have many pertinent questions to ask of it. Robinson's focus is mainly on the *inadvertent* error: he asks 'Is a poem's aesthetic wholeness damaged by a factual error?' He continues 'The aesthetic wholeness of a poem is composed of its internal context and all the aspects of external contexts legitimately assumed in, or implied by, the work itself' (p. 99). This wholeness 'is weakened by a mistake of fact; yet this weakening will only appear to happen if the work has already achieved sufficient distinctness for value to be attributed to it through attention'. 'Errors of fact or consistency may prevent a work from achieving such distinction . . . [but] the finding of errors can leave it untouched . . . however much we acknowledge the principle of value in factual accuracy.' These are careful and useful formulations, but we would surely want a definition of 'internal context' (especially) and 'external contexts'. It would need to be said, too, that the presence of factual errors would also weaken a work which may *not* already have achieved distinction.

But perhaps it is impossible to unravel the question further without attempting some rudimentary classification of the different kinds of factual error which are possible: a tentative listing would include the following:

- an error of fact which is unrecognised by the author
- an error of fact which is disregarded by the author
- an error of fact which is deliberately or strategically made by the author.

A well-known example of an error unrecognised by the author is the erroneous presence of 'stout Cortez' in Keats's sonnet 'On First Looking into Chapman's Homer', because, as Tennyson was the first to point out (see Rzepka, below), it was Balboa, not Cortez, who was the first European to see the Pacific. Robinson makes the 'wild surmise' that 'it is even possible that, as with a beauty spot, a flaw can enhance the value of a work of art' (p. 104), this being perhaps a kind of philatelic notion of literature, in which the flawed examples are the most interesting and valuable (or valued) ones. The Keats of this sonnet was another twenty-one-year-old, and he too is keen to let us know that he has read a lot of poetry ('Much have I travelled in the realms of gold'). He too might have taken the poultry yard defence if taxed with his error, and might well have let stout Cortez stand, so to speak. On the other hand, Andrew Motion[1] sees Keats as openly advertising the fact that he has only just come across Chapman ('On *first* looking into . . .), and the fact that he is reading Homer in translation draws attention to his lack of a Classical education, so there may be an element of defiant reverse snobbery in the declaration that, though he has been told of the existence of the Homeric continent, he has never been there till now. Given that the alternative to Chapman's Homer was Pope's, Keats's enthusiasm for the former is cognate with the Romantics' rejection of the Augustan smoothness of their immediate poetic predecessors, and their preference for the roughness of the Elizabethans and the balladeers – the 'message' of the poem, in a sense, is 'No Pope Here'. Thus considered, Keats's Chapman poem says much more briefly what Wordsworth and Coleridge said at some length in their preface to *Lyrical Ballads*. So it has been argued that Keats *meant* to say Cortez, not Balboa (making it a *strategic* error), in order to indicate his own 'belatedness' as a reader of Homer – he is reading it in translation, and so isn't a Balboan 'first-comer' to the Homeric (pure serene) scene.[2] But the change wouldn't add anything that the poem hasn't already said (even if the reader recognises the error as strategic). Even if the slip/error/substitution *is* inadvertent, it doesn't sink the poem, because the poem isn't primarily about the earliest European encounters with the Pacific. On the other hand, if the proper name which Keats had confused had been Chapman's, the case would be different: a sonnet wrongly entitled 'On First Looking into Ben Jonson's Homer' could not have survived *that* error, for its internal logic (perhaps its internal context in Robinson's terms) would be destroyed by claiming as a revelation a work by an author whose name the poet cannot even remember. The poet, then, may get away with the mistaken 'fact' if it is marginal to the central poetic concern of the piece under scrutiny.

Sometimes the borderline between the unrecognised (the first type in my list) and the disregarded error (the second type) can be rather blurred, as in the case of several well-known instances of this marginal or tangential kind: in *The Winter's Tale*, we can live with the fact that Bohemia actually has no sea-coast: it isn't germane to the action that the geography should be accurate; in *Julius Caesar* we can tolerate the anachronistic striking clock in Act 2 Scene 1, and Brutus reading an anachronistic bound book in Act 2 Scene 3 ('let me see; is not the leaf turned down / Where I left reading?'). Again, these details are not germane to the progress of the action, whether or not the errors are unwitting. But if *Julius Caesar* were a detective story in which the clock and the book were vital clues, then we would surely feel differently. The error would no longer be tangential, but 'germane to the topic'.

But there can be 'marginal' examples of this kind of marginality: Tennyson's phrase the 'noble six hundred' in 'The Charge of the Light Brigade' doesn't detract from the effectiveness of the poem when it is learned (as Tennyson did learn, but without feeling it necessary to change the poem) that 673 men actually made the charge. So this is an example of a disregarded error, but perhaps the matter really is germane to the topic of the poem, for the poem is centrally about the charge, and a key detail about the charge is wrong. However, the internal reasons for leaving the figure as it is are cogent, for numbers are always tricky things to handle in fixed-metre poems, and if a rhymed and metrical poem like that one *had* managed to incorporate the exact numeral, the effect would probably have been inadvertently comical – only a reckless, McGonagall-like poet would attempt it. So Tennyson's is a knowing adjustment of a material fact which is in the public domain, justified by internal poetic reasons, and not a careless and unnoticed slip, so we can issue a poetic licence for it without any qualms.

But there are circumstances where the strategic adjustments of fact made by the poet raise ethical issues. To take a very marginal instance, and coming back to Wordsworth's 'Daffodils' poem, the poem opens with the line 'I wandered lonely as a cloud', even though he was not on his own at all when he saw the daffodils, but walking with his sister Dorothy, whose journal observations and phrasing he borrowed in order to write the poem. Dorothy's contribution to the poem is completely written out – is this legitimate practice? A footnote thanking her for her contribution would have been nice, but poets are not obliged to write verse autobiography, any more than novelists are, and the facts of personal and private life are quite different from material facts which are in the public domain. There may, of course, be shades of the poultry yard in this defence, but it surely has to stand.

More problematical ethical issues are raised by another of Tony Curtis's poems about the artist William Orpen, entitled 'William Orpen & Yvonne Aubicq in the Rue Danon' (pp. 17–19 in *Tony Curtis: Selected Poems*, 1986). In this poem, set during the First World War, Orpen contemplates denouncing his mistress, Yvonne Aubicq, to the authorities as a spy. He imagines her facing a firing squad in a fur coat which she slips from her shoulders, revealing herself naked, as officer and soldiers raise phallic sword and rifles to execute her – 'It seems a lifetime before they fire', the poem ends. The source of the poem is Orpen's invention of a mythical story about the execution of a female spy who bares herself in this way before the firing squad. Orpen had alleged that his painting of Aubicq was actually a portrait of this (mythical) woman spy. The myth of the nude, fur-coated female spy was widely circulated and widely believed, and it is clearly cognate in spirit with other myths of the time, such as that of the Angel of Mons, and Arthur Machen's story 'The Bowmen', which were taken as fact by contemporaries.[3] Orpen's fantasy seems to attempt to romanticise what was in fact a war of mechanised slaughter on an industrial scale. Of course, the story may well reveal a great deal about the sexual attitudes of the British patrician class, but the problem is that Curtis's poem is unannotated, and as it stands it reads as if Sir William Orpen – a real person, not a poetic 'persona' – seriously contemplated disposing of Aubicq by denouncing her as a spy. Is it all right for a poet to do this, or should there be some indication that the poet, though using the lives of actual people, has parted, at some point in the poem, from known facts and logical inferences, and is presenting 'a scene from the mind' (to quote a phrase from the Curtis poem discussed earlier)? Though it is difficult to imagine that general agreement would be attainable on this kind of example, the 'strategic' factual error will often seem (at best) somewhat uncomfortable: in the case of certain examples, the adjustment of the facts which is made within the 'safety' of a poem is perhaps a little like the slander made in the House of Commons, and therefore protected by parliamentary privilege. Facts could not be altered in this way in an article, but the parallel world of literature is felt to be different, and the writ of the poetic licence is upheld, even at the risk of debasing the truth status of literature as a whole.

In the light of all this, let us return to the 504/534 case. To decide whether the mistake matters we have to think about the context rather than the text, for poems like the '504' piece are 'content-specific' – they include precise social and historical data, mentioning specific names, times, places, events, personalities, and so on. Content-specific poems don't respond very well to our familiar 'unseen close reading' techniques – they need an approach which might be called 'documentary close reading', in which the cited documentary facts are placed alongside the poem and read in combination with it. In the era of the internet, it is very easy to do this, and a Google search along the lines of '534 + "Queen Mary" + Clydeside + Depression' will produce most of the data used in the poem. So we can find out that the keel was laid on 1 December 1930, and that work on the ship was suspended for over two years because of the economic Slump. Throughout those two years, the unnamed, rusting hull of 'Number 534' was constantly referred to in the newspapers, and became a vivid emblem of the national sense of helplessness during that era of still-remembered unemployment. A poem about the 1930s which gets this number wrong makes an error which is central and germane to its subject matter, not one which is marginal or tangential. It's like forgetting Chapman's name in the act of offering him poetic praise. So if the poet doesn't know about 534 the reader immediately wonders what else he doesn't know about, and in what other ways the world of the poem might be different from our own. The '504' slip, then, takes us into a reading of the poem which foregrounds context, but context in this sense is really content. This, I think, is what Peter Robinson means by 'all the aspects of external contexts legitimately assumed in, or implied by, the work itself' (*Poetry, Poets, Readers*, p. 99). '504', to be blunt, is just boringly and uninterestingly wrong. No purpose could be served by getting it wrong; it isn't possible to conceive of a defence like Rzepka's of Keats's Balboa slip (that Keats, in some deeper thematic way, *meant* Cortez), and poets are not entitled to be careless with facts in that aimless way. A poet, in reply, might plead the 'poultry yard', maintaining that poets would demean themselves by checking such details – 'As to the numbers in tradesmen's order books, with them we have no concern' (though I have no evidence that Imlah would do so). But playing the poultry yard card when it isn't called for would seriously damage the relationship of trust between reader and writer.

Facts in poems

The argument about poetry and facts is usually conducted (as so far in this chapter) by looking at examples of errors. But if context is content, then we should also consider how poems make use of external facts. Throughout the book a distinction has been made between 'deep' context and 'broad' context. The former is explicit in some way in the text – it's mentioned or alluded to – indeed, we have said that it's the kind of con*text* which is really con*tent*. Broad context, on the other hand, has no such unambiguous warranty in the text. As an example of a poem that uses a very specific deep context, I will look at the late Michael Donaghy's fine poem 'A Sicilian Defence' (in *New Writing 9*, ed. A. L. Kennedy and John Fowles (2000), p. 15):

A Sicilian Defence

It's another story altogether
by lanternlight, beneath two birches
and the sound of a shallow river
where two men are playing chess
for as long as either will remember,
opening King's pawn on e4 . . .
It's not a question of either/or –

One might be my father, or me at sixty.
The other might as well be me
thinking: his right's my left, my left
his right. I see it now in a different light.
I know it now by another name.

Is it any wonder then this game
runs on through this and every night
forever, lit by lanternlight, two birches
and the sound of a river?

This poem uses the motif or image of chess. The 'Sicilian' defence is an opening sequence of moves which starts by moving the King's pawn to e4, just as the poem says. If you didn't know, as a reader of the poem, what the Sicilian is, then you might assume that the world of Mafia assassins is being evoked, and indeed, it is, but only as a secondary or supportive image, suggesting the violent undercurrents of every chess game. The Exeter Chess Club, for instance, heads its web page on the Sicilian with a quotation from a song which offers the advice 'Never go in against a Sicilian when "death" is on the line', and it remarks that chess magazines 'are full of quick White kills against the Sicilian'. To play the Sicilian as Black (White always opens in chess, of course) is to invite an immediate all-out assault on your defensive position, but, if that fails, then it's all up for grabs, and the game could go on for a long time, just like the one in the poem, which 'runs on through this and every night / forever'.

Chess is full of archetypal undertones like those in the poem; every game enacts an Oedipal 'family drama' in which the object is to take the Queen and destroy the King, and victory is short-lived, for the winner is always waiting for the inevitable moment when the next challenger arrives (as in a comparable poem by Carol Rumens, 'A Poem for Chessmen', in *The Penguin Book of Contemporary British Poetry*, ed. Morrison and Motion, p. 161). In Ingmar Bergman's 1956 film *The Seventh Seal*, the Knight Antonius plays a chess game against Death, on a remote beach, an archetypal landscape which is like that of the river and two birches that is the setting for the endless chess game in Donaghy's poem. The more we know, then, about the way chess has been put to allegorical and symbolic uses in literature and in other arts, the more resonance Donaghy's poem will have for us. Indeed, it is with all *that* that the poem is intended to reverberate, for such facts and instances are the poem's deep context. Clearly, then, as in all poems, the words *on* the page are in dialogue with the words (and images) *off* the page. But all this data is an area of factual knowledge which is directly 'triggered' by the words of the poem, and is hardly distinguishable from its content: the poem gives it explicit resonance and relevance, and can't really be read adequately without it. Poems are responses to a real world that we share with the poets, not mystical and abstract verbal icons floating in inner space. That notion of poetry has done untold damage, and we need to bring our poetry reading back to earth. The technique used here, then, isn't the old kind of 'unseen close reading', but the process of 'documented close reading'. It reinstates the poet's sources, and uses them as a parallel text to the text itself. It might seem at first a close relative of Jerome McGann's 'historicist close reading'[4] but it isn't attempting to reconstruct historical paradigms, and McGann's close reading is concerned with broad rather than deep context, the kind which sees no need for a verbal 'trigger' within the poem itself. Contrary to McGann, the present book asserts that the aim of contextualisation should always be to construct the narrowest and most text-specific kind of context which is possible. It advocates the need for precision of interlock between text and context, such that a given context will fit one work only.

Message in a bottle – Adrian Henri's *Lowlands Away*[5]

I will consider a final example of 'poetry and facts' in a more sustained way, since it is a poetic sequence which is built into several different contexts, having ekphrastic elements, a precise personal and biographical deep context, a multi-layered intertextual relationship with other texts of various kinds, and what might be called a musical co-text. Hence, it seems a fitting final example. In 1990 Richard Gordon-Smith, a young musician and composer with the Liverpool Philharmonic Orchestra, visited relatives in Maldon, Essex. He was shown the last letter written by his great-grandfather, Captain George Gentry, in 1895. It hadn't been delivered to his wife by the postman – it reached her via the British Consul in Dunkirk, the Consul having received it from a Monsieur DeBaecker who had spotted it and picked it up while walking on the beach. It was a real-life 'message in a bottle'. George Gentry was captain of a Thames and Medway barge called the *Cynthia*. There were thousands of these small, single-masted sailing ships, trading round the British coasts, right up to the Second World War. They usually had a crew of three, and carried about 100 tons of freight, which they loaded in the docks from big sea-going cargo ships, and then did river, canal or coastal trips to make pinpoint deliveries. They had a large single hatch about 20 feet long – ideal for easy loading, but vulnerable in high seas, since, fully loaded, the water was only 6 inches below the main deck level of these craft. Because of the shallow draght, the rudder was exposed and vulnerable in bad weather. They were fine craft for river and coastal trips – adequate, even, for crossing the North Sea, provided the weather kept fine – 'Lowlands' in the title is a general term for Holland and Belgium, and for sailors the Lowlands Sea was the North Sea.

Cynthia loaded cargo in London, 12–13 May 1895, then set sail for the Rhine. The following day ferocious gales blew up in the North Sea. *Lloyd's List* (the specialist maritime newspaper) reported *Cynthia* as missing. Back home at Maldon, Essex, the family watched the weather anxiously and waited for news. They probably didn't know that the *Cynthia*'s cargo on that trip was empty mineral-water bottles, being taken back to the Apollinaris bottling plant on the Rhine. The letter in the bottle picked up on the beach read as follows:

Thursday night May 19th
    Barge *Cynthia*

We are sinking   rudder head
gone – boat and hatches   we are
off the Weiligen   have had
distress signal flying all
day. Farewell to all we love

Capt Gentry. Maldon
T Carrington. Mistley
A Brown. London

should this be picked
up please send on to
66 Wantz Rd. Maldon. Essex.

The composer says that the phrase 'Farewell to all we love' haunted him for months: he seemed to be looking down a 'time tunnel', 'watching the century-old tragedy unfold'.[6] 'As the copper plate writing of the beginning of the letter gives way to a more desperate hand, I could almost see the water lapping round the writer's boots and hear the howling gale.' The main thematic material of the music of the oratorio *Lowlands Away*, which the letter inspired Gorton-Smith to compose, is based on the *Cynthia's* registration number – 21361 – as applied to a major scale, 'These five digits add up to thirteen, the number of dangerous omen; there are thirteen sections in the piece, and this number is also used rhythmically' (sleeve notes). The poet Adrian Henri worked collaboratively with the composer on the libretto of the oratorio. The thirteen pieces of text which were used can be summarised as follows, the asterisks being explained later:

(1) *Invocation*: a stanza taken from the traditional ballad 'Lowlands Away', which tells of a woman's premonitory dream of a sweetheart lost at sea.

(2) *Barge Ballad I*: three stanzas listing the names of Thames & Medway barges, alphabetical, with names beginning A, B, and C, respectively in the first three stanzas.*

(3) *Capstan Song*: 'Here we ride at the harbour side' – casting-off shanty composed by Henri with a counter-verse representing the voice of the sea.*

(4) *Barge Ballad II*: continuation of the composite piece of alphabetical listing of barge names – four stanzas, D to M in total.*

(5) Brief extract from Psalm 107: 'They that go down to the sea in ships . . .'

(6) *Sea Challenge*: two stanza poem about facing the dangers of the sea.★

(7) Brief extract from the 'Song of Songs': 'Many waters cannot quench love . . .'

(8) *Dreamwreck*: poem 'In our separate worlds / we call each other lover'.★

(9) *Song of the Dark Lady*: 'fear death by water' – images of fate and Tarot.★

(10) *Storm*: poem imaging destructiveness of the sea (using 'Break Break Break').★

(11) *Bottle Message*: the text of the message in the bottle.

(12) *Lowlands Away*: three-verse version of the traditional ballad.

(13) *Barge Ballad III*: names alphabet concludes with three stanzas covering N to W: quotation from Revelation 21 ('And I saw a new heaven and a new earth'): concluding chorus to the Barge Ballad listing types of small trading boat ('Ketches Shrimpers Tramps and Bawleys).★

One striking fact about the material is the extent to which the poet seems to minimise the presence of his own words in the libretto. In the preface to his work in *Seven Poets and a City* he describes his poetics as having been 'formed from the concept (ultimately derived from Williams, Olson and the Black Mountain poets) of writing for, and in, one's own voice' (p. 37), but in the 1980s this modulated (because of writing poems for children and writing for the theatre) into the practice of writing dramatic monologues, which he describes as 'one's own voice using a borrowed voice'. He goes on to mention his long-standing practice of working with music as a context for poetry, and then the experience with *Lowlands Away* of working 'within the extended forms of classical music, and yet within the limitations of the composer's needs' (p. 38). This describes a trajectory in which there is a gradual movement away from 'own voice', through a 'borrowed voice', and arriving finally at 'other voices' (though this last phrase isn't used by Henri). This process I would read as a movement from a stance of individualism to one of collectivism, or from seeing the poet as the lone Romantic original, to a notion of the poet as channelling the voices and experiences of others (so that this sequence expresses 'the lives and tragedies of Liverpool's mariners over the centuries', even though the location of this particular tragedy is elsewhere). Hence, the 'deep context' is given maximum room in the poem, and one indication of this is that the words of others take precedence over the poet's own words. The eight items marked with an asterisk in the list of the thirteen sections of *Lowlands Away* are the ones which are poems composed by Henri (2, 3, 4, 6, 8, 9, 10, 13). But three of these (2, 4, and 13) are really 'found poems' (since they are mainly just alphabetical listings of the names of Thames and Medway barges), each of these four-line stanzas having three lines of names, followed by a refrain line, on the pattern:

Aidie Ailsa Agnes Mary
Abergavenny Alice Ash
Ashpodel Atlantic Atlas
Beyond the bay where breakers splash

Even the remaining five 'composed' sections (3, 6, 8, 9, 10) contain extensive elements of allusion, parody, or quotation, such as traditional shanty elements in 3 and quotations from a children's rhyme about the seashore, and echoes and quotations from *The Waste Land* in 9, a quotation from Tennyson in 10 and marked affinities with Hopkins's way of describing the sea in 'The Wreck of the *Deutschland*', and a biblical quotation in 13. This leaves only two short pieces (6 and 8) as 'one's own voice' poems in the full sense, and in all the rest it is the 'facts' which take precedence over the 'interpretations'. The poet isn't *professing* a theory of impersonality here but *enacting* one. It isn't always entirely clear to me which came first, the words or the music, but mostly it seems to have been the former: Henri wrote eleven poems, of which seven were eventually used in the libretto (sleeve notes), and Henri's comments in *Seven Poets and a City* record that ' "Write me a storm" is one of the strangest requests of my career' (p. 36). Indeed, the libretto taken as a whole is a joint composition/compilation, with the composer selecting the version of the ballad 'Lowlands Away' which will be used, plus the three scriptural texts and the children's rhyme, and Henri supplying 'seven specially-written poems' (sleeve notes).

Nowadays, it would seem odd, on hearing about an air-crash, let's say, to decide to write a poem about it. The events of '9/11', for instance, did not result in any new poems, so far as I know, only the revival of a couple of old ones, like W.H. Auden's 'September 1, 1939', because it happens to be about being in New York and hearing of an event which presages disasters to come.[7] By contrast, when Gerard Manley Hopkins, in 1875, told his Rector how affected he had been by reading the account of the wreck of the immigrant ship *Deutschland*, the rector 'said that he wished someone would write a poem on the subject', as if this were the natural response to such an event. In 'Lowlands Away' the poet uses the words of the last message sent by the victims of the shipwreck. I suppose this is a kind of nineteenth-century equivalent to the mobile phone messages sent by some of the '9/11' victims. The poet in this case avoids as far as possible composing words of his own. Instead, he mainly uses words which are already there in the situation, or words which have traditionally been used of situations of this kind.

The ultimate 'deep' context – in this instance as in any other – is provided by the facts which are in the poem, and that is the context which the poem speaks. In Henri's case, the sequence pushes the poet himself to the margins and allows other words, and others' words, to speak for him. The historicist impositions which have become common in recent years seem to be driven by something *opposite* to that impulse, that is, by a desire to 'revoice' the poem, so that it speaks *our* concerns rather than its own. Of course, it is probably not possible to entirely escape that impulse when reading poetry, and that may be one of the things I have inadvertently demonstrated in the present book. But we can at least learn to be sceptical and wary of that appropriating impulse by seeking to allow the deep context of literature to speak, and rather than burying it in the cumbersome weight of our half-acre broad contextual tombs.

Notes

1 'It's a poem about exclusion as well as inclusion. Its title suggests that Keats felt he had come late to high culture. It draws attention to the fact that he couldn't read Homer in the original Greek. It's Chapman's Homer, not Homer's Homer' – from the transcript of a 1998 New York lecture – see http://www.abc.net.au/rn/arts/bwriting/stories/s122753.htm.
2 See Charles Rzepka, 'Cortez – or Balboa, or Somebody Like That: Form, Fact, and Forgetting in Keats's "Chapman's Homer" Sonnet', *Keats–Shelley Journal*, vol. 51 (2002), pp. 35–75.
3 As detailed in the introduction to Trudi Tate's collection *Women, Men and the Great War: An Anthology of Stories* (Manchester University Press, 1995), p. 3.
4 See 'Keats and the Historical Method in Literary Criticism', in *The Beauty of Inflections* (Oxford University Press, 1985).
5 *Lowlands Away* is an oratorio with music by Richard Gordon-Smith and words by Adrian Henri. The first performance, by the Royal Liverpool Philharmonic Orchestra, took place on 27 April 1996. A CD recording was released in 2001 (*Lowlands Away* – poetry by Adrian Henri, Royal Liverpool Philharmonic Choir & Orchestra / RLPO *Live* RLCD 303), printing the full text in the sleeve notes. A book version of *Lowlands Away*, with eight pastel images by the poet, was published by The Old School Press (run by Martin Ould, at Hinton Charterhouse, nr Bath, UK), in 2000, in an edition of 410. Substantial selections from the work were included in *Liverpool Accents: Seven Poets and a City*, ed. Peter Robinson (Liverpool University Press, 1996), pp. 39–45, but the order, selection, and presentation of the material are somewhat different.

6 The letter, and the composer's comments, are taken from the sleeve notes.
7 The choral work *On the Transmigration of Souls* (Audio CD, 2004, Nonesuch, ASIN: B0002JNLNM) by the American composer John Adams, which provides what he calls a 'memory space', rather than a memorial, for those who died in the events of '9/11', similarly avoids the use of 'composed' words. Instead it employs 'documentary' words, such as the word 'missing' used repeatedly, fragments found on missing person posters, phrases from newspaper memorials, and lists of the names of victims of the attack.

References

Abbott, Claude Colleer, ed., *The Correspondence of Gerard Manley Hopkins and Richard Watson Dixon*, Oxford University Press, revised edition, 1955.

Abbott, Clande Colleer, ed., *The Letters of Gerard Manley Hopkins to Robert Bridges*, second revised impression, Oxford University Press, 1955.

Abbott, Claude Colleer, ed., *Further Letters of Gerard Manley Hopkins*, Oxford University Press, 1956.

Allen, Graham, *Intertextuality* (New Critical Idiom series), Routledge, 2000.

Armstrong, Isobel, *Victorian Poetry: Poetry, Poetics, and Politics*, Routledge, 1993.

Arnold, Bruce, *Orpen: Mirror to an Age*, Cape, 1981.

Ashfield, Andrew, ed., *Romantic Women Poets, 1788–1848*, Manchester University Press, 1998.

Atwood, Margaret, *The Circle Game*, Contact Press, Toronto, 1966.

Auerbach, Erich, *Mimesis: The Representation of Reality in Western Literature*, Princeton University Press, 2003.

Backhouse, Robert, ed., *The Spiritual Exercises of St Ignatius Loyola*, Hodder and Stoughton, 1989.

Barrell, John, *Imagining the King's Death: Figurative Treason, Fantasies of Regicide, 1793–1796*, Oxford University Press, 2003.

Barry, Peter, *Contemporary British Poetry and the City*, Manchester University Press, 2000.

Barry, Peter, *English in Practice*, Arnold, 2002.

Bateson, F. W., *Essays in Critical Dissent*, Longman, 1972.

Batho, Edith, and Bonamy Dobrée, *The Victorians and after, 1830–1914*, Cresset, 1938.

Bennett, Andrew, *Keats, Narrative and Audience: The Posthumous Life of Writing*, Cambridge University Press, 1994.

Bertram, Vicki, *Gendering Poetry: Contemporary Women and Men Poets*, Pandora, 2005.

Breen, Jennifer, *Women Romantic Poets 1785–1832*, Everyman, 1994.

Brown, Christopher, and Peter Sutton, *Masters of Seventeenth-Century Dutch Genre Painting*, Philadelphia Museum of Art, 1984.

Brooks, Cleanth, *The Well Wrought Urn: Studies in the Structure of Poetry*, Dobson Books, 1949.

Butler, Marilyn, *Romantics, Rebels and Reactionaries: English Literature and its Background, 1760–1830*, Oxford University Press, 1981.

Bygrave, Stephen, *Coleridge and the Self: Romantic Egotism* (Studies in Romanticism), Palgrave, 1986.

Chandler, James, *England in 1819: The Politics of Literary Culture and the Case of Romantic Historicism*, University of Chicago Press, 1999.

Coleridge, E. H., ed., *Coleridge: Poetical Works*, Oxford University Press, 1967.

Critchley, Simon, *The Ethics of Deconstruction: Derrida and Levinas*, Blackwell, 1992.

Crystal, David, *Language Death*, Cambridge University Press, 2002.

Curtis, Tony, *How to Study Modern Poetry*, Macmillan, 1990.

Curtis, Tony, *Selected Poems*, Poetry Wales Press, 1986.

Davey, Frank, *Margaret Atwood: A Feminist Poetics*, Talon Books, Vancouver, 1984.

Derrida, Jacques, *Limited Inc*, Northwestern University Press, 1988.

Devlin, Christopher, ed., *The Sermons and Devotional Writings of Gerard Manley Hopkins*, Oxford University Press, 1959.

Donoghue, Denis, *Ferocious Alphabets*, Faber & Faber, 1981.

Dunne, Tom, *Gerard Manley Hopkins: A Comprehensive Bibliography*, Oxford University Press, 1976.

Elton, Oliver, *Survey of English Literature*, Arnold, 1912.

Everest, Kelvin, *Coleridge's Secret Ministry: The Context of the Conversation Poems, 1795–1798*, Harvester, 1979.

Feldman, Paula R., ed., *Records of Woman, With Other Poems, Felicia Hemans*, University Press of Kentucky, 1999.

Fleishman, Avrom, *A Reading of Mansfield Park: An Essay in Critical Synthesis*, Johns Hopkins University Press, 1970.

Flint, Kate, *The Victorians and the Visual Imagination*, Cambridge University Press, 2000.

Ford, Jennifer, *Coleridge on Dreaming: Romanticism, Dreams, and the Medical Imagination*, Cambridge, 1998.

Foucault, Michel, *The Archaeology of Knowledge*, Routledge, 2002.

Gallagher, Catherine, and Stephen Greenblatt, *Practicing the New Historicism*, University Chicago Press, 2000.

Geertz, Clifford, *The Interpretation of Cultures*, Basic Books, 1977.

Genette, Gérard, *Narrative Discourse: An Essay in Method*, Cornell University Press, 1983.

Graff, Gerald, *Professing English: An Institutional History*, Chicago University Press, 1987.

Hadfield, Andrew, *Edmund Spenser's Irish Experience: Wilde Fruit and Salvage Soyl*, Clarendon Press, 1997.

Hadfield, Andrew, ed., *The Cambridge Companion to Spenser*, Cambridge University Press, 2001.

Herbert, W. N., *The Luarelude*, Faber & Faber, 1998.

Holderness, Graham, *Textual Shakespeare: Writing and the Word*, University of Hertfordshire Press, 2003.

Hollander, John, *The Gazer's Spirit: Poems Speaking to Silent Works of Art*, University of Chicago Press, 1995.

Holmes, Richard, *Footsteps: Adventures of a Romantic Biographer*, Viking Penguin, 1985.

Jack, Ian, *English Literature, 1815–1832*, Oxford University Press, 1963.

Kay, Jackie, *The Adoption Papers*, Bloodaxe, 1991.

Kennedy A.L., and John Fowles, eds, *New Writing 9*, Vintage, in association with the British Council, 2000.

Kennedy, John, *St Francis Xavier's, Liverpool, 1848–1998*.

Kenny, Anthony, *God and Two Poets: Arthur Hugh Clough and Gerard Manley Hopkins*, Sidgwick & Jackson, 1988.

Kermode, Frank, *The Genesis of Secrecy: On the Interpretation of Narrative*, Harvard University Press, 1979.

Kitchen, Paddy, *Gerard Manley Hopkins: A Life*, Carcanet, 1978.

Krieger, Murray, *Ekphrasis: The Illusion of the Natural Sign*, Johns Hopkins University Press, 1992.

Leader, Zachary, *Revision and Romantic Authorship*, Clarendon Press, 1996.

Lewis, Gwyneth, *Keeping Mum*, Bloodaxe, 2003.

Lichtenstein, Rachael, and Iain Sinclair, *Rodinsky's Room*, Granta, 1999.

McFarland, Thomas, *William Wordsworth: Intensity and Achievement*, Oxford University Press, 1992.

McGann, Jerome, *The Beauty of Inflections: Literary Investigations in Historical Method and Theory*, Oxford University Press, 1988.

McGann, Jerome, *The Poetics of Sensibility*, Oxford University Press, 1986.

McGann, Jerome, ed., *New Oxford Book of Romantic Period Verse*, 1993.

MacIntyre, Donald, *Jutland*, Evans Bros, 1957.

Magnuson, Paul, *Reading Public Romanticism*, Cambridge University Press, 1998.

Marcus, Laura, and Peter Nicholls, eds, *The Cambridge History of Twentieth Century Literature*, Cambridge University Press, 2004.

Martz, Louis L., *The Poetry of Meditation: A Study in English Religious Literature of the Seventeenth Century*, Yale University Press, 1954.

Mays, J. C. C., ed., *Collected Works of Samuel Taylor Coleridge: Poetical Works Volume 16*, Princeton University Press, 2001. *Poetical Works I: Poems (Reading Text). Poetical Works II: Poems (Variorum Text)*.

Mellor, Anne K., ed., *Romanticism and Feminism*, Indiana University Press, 1988.

Mellor, Anne K., *Romanticism and Gender*, Rontledge, New York, 1993.

Moi, Toril, ed., *The Kristeva Reader*, Columbia University Press, 1986.

Morrison, Blake, and Andrew Motion, eds, *The Penguin Book of Contemporary British Poetry*, Penguin, 1982.

Motion, Andrew, *Secret Narratives*, Salamander Press, 1983.

Motion, Andrew, *Keats*, Faber & Faber, 1997.

Nunberg, Geoffrey, and Umberto Eco, eds, *The Future of the Book*, University of California Press, 1996.

Orr, Mary, *Intertextuality: Debates and Contexts*, Polity, 2003.

O'Connor, Freddy, *Liverpool: Our City, Our Heritage*, Printfine Ltd, 1990.

O'Neill, Michael, ed., *Literature of the Romantic Period: A Bibliographical Guide*, Oxford University Press, 1998.

O'Neill, Michael, *Romanticism and the Self-Conscious Poem*, Clarendon Press, 1999.

O'Sullivan, Maggie, ed., *Out of Everywhere: Linguistically Innovative Poetry by Women in North America & the UK*, Reality Street Editions, 1996.

Parker, Reeve, *Coleridge's Meditative Art*, Cornell University Press, 1975.

Phillips, Catherine, ed., *Gerard Manley Hopkins*, Oxford University Press, 1995.

Pope, Rob, *The English Studies Book*, Routledge, 1998.

Prince, Gerald, *Dictionary of Narratology*, revised edition, University of Nebraska Press, 2003.

Raine, Craig, *The Onion, Memory*, Oxford University Press, 1978.

Raine, Craig, *A Martian Sends a Postcard Home*, Oxford University Press, 1979.

Rees-Jones, Deryn, *Quiver*, Seren, 2004.

Rich, Adrienne, *A Wild Patience Has Taken Me This Far: Poems 1978–1981*, Norton, 1981.

Ricks, Christopher, *Essays in Appreciation*, Oxford University Press, 1998.

Riley, Denise, ed., *Poets on Writing: Britain 1970–1991*, Macmillan, 1992.

Rivkin, Julie, and Michael Ryan, eds, *Literary Theory: An Anthology*, Blackwell, 2004.

Roberts, Warren, *Jane Austen and the French Revolution*, Macmillan, 1979.

Robinson, Peter, ed., *Liverpool Accents: Seven Poets and a City*, Liverpool University Press, 1996.

Robinson, Peter, *Poetry, Poets, Readers: Making Things Happen*, Oxford University Press, 2002.

Roe, Nicholas, ed., *Keats and History*, Cambridge University Press, 1995.

Rookmaaker, Jr, H. R., *Towards a Romantic Conception of Nature: Coleridge's Poetry up to 1803: A Study in the History of Ideas*, John Benjamins, Amsterdam, 1984.

Rylance, Rick, and Judy Simons, eds, *Literature in Context*, Palgrave, 2001.

Sampson, Fiona, *The Distance Between Us*, Seren, 2005.

Said, Edward, *Culture and Imperialism*, Vintage, 1995.

Said, Edward, *Orientalism: Western Conceptions of the Orient*, Penguin, 2003.

Saintsbury, George, *A History of Nineteenth Century Literature: 1780–1895*, Macmillan, 1896.

Simpson, Matt, *Cutting the Clouds Towards*, Liverpool University Press, 1998.

Steiner, George, *On Difficulty, and Other Essays*, Oxford University Press, 1978.

Stillinger, Jack, *Multiple Authorship and the Myth of Solitary Genius*, Oxford University Press, 1991.

Stillinger, Jack, *Coleridge and Textual Instability: The Multiple Versions of the Major Poems*, Oxford University Press, 1994.

Sutherland, John, *Is Heathcliff a Murderer? Great Puzzles in Nineteenth-Century Fiction*, Oxford University Press, 1998.

Sweet, Nanora, and Julie Melnyk, eds, *Felicia Hemans: Reimagining Poetry in the Nineteenth Century*, Palgrave, 2001.

Tate, Trudi, ed., *Women, Men and the Great War: An Anthology of Stories*, Manchester University Press, 1995.

Thomas, Alfred, S. J., *Hopkins the Jesuit: The Years of Training*, Oxford University Press, 1969,

Todd, Janet, ed., *Jane Austen in Context*, Cambridge University Press, 2005.

Trinder, Peter W., *Mrs Hemans*, University of Wales Press, 1984.

Tuma, Keith, *Fishing by Obstinate Isles: Modern and Postmodern British Poetry and American Readers* (Avant-Garde & Modernism Studies), Northwestern University Press, 1999.

Tuma, Keith, *Anthology of Twentieth-Century British and Irish Poetry*, Oxford University Press, 2001.

Warner, Val, *Tooting Idyll*, Carcanet, 1998.

Wheeler, K.M., *The Creative Mind in Coleridge's Poetry*, Heinemann, 1981.

Williams, Raymond, *Marxism and Literature*, Oxford University Press, 1977.

Wolfreys, Julian, ed., *Literary Theories: A Reader & Guide*, Edinburgh University Press, 1999.

Index